KATIE'S DIARY

The Series in Death, Dying, and Bereavement
Consulting Editor
Robert A. Neimeyer

Davies—Shadows in the Sun: The Experiences of Sibling Bereavement in Childhood
Harvey—Perspectives on Loss: A Sourcebook
Klass—The Spiritual Lives of Bereaved Parents
Leenaars—Lives and Deaths: Selections from the Works of Edwin S. Shneidman
Lester—Katie's Diary: Unlocking the Mystery of a Suicide
Martin, Doka—Men Don't Cry...Women Do: Transcending Gender Stereotypes of Grief
Nord—Multiple AIDS-Related Loss: A Handbook for Understanding and Surviving a Perpetual Fall
Roos—Chronic Sorrow: A Living Loss
Rosenblatt—Parent Grief: Narratives of Loss and Relationship
Werth—Contemporary Perspectives on Rational Suicide

FORMERLY THE **SERIES IN DEATH EDUCATION, AGING, AND HEALTH CARE**
HANNELORE WASS, CONSULTING EDITOR

Bard—Medical Ethics in Practice
Benoliel—Death Education for the Health Professional
Bertman—Facing Death: Images, Insights, and Interventions
Brammer—How to Cope with Life Transitions: The Challenge of Personal Change
Cleiren—Bereavement and Adaptation: A Comparative Study of the Aftermath of Death
Corless, Pittman-Lindeman—AIDS: Principles, Practices, and Politics, Abridged Edition
Corless, Pittman-Lindeman—AIDS: Principles, Practices, and Politics, Reference Edition
Curran—Adolescent Suicidal Behavior
Davidson—The Hospice: Development and Administration. Second Edition
Davidson, Linnolla—Risk Factors in Youth Suicide
Degner, Beaton—Life-Death Decisions in Health Care
Doka—AIDS, Fear, and Society: Challenging the Dreaded Disease
Doty—Communication and Assertion Skills for Older Persons
Epting, Neimeyer—Personal Meanings of Death: Applications for Personal Construct Theory to Clinical
    Practice
Haber—Health Care for an Aging Society: Cost-Conscious Community Care and Self-Care Approaches
Hughes—Bereavement and Support: Healing in a Group Environment
Irish, Lundquist, Nelsen—Ethnic Variations in Dying, Death, and Grief: Diversity in Universality
Klass, Silverman, Nickman—Continuing Bonds: New Understanding of Grief
Lair—Counseling the Terminally Ill: Sharing the Journey
Leenaars, Maltsberger, Neimeyer—Treatment of Suicidal People
Leenaars, Wenckstern—Suicide Prevention in Schools
Leng—Psychological Care in Old Age
Leviton—Horrendous Death, Health, and Well-Being
Leviton—Horrendous Death and Health: Toward Action
Lindeman, Corby, Downing, Sanborn—Alzheimer's Day Care: A Basic Guide
Lund—Older Bereaved Spouses: Research with Practical Applications
Neimeyer—Death Anxiety Handbook: Research, Instrumentation, and Application
Papadatou, Papadatos—Children and Death
Prunkl, Berry—Death Week: Exploring the Dying Process
Ricker, Myers—Retirement Counseling: A Practical Guide for Action
Samarel—Caring for Life and Death
Sherron, Lumsden—Introduction to Educational Gerontology. Third Edition
Stillion—Death and Sexes: An Examination of Differential Longevity Attitudes, Behaviors, and Coping
    Skills
Stillion, McDowell, May—Suicide Across the Life Span—Premature Exits
Vachon—Occupational Stress in the Care of the Critically Ill, the Dying, and the Bereaved
Wass, Corr—Childhood and Death
Wass, Corr—Helping Children Cope with Death: Guidelines and Resource. Second Edition
Wass, Corr, Pacholski, Forfar—Death Education II: An Annotated Resource Guide
Wass, Neimeyer—Dying: Facing the Facts. Third Edition
Weenolsen—Transcendence of Loss over the Life Span
Werth—Rational Suicide? Implications for Mental Health Professionals

KATIE'S DIARY

Unlocking the Mystery of a Suicide

Edited by

David Lester

Brunner-Routledge
New York and Hove

Published in 2004 by
Brunner-Routledge
29 West 35th Street
New York, NY 10001
www.brunner-routledge.com

Published in Great Britain by
Brunner-Routledge
27 Church Road
Hove, East Sussex
BN3 2FA
www.brunner-routledge.co.uk

Brunner-Routledge is an imprint of the Taylor & Francis Group.
Printed in the United States of America on acid-free paper.

10 9 8 7 6 5 4 3 2 1

Library of Congress Cataloging-in-Publication Data

  Katie's diary : unlocking the mystery of a suicide / edited by David Lester.
     p. cm. — (Series in death, dying, and bereavement)
   Includes bibliographical references and index.
     ISBN 0-415-93501-6 (alk. paper) — ISBN 0-415-93500-8 (pbk. : alk. paper)
   1. Katie, d. 1995. 2. Suicide—Psychological aspects. 3. Suicide victims—
Diaries. I. Lester, David, 1942- II. Series.

RC569.K37 2003
616.85′8445′0092—dc21

                                                          2003010051

This book is dedicated to "Katie"

as both a memorial to her life

and in the hope that her life and death

increase our understanding of suicide

CONTENTS

Conclusions

CONTRIBUTORS

SILVIA SARA CANETTO, Ph.D., is Associate Professor of Psychology at Colorado State University in Fort Collins. She has doctoral degrees from the University of Padova (Italy) and Northwestern University Medical School (USA) and an MA from the Hebrew University of Jerusalem. She is internationally known for her research on gender, culture, and suicidal behavior. Among her publications is the 1995 book *Women and Suicidal Behavior*, which she coedited with David Lester. She is the recipient of the 1997 Shneidman Award of the American Association of Suicidology and an elected member of the International Academy for Suicide Research.

THOMAS E. ELLIS, Psy.D., ABPP, is Professor of Psychology at Marshall University. He is coauthor of *Suicide Risk: Assessment and Response Guidelines* and of *Choosing to Live: How to Defeat Suicide through Cognitive Therapy*. His other publications focus on cognitive therapy with suicidal patients, cognitive features of suicidal patients, and classification of suicidal behaviors. He is a consulting editor for *Suicide and Life-Threatening Behavior* and the *Journal of Rational-Emotive and Cognitive-Behavioral Therapy*, and he is past Director of the Clinical Division of the American Association of Suicidology.

LISA FIRESTONE, Ph.D., is Program and Education Director of the Glendon Association and an adjunct faculty member at the University of California, Santa Barbara. Since 1987, she has been involved in clinical training and applied research in the areas of suicide and violence, and she developed the *Firestone Assessment of Self-Destructive Thoughts* (FAST) as a result of her research. Dr. Firestone is an active presenter at national and international conferences and is coauthor of *Conquering Your Critical Inner Voice*.

DR. ROBERT R. FOURNIER is a resident of Cape Cod, living there with his wife of 25 years, and father to three adult children, all relatively close in age to that of "Katie" at the time of her death. He is a clinical social worker, a specialist in individuals and group psychotherapy with victims of trauma and with persons either at risk for suicide or those bereaved by the loss of a loved one. He has a long-standing interest in the relation of suicide to spirituality. He works in both private practice and with the Department of Veterans Affairs.

JAMES HOLLIS, Ph.D., is a Zurich-trained Jungian analyst in practice in Houston, Texas, where he is also Executive Director of the Jung Educational Center. He is the author of nine books, the latest being *On This Journey We Call Our Life*.

ANTOON A. LEENAARS, Ph.D., C.Psych., CPQ, is a psychologist in private practice in Windsor, Canada, and was a member of the faculty at the University of Leiden. He was the first Past President of the Canadian Association for Suicide Prevention (CASP), and is a Past President of the American Association of Suicidology (AAS). He has published ten books, most recently, *Lives and Deaths: Selections from the Works of Edwin S. Shneidman*, and is editor-in-chief of the *Archives of Suicide Research*. Dr. Leenaars has received the International Association for Suicide Prevention's Erwin Stengel Award, CASP's Research Award, and AAS's Edwin Shneidman Award.

DAVID LESTER has Ph.D. degrees in Psychology (Brandeis University, USA) and in Social and Political Science (Cambridge University, UK). He has been President of the International Association for Suicide Prevention and is presently Professor of Psychology at the Richard Stockton College of New Jersey. His research interests focus on suicide, murder, and thanatology.

JAMES W. PENNEBAKER received his Ph.D. in 1977 from the University of Texas at Austin. He taught at the University of Virginia and Southern Methodist University before returning to the University of Texas in 1997. His research focuses on how individuals think, talk, and behave in the aftermath of traumatic experiences.

LORI D. STONE is completing her Ph.D. at the University of Texas at Austin, working with James W. Pennebaker. Her research interests include the social psychological aspects of language use, focusing on individual differences, health outcomes, and interpersonal processes.

SERIES EDITOR'S FOREWORD

"In every man's writings," Goethe once observed, "the character of the writer must lie recorded." Certainly this is true of the self-revelatory writing of Katie's intimate journal, in which the author writes searchingly, hopefully, and despairingly about herself and to herself in the context of an anguished life that ultimately becomes unlivable. This remarkable book takes Katie's searing prose as its starting point, sifting through its painful particulars in an effort to winnow insights from her unique struggle that could yield a broader understanding of how frustration in the universal human quest for coherence and connectedness can often have tragic consequences. In this sense, Katie's diary, bequeathed to David Lester by her sister, is a generous if unsettling gift to all those who strive to understand the dynamics of self-destruction.

It is the rare document that captures the conflict and complexity of an individual's stream of consciousness, as it alternately flows, is impeded, and torrentially cascades onward toward an end that can be envisioned confidently only in retrospect. Katie's diary charts this dramatic inner course, and it is into this often-turbulent current that Lester and his eight contributors wade in an effort to understand the forces that give it its tragic momentum. In the course of their reflective and deep-going analysis, they draw on sociological, feminist, developmental, linguistic, cognitive, psychological, literary, psychiatric, archetypal, spiritual, and psychodynamic perspectives to reveal the dominant internal and external structures and processes with which Katie contends, and in doing so, reveal as much to the reader about the possible utility of these conceptual frameworks as they do about Katie's ultimate suicide.

Indeed, it is this interaction between a tragic text and its respective readers that makes *Katie's Diary* a singular contribution to suicidology. No other book in the field is so concretely anchored in the subjective realities of a single suicidal subject, and few bring to bear such a panoply of probing perspectives as those Lester has assembled. The result is a remarkably well-grounded approach to the abstract conceptualization of suicide, one that allows the reader to identify both common factors in the diversity of contemporary theories, and their novel points of departure. Perhaps of even greater value, the wide-ranging commentaries on Katie's diary captured in these chapters suggest empathic and informed inroads into her torment, encouraging professional readers both to grasp the depth of her despair, and to discern possible paths through and beyond it. In the end, this might turn out to be the silver lining in the dark cloud of Katie's fatal struggle, as she compels each of us to examine and extend our understandings of and responses to circumstances in which life no longer seems worth living.

Robert A. Neimeyer, Ph.D.
The University of Memphis
Series Editor

PREFACE

It is not easy to understand why people kill themselves. The twentieth century witnessed tremendous growth in the number of books and articles written on suicide, but, despite the fact that I have perused most of these publications, including the theories and the research, I am still at a loss to understand why any person commits suicide. What might be the source of my ignorance?

Suicide is a very rare behavior. Even among those with the highest rate of suicide, it is a statistical anomaly. The highest suicide rates in the world are found in the Baltic states Latvia and Lithuania and in Sri Lanka, with rates of 50 per 100,000 per year. That means that, out of every 100,000 people each year, 99,950 do not commit suicide!

I recently was able to estimate the suicide rate of European Jews, mostly Polish, locked up behind barbed wire in the ghetto in Lodz, Poland, during the Second World War. The conditions in this ghetto were horrible, with the people living in squalid and overcrowded conditions, starving and in poor health. The suicide rate peaked in 1942 at about 90 per 100,000 per year. Of the roughly 150,000 people in the ghetto that year, about 135 committed suicide, but that means that 149,865 did not!

No matter how bad the conditions of life become, the vast majority of people struggle to stay alive.

I have published many books and hundreds of articles on suicide, and I sometimes think that I have not increased my understanding of why people kill themselves much at all. I have discovered a few simple facts. In psychological research, we sometimes find that a sample of people who have committed suicide took a psychological test a few months or years prior to their death—perhaps a scale to measure how depressed or hopeless they were, or a test such as the Minnesota Multiphasic Personality Inventory (MMPI) to measure how psychiatrically disturbed they were. We find from these records that they were very depressed, hopeless, and disturbed. We then realize that we could have anticipated the results before we carried out the research. We appeared to have confirmed the obvious, a common criticism of psychological research.

Suicides sometimes leave notes, and there has been a great deal of research on these notes in the hope that their content would give us clues as to the suicidal mind. Indeed, study of these notes has revealed a few such clues. For example, suicide notes can be found to include the motives for suicide first identified by Karl Menninger (1938): to die (escape), to kill (anger felt toward others), and to be killed (feelings of guilt and a desire to atone). But suicide notes are typically brief, and do not provide rich material for analysis.

Serendipitously, I was given a diary of a young woman who had killed herself. I have called her "Katie" in this book. The diary covered the last year of her life and was in five separate books. The diary was given to me by her younger sister, whom I have called "Laura" here, who had never read the diary. Laura thought that, as a suicide expert, I might find it interesting. I was astonished. I had in my hands a source of data on suicide that was extraordinarily rare. Compared to a suicide note of a paragraph or two, I had over two hundred single-spaced pages of introspection! I had the opportunity to look into the mind of a suicide in greater depth than ever before, and perhaps it would be possible to obtain insights into the suicidal mind that conventional research has failed to provide.

I thought of colleagues who could read this diary and comment on it from their differing perspectives, and I explained to Laura that I could produce a book based on this diary, a book that would serve as a memorial to Katie and would contribute to our understanding of suicide. Laura permitted me to embark on this project, the result of which is this book. The aim of the project was to explore what new insights into suicide an in-depth examination of the diary of a suicide could provide.

I have worked and collaborated with some of these colleagues before; others I chose because they had not written on suicide in the past, yet I thought that they would provide fresh insights into suicide. There were, of course, many others I could have approached to participate in this project, offering additional perspectives, but page limitations prevented me from inviting them. Each contributor read all five books of the diary, covering a one-year period.

Silvia Canetto has written extensively on suicide from a feminist perspective. In chapter 4, she writes a moving letter to Katie and, in the course of this, addresses the issues of suicide in women. Lori Stone and James Pennebaker put Katie's diary through a computer program that analyses texts for linguistic patterns. In chapter 5 they report the features identified and how these features changed as the date of Katie's suicide drew closer. Thomas Ellis in chapter 6 discusses Katie's thinking processes and how these contributed to her decision to commit suicide.

Antoon Leenaars has developed a coding system for the content of suicide notes, and in chapter 7 he applies his coding system to Katie's diary.

In chapter 8, I cast Katie's self-destructive behavior as a type common to young women, and I labeled this the "Ophelia Complex." Throughout her diary, Katie makes many references, even appeals, to God. In chapter 9, Robert Fournier discusses this aspect of Katie's diary, focusing on the spiritual issues that her writing addresses.

James Hollis, a former colleague of mine at the college where I teach, has trained as a Jungian analyst. In chapter 10, he looks at Katie's suicide from a Jungian perspective, a perspective which is not often used to analyze suicidal behavior, but which has the potential to offer new insights. In chapter 11, Lisa Firestone discusses how a psychotherapist might have helped Katie had she sought counseling, and Lisa provides a fascinating transcript of how a counseling session might have proceeded. Finally, in chapter 12, I discuss the issue of whether writing the diary helped or hindered Katie and examine the clinical implications of the insights presented by the contributors.

All of the identifying information in the diary has been changed—names and places. There is no mention of the year. The fifth and final volume of the diary is included in this book (as chapter 3). The remaining volumes are available to qualified professionals who have explicit research proposals and may be obtained by writing to me.

I should like to thank Laura for permitting me to read Katie's diary and for allowing me to proceed with this project. I wish I could thank Katie, too. Indeed, I wish that she had not killed herself but had been able to find the counseling that would have enabled her to face the stress of life. But I am glad that, in some small way, her life and death may help us understand suicide so that we may be better prepared to help others in the future.

David Lester
The Richard Stockton College of New Jersey
Pomona, NJ

☐ Reference

Menninger, K. (1938). *Man against himself.* New York: Harcourt, Brace & World.

David Lester

Introduction: The Study of Personal Documents

There is a long history of using written texts in general to illustrate and sometimes test psychological theories (Lester, 1987). For example, theories of suicide have been tested using the content of suicide notes (Leenaars, 1988a). Occasionally, suicides (for example, Sylvia Plath) leave a book or poem describing their behavior, and this kind of material may be of use in exploring the unconscious psychodynamics of the suicidal act. In other fields of psychology, folk tales of primitive societies have been studied, for example, for evidence of the societal needs for achievement and power (McClelland, Davis, Wanner, & Kalin 1966), and literary stimuli have been used in studies of people's preference for differing degrees of complexity (Kammann, 1966).

Let us first briefly review the ways in which literature has been used to throw light on the individual and society.

☐ Psychology and Literature[1]

Understanding Human Behavior in Historical Times

The psychological study of history has created a new discipline, called psychohistory. Psychohistory seeks to enlarge our understanding of historical events and persons by applying psychological theory and knowledge (Hoffer, 1979). Crosby (1979) defined the field as "the form of history which makes explicit use of the concepts, principles, and theories of psychology in order to enhance our understanding of particular people and events in the past" (p. 6).

This joining of psychology and history had long been advocated (Barnes, 1925, Smith, 1913) but developed in depth only in the 1970s. The major psychological theory applied to history has been psychoanalysis (for example, Erikson's study of Martin Luther [1962]), but other theories, such as cognitive theory and trait theory, have been utilized. Although psychohistorians can use a variety of materials in order to make inferences about the psychological state of historical individuals and cultures, occasionally literature has been used.

For example, Hoffer (1974) analyzed school textbooks in the first half of the nineteenth century to show how threats to national unity appeared to influence school textbook writers to minimize divisive and unruly episodes in earlier American history, a decision which Hoffer saw as consistent with Festinger's (1957) theory of cognitive dissonance.

McClelland (1958) illustrated the possibility of incorporating quantitative methods into psychohistory. For example, McClelland scored a variety of Greek writings for the need to achieve and found that this need declined steadily in Greece from 700 B.C. to 250 B.C., which fits with the historical events of that period. Hull, Allen, and Hoffer (1978) used the manuscripts left by loyalists and revolutionaries in Revolutionary New York to identify differences in a variety of traits, including need for order, submissiveness, and conformity, and they related this to the writers' political affiliation.

Psychological Analyses of Literature

Psychoanalytic theory (and other psychodynamic theories) have been applied in order to understand better the unconscious motivations of the fictional characters. For example, Faber (1970) used psychoanalysis to analyze the suicides in the Greek tragedies written by Sophocles and Euripides.

A frequent task in the psychological study of literature has been the tracing of a significance of a symbol or an idea through its many manifestations, perhaps identifying in the process a Jungian archetype. For example, McClelland (1963) started with the idea that not all people fear death. Indeed, some people, often women, actually seem to look forward to death, with a sense of excitement in addition to fear, as if death could be an unconscious equivalent for the final sexual union with the ideal mate (Bromberg & Schilder, 1933). McClelland's student, Greenberger (1965), found that dying women were more likely to give stories involving illicit sexuality to cards from the Thematic Apperception Test than women who were not dying. Women students in his classes rated "a gay seducer" as more appropriate as a description of death than did the men.[2] Stimulated by these findings, McClelland traced the development of the Harlequin theme in literature. In the typical Harlequin story, Harlequin pursues Columbine, his love, despite obstacles placed in his way by her father, guardian, or suitor, Pantaloon. In the dark scenes, Harlequin is definitely connected to underworld figures, and often Columbine dies at the end of the story.[3]

Psychological Studies of the Author and the Reader

Psychoanalysis (and other psychodynamic theories) have often been applied to fictional works in order to better understand the author. The first example of the use of psychoanalysis to this end was by Freud (Niederland, 1960), who applied his psychoanalytic theory to the novel *Die Richterin* by the Swiss writer Conrad Ferdinand Meyer (1825–1898). Freud sent an essay to his friend, Wilhelm Fliess, on June 20, 1898, in which he suggested that the novel was an unconscious defense against the writer's memory of an affair with his sister (Freud, 1954). In the novel, a mother murders her husband and rules in his place until her stepson returns and unmasks his stepmother as the murderer. The stepmother thereupon commits suicide, but, in the course of the novel, the avenging stepson has an affair with his half-sister. Niederland notes that Meyer's father died when Meyer was fifteen. Meyer's early efforts to write were thwarted by his mother but encouraged by his sister. After his mother's suicide, Meyer lived with his sister in a close and personal relationship, until he married in his late forties. She acted as his housekeeper, companion, secretary, and advisor.

There have been several studies of the psychological state of individual authors. Bellak (1963), for example, treated the short stories of Somerset Maugham as if they were stories written to stimuli such as those in the Thematic Apperception Test, scoring the stories to measure Maugham's psychological needs. For example, the *descriptive theme* in "Footprints in the Jungle" is that Bronson brings Cartwright home because he is temporarily in hard circumstances. Bronson's wife has an affair with Cartwright and persuades Cartwright to murder her husband. Though the police discover the crime, they do not have enough evidence to try the couple, who then live happily ever after. Bellak saw the *interpretive theme* here as that women can come between men and cause trouble and that sexual passion can motivate murder even in decent people, who may not even suffer remorse. At the *diagnostic level*, Bellak suggested that Somerset

Maugham viewed, perhaps unconsciously, women as sources of trouble for men, separating them and destroying them. There is also an Oedipal theme here in which a man has to kill another man in order to obtain a mate; and, finally, passion can overpower the superego, leading to lack of control over aggression.

In general, after an analysis of ten of Maugham's ninety-one short stories, Bellak suggested that Maugham had a continuous struggle with his sexual and aggressive impulses. To control them, Maugham sought emotional isolation and detachment, playing the role of an onlooker toward others. His resulting self-image is that of a mildly ineffective person pushed around by external forces. Maugham saw women as domineering and demanding, leading men to feel inadequate, a view which is perhaps a projection of his own strong unconscious aggressive drives. Maugham suffered from a conflict between activity and passivity, conformity and nonconformity, and male and female identification, leading to embarrassment and shame, a feeling of inadequacy and a fear of failure. Bellak noted that his conclusions from his thematic analysis of Maugham's short stories was consistent with biographies of Maugham's life.[4]

☐ Studying Suicide by Means of Literature

In addition to studying the suicides that occur in fiction, such as Faber's studies mentioned above of suicides in Greek tragedies, another approach to understanding suicide through literature is to study the writings of writers who killed themselves. Not all such suicides provide clues to suicide in their writings, but there are several suicidal writers whose fiction appears to be somewhat autobiographical and, therefore, provides us with some insights into their unconscious psychodynamics, which increases our understanding of them, authors such as Ernest Hemingway and Cesare Pavese. However, Sylvia Plath (1981, pp. 183–184) wrote a poem ("Daddy") four months prior to her suicide which provides a startling insight into the unconscious psychodynamics of her suicide.

In "Daddy" Plath casts herself as a Jew in a concentration camp versus her father as a Panzer man and as a devil who bit her heart in two. She says that she has always been scared of him, and she calls him a bastard. Yet she says that her suicide attempt at age twenty was an attempt to be reunited with him. She then made a model of her father and married him, but she calls this person a vampire who drank her blood for seven years. Indeed, her marriage to the British poet, Ted Hughes, lasted about seven years. At the end of her poem, she tells her father that he can lie back now, perhaps because, as she says a few lines earlier, she is finally through.

The Oedipal theme in the poem is clear. The motivation for her first suicide attempt was to be reunited with the father who died when she was eight (though the poem says ten). And, in case he is jealous of her marriage to Ted Hughes (why else is Daddy sitting up in his grave?), she is now finally through and, presumably, going to be reunited with Daddy this time (and so he can lie back down to await her).

In addition, though, there are other elements in the poem. The ambivalence toward her father is evident throughout the poem, but most exquisitely expressed in the final line where she writes, "Daddy, daddy, you bastard . . . ," a juxtaposition of affection (daddy) and anger (you bastard). Plath also says, "If I've killed one man, I've killed two." Who are these two? Daddy and her husband? Plath's father died of natural causes when she was eight, but perhaps Sylvia had wished for his death when she was angry at him and believes, magically, that her death wish for him contributed to his death, a common belief in children. Or perhaps she feels guilty over other behaviors? But then, how did she kill her husband? Perhaps psychologically as her stature as a poet grew to equal, and perhaps surpass, the stature of Ted Hughes?

There is an interesting feature to this poem in that Plath uses the word "black" six times, a frequency much higher than in her first book of poems (Lester, 1989b). According to Piotrowski's (1974) method for interpreting the Rorschach ink-blot test, the use of dark shading predicts a tendency to act out, rather than quieten down, when anxious or under stress.[5]

☐ The Use of Personal Documents (Rather Than Literature)

The study of personal documents in psychology also has a long history, but it received strong support from Gordon Allport, who urged such study in general (Allport, 1942) and who provided many illustrations. For example, Allport (1965) reprinted a series of letters from a woman, whom he named Jenny, to a friend in order to see whether they could "explain" Jenny.

> Why does an intelligent lady behave so persistently in a self-defeating manner? When and how might she have averted the tragedy of her life? . . . Was the root of her trouble some wholly unconscious mechanism? (Allport, 1965, p. viii)

In the book, Allport used the letters to provide psychodynamic, existential, learning, and trait descriptions of Jenny.

The use of personal documents in the study of suicide has played a prominent role because there are so few data available on suicides. Most suicides leave no clinical records, and when they do, perhaps as a result of being in psychotherapy or being hospitalized in a psychiatric facility, the records are not standardized. As a result, it is difficult to collect comparable data or psychological test scores from a sample of such suicides.

However, a good proportion of suicides, perhaps as many as 40 percent, do leave suicide notes. In the 1950s, Edwin Shneidman and Norman Farberow (1957) published their first study of a sample of suicide notes that they found in the files of the Los Angeles medical examiner's office. Since then, many studies have examined the content of suicide notes, most recently by Antoon Leenaars in a innovative attempt to test psychological theories of suicide using the content of suicide notes (Leenaars, 1988a).

The study of suicide notes presents several problems. First, suicide notes are typically brief. Many are simply sets of instructions or "last wills and testaments." Only a few may give some clues as to the precipitating stressors that led to the suicide and to the psychodynamics underlying the choice of this solution.

The second problem is the choice of written communications with which to compare the suicide notes. Unfortunately, Shneidman and Farberow in their seminal book chose to compare genuine suicide notes with "simulated" suicide notes written by men who were not suicidal. They published 33 pairs of these genuine and simulated suicide notes in their 1957 book, and more than two dozen papers have appeared since then comparing these genuine and simulated suicide notes.

Lester (1988) has argued that this comparison does not shed light on the mind of suicidal individuals but rather examines whether nonsuicidal individuals have any insight into the suicidal mind. Since many studies find differences between the genuine and the simulated suicide notes, the evidence is that nonsuicidal individuals do not have good insights into the suicidal mind. For example, a small proportion (15%) of the genuine suicide notes in Shneidman and Farberow's sample have anger in them directed toward a significant other, while none of the simulated suicide notes do so (Lester, 1989a). All this tells us is that nonsuicidal individuals do not realize that a small proportion of suicidal individuals are angry.

Instead, Lester suggested that simulated suicide notes are a good way to study the opinions and myths that people in the general population have about suicides and suicidal behavior. For example, he found that women more often addressed their simulated suicide note to someone than did the men, apologized and asked forgiveness, stated that they were unhappy, and said that others would be better off if they were dead. Thus, men and woman appear to have different conceptions about the motives for suicide.

What might make a better comparison group for genuine suicide notes? Ideally, we need letters and notes written by these suicides at an earlier time when they were not suicidal. Then we could see how their psychological state had changed from the nonsuicidal period to the suicidal period. Unfortunately, most individuals do not have collections of letters and notes written over the course of their lifetime. Furthermore, regrettable though it is, researchers are sometimes lazy. It is easy to collect a sample of simulated suicide notes. For example, Shneidman and Farberow went to labor unions and fraternal groups and asked groups of men to write simulated suicide notes. I have asked students in my courses on suicide to write such notes. A captive group of people can write simulated suicide notes in ten minutes. To collect letters from deceased suicides requires tracing the significant others of each suicide, visiting them, explaining the purpose of the research, and seeing if they will cooperate by searching out earlier letters, if any exist.

The better research using genuine suicide notes looks for differences among the genuine suicide notes. For example, Jacobs (1967) classified genuine notes into different types, Leenaars looked for differences between the suicide notes of men and women (Leenaars, 1988b) and between those of different ages (Leenaars, 1989), while Brevard and Lester (1991) compared suicide notes from completed suicides (who died as a result of their suicidal action) and attempted suicides (who survived). Other studies have compared suicides notes from different nations (e.g., Lester, 1997) and the method used for the suicidal act (e.g., Leenaars, 1990).

The Use of Diaries

Diaries may provide an excellent way of delving into the psychodynamics of people's lives. Culley (1985) thought that a diary gives shape and meaning to the writer's life, and so a reading of the diary should give us insights into this meaning. Kagle (1979) argued that diaries would be affected by tensions and disequilibria in the life of the writer that need to be resolved. Such diaries may prove to be more of a "royal road to the unconscious" than are dreams.

An example of the use of diaries in the exploration of psychodynamics is Brumberg (1997), who studied diaries from young girls to show how a focus on the development of internal character in the late 1800s changed to a focus on the shape and appearance of their bodies in the late 1900s.

Some suicides leave diaries. The most accessible diaries of this kind are those written by famous writers who have committed suicide. The diaries of Sylvia Plath have been published (Plath, 2000) although, unfortunately, her husband, Ted Hughes, destroyed one diary and lost another which, together, covered the last three years of her life. The diaries of Cesare Pavese have also appeared in print (Pavese, 1961).[6] Occasionally, diaries of others, less famous, have appeared in print, such as those of Arthur Inman (1985).[7]

But what of the diaries of ordinary individuals, more representative of the typical suicide, but not sufficiently famous as to warrant publication? I know of only one study. Peck (1988–1989) reported on a diary left by a 48-year-old woman who killed herself. He presented extracts from the last week of the diary to try to illustrate that her suicide was rational, that is, that she had the ability to reason, a realistic worldview and adequate information, and that she was avoiding harm and achieving goals. Peck is not convincing in arguing that these criteria are met, but the extracts from the diary he provides do mention the stressors that the woman was experiencing, her low self-esteem, her perception of herself as ineffectual and inadequate, and the pain, both physical and psychological, that she was experiencing as a result of her situation.[8]

☐ Katie

The present volume is based on the examination of a 200-page diary kept by a young woman for the year preceding her suicide. This diary is rich in psychodynamic-relevant material and stops just one week before her suicide. We thus have the opportunity, not only to study the psychology of a suicidal individual, but also to see whether changes occur in the content of the diary (and the corresponding psychodynamics) as her eventual suicide draws near.

In the next section, I will briefly review what is known of Katie's early life and then include the fifth and final book of her diary. Katie's diary covers five books and, when typed for the commentators to read, some 200 single-spaced typed pages. The fifth book covers the period of May 30th to June 20th and stops nine days before Katie's body was discovered. Katie wrote nothing in her diary during the final few days of her life, and so we do not know what her state of mind was during that time.

Because one clinician might be limited in what she or he perceives in this material, I have invited several colleagues with different backgrounds to read and comment on the diary. Some commentators explore the content of the diary and how the content changes over time; other commentators examine aspects of Katie's personality—her desires, emotions, and thoughts; and finally some ideas are proposed for how a psychotherapist might have helped Katie choose life over death.

☐ Notes

1. This section is based on Lester (1987, 1996).
2. It should be noted that subsequent research has not always confirmed these empirical findings (Lester, 1966; Lester & Schumacher, 1969).
3. For a recent review of content analyses of written archival data, see Lee and Peterson (1997).
4. Of course, Bellak's knowledge of Maugham's life may have affected the conclusions he drew from his thematic analysis of Maugham's short stories!
5. Lester (1991) noted a similar tendency in the poems of Anne Sexton, who also committed suicide.
6. Some comments on Pavese based on his diary have been made by Shneidman (1979, 1982).
7. Some reflections on Inman's diary have been made by Shneidman (1994) and Leenaars and Maltsberger (1994).
8. A stroke had left her partially paralyzed, and a traffic accident had resulted in leg and facial injuries. She suffered from severe headaches after these events. She was also in love with a man with whom she was living who did not love her in return.

☐ References

Allport, G. (1942). *The use of personal documents in psychological science*. New York: Social Science Research Council.

Allport, G. W. (1965). *Letters from Jenny*. New York: Harcourt, Brace & World.

Barnes, H. E. (1925). *Psychology and history*. New York: Century.

Bellak, L. (1963). Somerset Maugham. In R. W. White (Ed.), *The study of lives*, pp. 142–159. New York: Atherton.

Brevard, A., & Lester, D. (1991). A comparison of suicide notes written by completed and attempted suicides. *Annals of Clinical Psychiatry*, 3, 43–45.

Bromberg, W., & Schilder, P. (1933). Death and dying. *Psychoanalytic Review*, 20, 133–185.

Brumberg, J. J. (1997). *The body project*. New York: Random House.

Crosby, F. (1979). Evaluating psychohistorical explanations. *Psychohistory Review*, 7(3), 6–16.

Culley, M. (1985). *A day at a time*. New York: Feminist Press at CUNY.

Erikson, E. (1962). *Young man Luther*. New York: Norton.

Faber, M. (1970). *Suicide and Greek tragedy*. New York: Sphinx Press.

Festinger, L. (1957). *The theory of cognitive dissonance*. Palo Alto, CA: Stanford University Press.

Freud, S. (1954). *The origins of psychoanalysis: Letters to Wilhelm Fliess, drafts and notes, 1887–1902*. Ed. by M. Bonaparte, A. Freud, & E. Kris. New York: Basic Books.

Greenberger, E. (1965). Fantasies of women confronting death. *Journal of Consulting Psychology*, 29, 252–260.

Hoffer, P. C. (1974, April). A case study of the reduction of cognitive dissonance. Paper read at the Ohio Academy of History.

Hull, N. E. H., Allen, S. L., & Hoffer, P. C. (1978). Choosing sides. *Journal of American History*, 65, 344–366.

Inman, A. C. (1985). *The Inman diary*. Ed. by D. Aaron. Cambridge, MA: Harvard University Press.

Jacobs, J. (1967). A phenomenological study of suicide notes. *Social Problems*, 15, 60–72.

Kagle, S. E. (1979). *American diary literature, 1620–1799*. Boston: Twayne.

Kammann, R. (1966). Verbal complexity and preferences in poetry. *Journal of Verbal Learning and Verbal Behavior*, 5, 536–540.

Lee, F., & Peterson, C. (1997). Content analysis of archival data. *Journal of Consulting and Clinical Psychology*, 65, 959–969.

Leenaars, A. A. (1988a). *Suicide notes*. New York: Human Sciences Press.

Leenaars, A. A. (1988b). Are women's suicide notes really different from men's? *Women and Health*, 14(1), 17–33.

Leenaars, A. A. (1989). Are young adults' suicides psychologically different from those of other adults? *Suicide and Life-Threatening Behavior*, 19, 249–263.

Leenaars, A. A. (1990). Do the psychological characteristics of the suicidal individual make a difference in the method chosen for suicide? *Canadian Journal of Behavioural Science*, 22, 385–392.

Leenaars, A. A., & Maltsberger, J. T. (1994). The Inman diary. In A. A. Leenaars, J. T. Maltsberger, & R. A. Neimeyer (Eds.), *Treatment of suicidal people*, pp. 227-236. Washington, DC: Taylor & Francis.

Lester, D. (1966). Checking on the Harlequin. *Psychological Reports*, 19, 984.

Lester, D. (1987). Psychology and literature. *Psychology*, 24(1/2), 25–27.

Lester, D. (1988). What does the study of simulated suicide notes tell us? *Psychological Reports*, 62, 962.

Lester, D. (1989a). Menninger's motives for suicide in genuine and simulated suicide notes. *Perceptual and Motor Skills*, 69, 850.

Lester, D. (1989b). Application of Piotrowski's dark shading hypothesis to Sylvia Plath's poems written before her suicide. *Perceptual and Motor Skills*, 68, 122.

Lester, D. (1991). Dark-shading in the poems of Anne Sexton. *Perceptual and Motor Skills*, 73, 366.

Lester, D. (1996). The unconscious and suicide in literature. In A. A. Leenaars & D. Lester (Eds.), *Suicide and the unconscious*, pp. 93–106. Northvale, NJ: Jason Aronson.

Lester, D. (1997). Menninger's motives for suicide in suicide notes from America and Germany. *Perceptual and Motor Skills*, 85, 1194.

Lester, D., & Schumacher, J. (1969). Schizophrenia and death concern. *Journal of Projective Techniques and Personality Assessment*, 33, 403–405.

McClelland, D. (1958). The use of measures of human motivation in the study of society. In J. W. Atkinson (Ed.), *Motives in fantasy, action, and society*, pp. 518–552. Princeton: Princeton University Press.

McClelland, D. (1963). The Harlequin complex. In R. W. White (Ed.), *The study of lives*, pp. 94–119. New York: Atherton.

McClelland, D., Davis, W., Wanner, E., & Kalin, R. (1966). A cross-cultural study of folk tale content and drinking. *Sociometry*, 29, 309–337.

Niederland, W. G. (1960). The first application of psychoanalysis to a literary work. *Psychoanalytic Quarterly*, 29, 228–235.

Pavese, C. (1961). *The burning brand*. New York: Walker & Co.

Peck, D. L. (1988–1989). Evaluation of a suicide diary. *Omega*, 19, 293–309.

Piotrowski, Z. A. (1974). *Perceptanalysis*. Philadelphia: privately published.

Plath, S. (1981). *The collected poems*. New York: Harper & Row.

Plath, S. (2000). *The unabridged journals of Sylvia Plath*. Ed. by K. V. Kukil. New York: Anchor Books.

Shneidman, E. S. (1979). Risk writing. *Journal of the American Academy of Psychoanalysis*, 7, 575–592.

Shneidman, E. S. (1982). The suicidal logic of Cesare Pavese. *Journal of the American Academy of Psychoanalysis*, 10, 547–563.

Shneidman, E. S. (1994). The Inman diary. In A. A. Leenaars, J. T. Maltsberger, & R. A. Neimeyer (Eds.), *Treatment of suicidal people*, pp. 3–15. Washington, DC: Taylor & Francis.

Shneidman, E. S., & Farberow, N. L. (1957). *Clues to suicide*. New York: McGraw-Hill.

Smith, P. (1913). Luther's early development in the light of psychoanalysis. *American Journal of Psychology*, 24, 360–377.

PART

Katie

CHAPTER David Lester

Who Is Katie?

Katie's parents had emigrated from Europe to the United States. Her father was German and her mother Hungarian. The father, a carpenter, was a domineering husband, preventing his wife from learning English and from driving a car, for example. He was an alcoholic and abusive to his wife and children. Katie was the first-born child, followed just over a year later by a sister, Laura.

Katie's father sexually abused her. In her diaries, Katie refers to this abuse but does not give explicit details. It is possible that she does not remember the incidents clearly, but she may also be reluctant to describe the incidents in detail in her diaries. It seems reasonable to conclude that the sexual abuse involved genital or oral sexual acts. I do not know whether Laura, Katie's younger sister, was also sexually abused by her father.

Katie's mother threw her husband out of the house when Katie was nine years old. He sometimes returned to the house while the mother was out working (at a factory), and his daughters would have to call the police to have him removed. Two years later, when the mother was filing for a divorce, he died, possibly of a heart attack. Soon thereafter, the mother became schizophrenic. The state authorities decided that she was not competent to raise her two daughters, and they were then placed in foster homes.

Katie's mother received inpatient care and was released, but after living in the community for eight years in squalid conditions,[1] she was institutionalized in a state psychiatric hospital with her younger daughter named as her legal guardian.

The two daughters were placed in several foster homes during the next few years, only occasionally placed together. They went to different colleges in the state, Katie two years ahead of Laura. They kept in touch and were quite close. Laura felt that Katie was somewhat immature, and she became protective of Katie as the years passed.

Katie developed an eating disorder at the time that she was taken away from her mother and placed in foster homes. Her anorexia was severe enough that she was hospitalized on several occasions, often around Christmastime. She was also frequently depressed. There is no indication that Katie had attempted suicide in the past. The daughters had been raised as Catholics, but Katie developed eccentric religious ideas to the extent that Laura worried that Katie suffered from hallucinations.

Katie blamed her mother for all of the trauma that she had experienced, and she saw her mother as having been purposely vindictive to her children. She preferred to tell others that her mother was dead. Laura, on the other hand, loves her mother and does not hold her responsible for the trauma she suffered at the hands of her father.

From the diary, we learn that Katie has a boyfriend whom she loves, Mark. Their relationship is troubled. Mark seems to have had sexual intercourse with an ex-girlfriend while he was seeing Katie, and this causes anguish for Katie and friction between her and Mark. Katie has trouble getting good grades in her college courses, and she sometimes withdraws from courses before the semester ends. She has financial problems paying for her college education and in getting a job to help with the finances.

For the period covered by the diaries, Katie is overweight, and she is discouraged about this, continually trying to lose weight, but without success. She refers to attending group meetings for those who are overweight and for those who were victims of incest. She also mentions drinking and using recreational drugs, including marijuana.

On June 29, Katie's boyfriend Mark went to her college dormitory room (a single-story dormitory for disabled students[2]), but Katie did not respond. The light was on in the room, and Mark could see under the door that Katie was lying there. Mark went outside and broke the window so that he could enter the room, and he found that Katie had hung herself using a cloth belt hooked around the metal door-closing mechanism.

Others in the dormitory called campus security who in turn called the local police department. There was no disorder in the room, except for the broken window, and there were no signs of foul play. No suicide note was found.

Mark reported that he had last seen Katie on June 16 and that she had recently been depressed. No one in the dormitory had seen Katie for the last few days. However, an employee of the bookstore had seen Katie on the day before her body was found.

The autopsy report indicated that Katie was 20 years old and 65 inches tall and weighed 143 pounds.[3] There were no signs of any illness, disease, or trauma apart from the hanging. Toxicological analyses revealed no alcohol or drugs. The medical examiner did not report examining Katie's reproductive system, and so it may be assumed that she was not pregnant.

Five volumes of a diary were found, together with a book of poems and a scrapbook of magazine clippings. Laura took possession of these, but has never read them. As mentioned in the preface, Laura entrusted the volumes to me.

The fifth and final volume of Katie's diary is reproduced in the next chapter. It is the briefest of the five books, but it provides an example of the material that the contributors to this book used in order to write their commentaries.[4]

Notes

1. She failed to pay her real estate taxes and utility bills, so that she lived without heat and water, and she was unable to hold a job.

2. Katie had moved to this dormitory after having disagreements with her roommate.

3. Katie's weight was within the range for a woman of her height with a large frame. It was outside the range for women with small or medium frames.

4. Chapter 5 of the present book provides a count of the number of entries in each book of the diary and the average number of words in each entry.

The Diary: The Last Month

5 Weeks
Book of Reflection and Self-Healing Action and Growth

May 30: 2:00 a.m.
I've decided to take this journal back and throw out the Victorian one the W's gave me. I hated the way it was starting to sound—absolutely awful. Now I have a new one so I can start all over. I'm scared—really scared. The past week I've stayed at Mark's grandparents' home—it's truly beautiful here. However, it's been a horribly turbulent week (between Mark and me). I hate improper English. I just want to take a vacation for myself— make the next 5–6 weeks a very very spa experience. I decided to drop my summer bio class anyway, but I've decided not to tell a soul, till probably mid-through, and just concentrate on losing weight. I've never quite had an opportunity like this. I intend to shed so much weight that it is absolutely shocking by the end of the summer. I really don't have much else for any sense of security. I can't stand myself and my life anymore. The very things I believe in are starting to disappear. I'm really hurting, but I can't talk about it because there is nothing left to talk about. I've made amends with my dad and mom and [sister]—for the most part my parents. What I really hate is my body and I've decided to change it. I think not seeing Mark for about 2–3

weeks is a must, but I'll see when I get there. I am so sick of everything concerning my body. If I get rid of all this disgusting excess weight, it won't bother me or any relationship in my life ever again.

I've just freaked out because I don't have any control whatsoever in my life at all. It's absolutely terrifying. I have to just say for the record that I'm not going to try to kill myself by doing this—only perhaps the old Katie, so a new isolated individual one could rise up and emerge. I'm not doing it to get even with Mark or anybody else, but only to free myself. I am more intrinsically in tune with fasting than any other thing. I want all this to melt away—all of it. I will not end up in the hospital again. Maybe I will be listened to now—taken more seriously. Maybe now I will express my ruthless hatred for Joyce—stupid, valueless back-stabbing bitch. I refuse to ever see her face again. If I ever have to walk to Kelly again I will. I refuse to go to Myers again. It really fucking sickens me. She's been worse than Sara ever has been. I guess I'd better make a shopping list for tomorrow. Who knows if I'll be single or not. All I know I can't afford to let anyone close to me again to hurt me. My sincere love for my friends brings the most pain once it's been taunted. I have to tell Joyce off for my own self. Her own selfishness has somewhat made me think and act that what I have is not real with Mark—that he doesn't love me. Her actions and words have explained such. Now it's time to clean house to survive. Bitch. No, I've decided she's never meant that much to me, except being the embodiment of a valueless cheap slut. These words fit her perfectly and I won't lower myself by having a friendship with such an animal. And Mark, sweet Mark, well, if we will last or will not, whatever will happen? The point is I do trust him with other people this summer. I don't think I have anything to fret if we decide to stay together. But in the meantime, I'm going to call up Joyce and tell her what a complete asshole she is and that I think it's best we don't see each other anymore. I will not let Mama W lose me if she doesn't want to because I love her so dearly. But Joyce is just going to get it when she least expects it. She's so ruthless and cruel. She's got nothing on top of me, to destroy me with. I hate her so much that she's going to just get it.

4:34 p.m.

Mark liked the dinosaur I made him. Grandma W got me a Siamese fighting fish. I've decided to name him Rex. Mark and I are going out. He told his grandma the truth about my mom. Rex seems to be coming to life. I have a lot to write about, especially within the last week. I'm giving myself a vacation. I feel good instead of guilty about doing it. I need a break for this summer. I wonder what I got on my report card. If I got all B's I will Thank you God forever for putting me back on top where I belong. I think I'll take a little snooze.

9:05 p.m.

I need some real and good friends, really bad. I love Mark. He is my best friend in the whole world. I've worn him out, and it hurts me so badly, so I have to make a huge change. I want to get up at 6 AM and exercise. Then ask Patti if I can use the phone. Then let's see, make a copy for the Walchs of these herbs and write a letter to Mrs. Walch and then get my mail and check on my check and then take a hike to the store to get flavored seltzer water and laundry, money and stamps and Band-aids. This should average to about 3 hours of aerobics. I need to eat every four hours, but I can't, not tomorrow. Depends, it all depends. I said such wicked things to my dear Mark. A lot had to do with the fact that I think I'm pregnant. Well, I pray to God that I'm not pregnant. Please God have mercy. I'm really worried. I'm making an exercise tape for myself. I need to have courage to face myself and take some action. I'm going to make so huge changes to make my body drastically different. It looks like my mother's body with her life. But I'm me with my own body, life, and identity. I need to uncover it and discover it. I need to make myself free—free—that is what I want to be. I want to make all the people I've hurt free of my tormented parts, Just like Mrs. W said, I have to isolate myself from my past. I have to say goodbye for good—to Michael and the past pains and let the good feelings thrive in my soul.

I'm going to ask for two weeks to be alone away from Mark, not hurt him with myself but to let him go. I've almost suffocated him and us, but what was I trying to hold on to—hm? I guess him and his love. I was so afraid to lose him. I felt I was losing my life again and what I wanted with him in my dreams I wouldn't have. I was so outraged. Why, God? Why does he have to have pain too? It's not fair. What's going to become of this—of us? I want this to be forever, I truly do, but none and nothing lasts forever. But I can make it last forever by living it and letting it free.

Please God, forgive me of all the cruel things I've said and done concerning him. Please give me the strength to do what is right. Especially with my anger. I'll wait about three days or so before I speak with him. I need to discover things outside my small isolated world. Nature is healing; this is my parental heritage; the laws and realities of life I learned here, and there is where I must go as much as possible. This too shall pass, as Mr. Walch has said. I need to breathe, cry, feel, let go, scream, laugh, and etc.

Wow, 85° tomorrow. I'll do my stuff tomorrow, definitely exercise in the morning. I could go to the store about 3 or so. I sure love this flavored seltzer. Anyway, I feel anxious and anxiety-stricken. I'm not sure if they are the same thing. I'm not going to hurt Mark at all with my weight. The lowest I'll go is 115 lbs. I just need to. I can't explain it, except I have to. If I'm 5 lbs. underweight, that is not such a bad thing—but 10 lbs. is definitely security. I'd like to clean my room. I look forward to walking around outside, free of chemicals and makeup. I need to fit in somewhat, so I need to get skinny and it will make me very happy. Mark makes me happy, but I need to do something for myself.

6/1

I feel so torn up inside over Joyce and Mark. I wrote Joyce a letter something like this

> You have had no great respect for my affection, vulnerabilities, and self. You have hurt me very deeply. This will affect my relationship with your mom. I know I haven't done anything wrong. I was more vulnerable and passive with you because of my attachment to your mother—told her to only call me tonight and no[t] to change my mind because it's not going to happen. Blah, blah, blah!

I feel like I've lost everything inside. I'm so afraid Mark will write me a goodbye letter too. God, it kills me that I hurt him last week, and he hurt me too very much by the way he treated me and spoke to me. It was sincerely the worst week. It hurts me still today that I hurt him. He means so much to me, the most out of everyone. I love him so dearly. But I'm so afraid that I'm suffocating him. I'm so afraid that Joyce will use the things she knows against me—to hurt me at all.

I feel like I am stuck in a very bad pattern. It frightens me very much. I'm scared that Mark is right about my dependence. And I'm afraid I've realized he is right this week. I don't know how I could have grown so dependent on him. Probably because of my love for him. It is so hard to fall in love with him, make myself vulnerable, and make him responsible for my heart. It all just happened, without any thought. My emotions last week frightened me so much. It was pure rage, out of my control, absolutely awful. God, I still wished I stayed here. I wish I listened to my instincts more—their voice seemed to have been muffled quite much.

God, I'm so hungry. I have to go down to 130 lbs. by the end of the summer. It's actually quite reasonable. I'm so afraid that I've made myself lose everything. I could not bear to lose Mark, not now, not after everything I've given up and fought for. But he never asked for me to give up my dreams and self, and I must remember that foremost.

God, I feel like such a burden to everyone. It's awful. I feel a <u>bit</u>, just a bit more serene today than yesterday since this knocking out of Joyce and probably the W's. I will talk to Mama W later. She can't fix this, and I don't want her to, but I want to be able to see her still. I can't though. I know her children come first. I know this will be a lot less hassle, money and rides. It's ok. I understand very much about their situation. I still can't believe I'm taking a taxi. I have to get a normal job this summer. I hope I did well in school. I've been so restless the last few days. I've had such thoughts of starving myself.

I wish I could just melt away right now, but I have demands that I need strength for. It will all work out. Besides, I don't need to starve myself to lose weight at all. It's 9:30. Where is my taxi? I think I need about 3–4 weeks away from Mark. It's so much better that way. He needs time, and I need time to get my summer settled. I wish the taxi would get here.

6/2: 12:35 AM
I bought Mark 3 cards today. They were so beautiful. However, I miss Joyce already. It's all so awful. But I had to do it. I feel like I abandoned her. But I really don't have it in me to take on another family's problems. I love everyone from a distance—of course, except my sweet Mark.

I transferred so much of the attitude Joyce gave me towards Mark. I can't do that anymore. I need to be clear and focused. I will scream before I hurt his sweet heart again the way I have.

It hurts that I let go of Joyce, but I had to. She hurt me so badly. It's been so awful. Now I pray that I can remain safe— with Mark—and I pray that she will be no threat to my love and life with him. I really want to lose so much weight. I want to be 130 lbs. That's all, and I'll take it from where I am—145. I pray to God I get my period soon.

I want to work out with weights tomorrow, calisthenics and jog to the post office. Oh, I still have to write out a letter explaining my financial situation. Dear God, give me strength. I need to let myself cry and sleep. I'll treat myself to a bagel after I go swimming. I'm so tired, but I must remember to tell Sylvia to bring the book back on Tuesday night. Sleep calls me.

6/2: 11:16 PM
I'm going absolutely crazy. I've calmed down since I've spoken with Mark. I hate all the anxiety I feel. It is all absolutely awful. The turmoil, at times like this, seems absolutely endless. I haven't heard from Shirley all day. I really wanted to get out, but it worked out better this way. I got my period today, and I made it to the Post Office. I feel like I almost fainted the entire time there and back. I lost focus once or twice. I was a bit worried if I'd ever get back home. I've been thinking about old things again—Sara, Claudia—company stuff. I want my body to become so strong, not weak at all. I really want a strong body. I could care less about waifishness, but muscles make the human body (meaning women) absolutely beautiful.

Mark's so cute. He thinks I look like Betty Boop. I want to put my focus on building him up inside. I really want to. I know I'm very good with people this way. He certainly does deserve it more than anyone else I know. It does scare me so because I'm so afraid he will take advantage of it and hurt me like so many other people have.

I have a hard time placing Mark in my mind as a friend. I have a block to it—I don't know why. It might be because we have fought, because he is a boy, because we are having sex—I don't know. It feels as if I don't have a grip on things—how to relate, connect—because I feel it's too late, or because it will hurt more if he leaves. But all these fears are probably the cause of a wall, mentally and emotionally, sometimes between us. I have to force myself to be open and nice again with him, especially above all else.

I really hate all these Latin guys here. They are so stupid. They expect me to be all flirtatious or something with them, or friendly, but I don't want to be—never did—and enjoy snubbing them. I want to be left alone by dorks at the Frat—stupid idiots. Absolutely so stupid indeed.

I always had the answer for everything. What happened to me? I used to have a boldness and a strong character and have an edge on everything in my faith, and now that has all seemed diminished, that is, my faith. I don't know what to believe in, and everything seems and feels so alien to me. Maybe I've cut too many things off. I truly do not know. I may have once again lost my identity in something. It might be dieting, Mark, wanting to meet up to the image in my head of myself. I've been looking too far back into the past. It's very angering despite the positive concepts I believed in. I seem to have had a good wholesome sense of myself despite everything else around me. I know it's still in me. I hate the desperate ways I've actually acted because of its misplacement. It's all so awful. Mark said I act so self-absorbed. Maybe in some ways I have, especially with my body and looks. I think Julia is very, very attractive. However, these desperate things I've done that I've never believed in, these "worldly" things I use[d] to be above, I've done them, and in some respects I feel so very stained—maybe more real, I guess. I used to always feel angelic, used to behave and make myself look so angelic, as a person of higher spiritual and living example to the world. I lived as a teacher, as an example of something right. It always used to make me feel so good. It was a way to extend nurturing to the world. But now people are different, and I have changed too. I've become negative. There does not seem to be a route back to optimism at all. It seems all so unrealistic. I'm afraid.

But there has to be something out there that is right and able to be believed in. It actually feels nice to write. I should note my attempt to be meticulously good to Mark again. When I started dating him, I felt this way certainly. However, when he hurt me with Claudia, I forced myself to direct anger at him, even though it felt so alien at first. Well, I feel awful, but he came at a point in my life when I got in touch with my anger, and he was exposed to rage that had absolutely nothing to do with him. That was wrong, and I was always right before I took all these stupid degrading risks—they were all so awful, except dating Mark— and separating myself from religion. I learned no real big revelation from them at all. People used to tell me I was always wrong (foster parents). They were all so abusive to me. I kept fighting back spiritually, but my heart crumbled, and slowly it's been going up. I have to believe that my spirit and inner person is growing back rapidly. I need to focus and do things to nurture this growth process. The world has most definitely gotten to me to the core—raw one. I know I was naive in ways before, that I am more wise now. That is very important to see right now. However, I've seen and learned everything, and the hope for today is that I have the ability to change in my behavior and self and life the things I don't like. That is the hope I believe in, that I do have control over my fate now as a fully grown adult versus my circumstance as a child and nothing is hopeless, absolutely nothing. Many things, bad and good, have been bridges toward individual freedom and goodness, or rather a place that is much nicer to live in. I refuse to speak badly of another, but promise to be honest in my perceptions of them (objective). I promise to do what is right, speak my mind, surpass all insecurities and try strengthening the friendships I have and myself.

Objective realistic thinking is not bad at all, and reaching for better things is not bad at all, and doing what I feel is right in the face of life's circumstances with intuition makes someone truly beautiful and strong. But I must put this thought down that has been picking on me for the past few hours. See, I'm afraid, even though I won't try to stop him, that when Mark hangs out with these girls from high school or his high school friends (coed) that he may find that being with me makes him very sad, not happy, and that he is closer to them than myself. And how much easier things are with them (girls) and might be with one of them because of their favorable backgrounds. I see in my actions, I make things more difficult than they have to be. I've cut down, but I know I could cut it down cold turkey. It's really not that hard. "Nothing in life is that hard." That carefree statement makes me feel better in times of my life where I care to make great improvement and changes. I need to make pebbles of boulders, and thinking this way helps do just that. However, how helpful it seems to me, I seldom use it at all. Will I need to break things down where they are quite manageable to me?

weight	*exercising a lot and eat (low fat) less and healthy*
looks	*work for clothes to look better in; take good care of myself emotionally and physically*
future	*do work meticulously in school (do well)*
Mark	*be open, understanding and freeing; and work to promote changes in myself that make me better and stronger where I want to go; and be open and focused on making a connection and making him feel better—I can't do all of it, but I could do some of it since I'm so close to him.*

I realized today that many people, including myself, always want to do things differently, or make a change. They might say something that is supposed to change them or thought alone. However, the point is that no one makes a plan that makes things more attainable at all, and that is what I'm trying to do. Now I have a grasp in my feeling about myself, and my life is going up.

self-image   *think openly, right and strong; do things for myself
that are good; make a good nurturing relationship for
myself and share one with loved ones; work on my
body and skin and hair and grades; and help
myself socially (make and find good friends); and
keep the relationship full of energy on my end.*

Goodnight

12:15 AM

anger   *process it in a journal; take smart actions to deal
with it; separate past and present anger; deal with
everything appropriately as possible*

*Be happy, laugh and be free, Katie. I give you permission; be a
distinct individual; don't mesh and just live; and do what you
can to do what is right and smart.*
        Love
        Katie

6/7

*I made it to Mark—taxi cost $45—originally $66. Yuck. He finally
got a job.*
        *Saw Claudia yesterday. She was riding her bike. She
perked up when she saw Mark and wore red and tried to look
respectable. I've lost myself in Mark. God. I am separating
myself. I thought that is what he wanted and needed because he
was so depressed. I really put myself out for him. I couldn't help
but get defensive. I worked out today—good. Only ate tuna
fish—yeah! I will get so much thinner than her automatically. My
fish survived the weekend. He looks so lonely though. Need to
get him a friend.*
        *One thing with Claudia. She does take good care of herself.
God, please let me get in the 80th percentile. Please. I did try.*
        *I don't want to write any more about Mark and Claudia. It
sickens me. He is so selfish. He needs her as a security blanket.
Duh! I'll disappear one day right out of his life when he least
expects it. Then he can do whatever he really wants to do.*

Things seem so old with him in some ways. I really hate that part.

I bet she is toning up for John's party. Oh well. I hate everyone, especially them two. I'm so sick of all this shit. All of it. I wanted so much for him to be sincere from the beginning, but he was not at all. Maybe he will always love her. Well, I need to separate to save my own life. I'm so mad at them. They are still playing games with each other. I hate them both so much. I feel like really dissing him—them both—whatever. I just want to get away from them both—separate myself from him, through not calling him. I don't know what is going on inside of me right now. I feel somewhat lost. It is the most awful feeling in the whole world. I know I was obsessing concerning what I wrote before. I feel the world is so intangible, especially love and security for me. So I've found security in eating, especially lately. All this anxiety over everything is genuinely awful. I gave up everything for Mark. I forced myself to be close to him despite all the pain and trust he killed in me. I hate it all. I never really felt safe with him after that. I acted like it was all my fault or something. I don't really know if he deserves forgiveness for any of this at all. It comes in waves, this emotion. I'm so angry all over again. I hate all of this. I'm tired and dry inside. I've given everything I can. I don't have any more to give, and I refuse to be selfless at all. So sick of all of this. Shit! I never asked for any of it—never deserved it either.

I'll make $500 in three weeks

Clothes

Sale

Got a 3.6 last semester—not one C—and I got my refund cashed

I need to tell Mark I can't make it this weekend at all.

6/9

I got a job. I start Monday. I've decided just to throw myself into my studies, work and dieting for the next three weeks. We do need a break. Maybe then everything will be fresh again. Let's make it 3 1/2 weeks. I've made myself too accessible, and I don't think that is a very good thing. I want to throw myself into my stuff for once. I can't do everything for him at all. Anyway, I made myself a model scrapbook that I will take with me everywhere. I think having this break is very important to our relationship. He needs to do whatever he will do if I'm not there. I really want this separation for the next 3 1/2 weeks. I need a change, time to grow and do my own stuff and conquer some fears of my own. I intend to make this book my best friend and only confidante. I never did let Mark miss me at all. Well, I think now is a good time as any. I need to tell him that I can't make it this weekend at all, and that my class and work and study schedule is so hard—to just make plans to see me at break. It is better for us this way. I think I've been suffocating him as I feel with myself.

I'm starting to feel strong finally—independent—and I want to see that I can stay away from him for 3 1/2 weeks. I also want to spend time on healing myself, healing my connection with God and changing my life for the better. I do believe in God. I got some incredible strength from God last semester and all year. I don't want to spend my life to try to discover where He comes from or where He is. All I know is that what I can perceive of Him, and the touch of Him is real, and that is what I know. I will still try to discover and make sense of things since that is my nature. But I will focus on what I know to be real for extra help and support.

I need to pray now and cry.

I don't want to burden anyone at all anymore.

I'm so scared of losing everything and everyone I love.

I feel too tangled up in everyone else and my past. I need to pray to words that do not touch this page so they can be set free.

6/9

Mama W cashed my check for me, and she is supposed to call me at 4:00 PM, but still nothing happened.

I read an article on jealousy. It makes sense why I feel the way I do and why I am so oversensitive because of my background. However, the little fling didn't help. I don't understand why he expects all of this to be so damn easy. But I intend to live in reality here from now on.

What the FUCK! I always DO!

I want a very clean and fresh look this Summer and Fall. I like light and airy things mixed with drama and natural. I feel most comfortable with that. I need the next three weeks to myself—I really do. I like the pale makeup colors and the natural colors the best. God, I love all these fashions with hair and clothes. But oh, how I would love to fit in them all. But I won't let myself get so overwhelmed. I've done good so far. I did manage to lose fourteen pounds already. I would like to make it to an even 130 lbs. That would be the best. I would not be too uncurvy at all. Well, all I can do is obsess now. I'm so behind in everything.

There is no way I can just give this book to Sylvia. I really need to separate myself from Mark and get my own life going which very respectively I did last semester. I made Honors, I guess—whatever the school may call it. I would like to maintain this level of productivity. Why haven't they called me yet? I'd better call Sylvia. I'll do what I can now that I've unwound.

6/11
God! Mark's parents are such jerks. I hope he can come up tomorrow. But if not, it gives me more time to lose weight. I'm so excited. I'm already on my fifth day. It feels really great. God, where is Sylvia? It looks beautiful outside. I want to walk around casually. I want to shower so badly. Where the Hell are they?

breakfast	slim fast	120
	- - -	200
	milk	110
	2 wheat	180
	1 can tuna	210
	2 prunes	46
	1 cup AS	<u>100</u>
		966

She act so weird—Beatles. Really relaxes me. I hate the fact that Claudia is so small and thinner than me. It's obvious how competitive she is. I won't bother Mark with such pettiness. It's not his fault. At least I look like a woman, not a little—whatever.

I don't care anymore. Sincerely, I don't. I don't know why I did before. I guess she was a threat of sorts. But I don't care anymore because he will do what he will do and, if he does, duh, I'll move on.

I know I'm beautiful. I thank God above that I am. He was so kind to bestow this to me. But inside I know my heart is beautiful, and I once again thank God to give me such sincerity. I want to feel beautiful. When I don't feel such a way, I lose grasp as to who I am, that is. I lose grasp as my sense of self and strength and humor. I don't care about my past anymore. I really don't care. I can't believe I've written about this so much and thought about this so much. Well, I just care about now and make myself happy. I don't care about everyone else—in their long hair, complexion. I'm ok, not bad obviously. If they have to compete with me, duh, indeed.

I just don't give a fuck impressing people. I just care about being very natural in every aspect. That is freedom. That is being real.

6/18
I just spoke with Mark. I feel like I lied to him. Maybe it's because I'm not out of the dark waters yet, ice waters, ice sky. I'm feeling really scared. I'm telling Mama W she has to pay [for] the examination. I will pay for the booster.

> *money $500*
> *$140 for booster*
> *$100 clothes*
> *$100 food for two months*
> *$145 spending money, buses*
> *$15 collection agency*
> *book*

August get a job, Wednesday and Thursday, two days a week

I feel scared inside about everything—shaken up is more appropriate. I feel like I'm losing touch with everything, that I'm slipping away without choice—or everything else is slipping away. Maybe that's why I've focused on making my body smaller. Maybe that's what it is this time. It's something good to slip away. # numbers and school # good to go up. I pray I can get away with copying all 107 pages tomorrow. I'm going to be good and keep my mouth shut, except for my check.

Yesterday was nice spending time with Mark. We made love. It felt so foreign to me being with him. I felt so shy and quite uncomfortable. However, the rest of the evening seemed very nice. Spending time with him and eating and watching a movie. It was all so very nice. I felt so in control, especially since I lost weight. It is such a good thing, and I don't want to stop ever. I've made the attempt into healthy. However, being a waif wouldn't bother me at all. I don't want to get sick. I just want to be entirely different. All these night noises are scaring me. I'm so scared, as if someone is going to come in and kill me. I really wonder how much weight I lost this week. I weighed in at 142. God, I can't believe I weighed so much. It's all so damn awful. I will get to 130, then to 120 and then to 115 and then to 110, 100. Maybe then people will take me seriously. I want my weight to drop, not my grades.

Well, what I was going to write about was that situation in the movie theater. Mark has a lot of dreams for himself, and I think it's all very wonderful. However, I felt a big emotion of abandonment and neglect coming on. I know I will not be able to deal with abandonment and neglect emotionally from him. Sometimes I feel neglected now by him in the very important ways. Emotionally I feel so alienated—still being with him is sometimes so foreign.

I know he cares about me. And I know it is my job to fill my heart and life with things. I know most likely Sylvia will marry Alan or someone else because she is so suave. Any man would go out of his way to keep her and make her part of his life, and Alan seems to have that sort of passion for her.

And I guess I secretly wish for that sort of love from Mark— to want to give me a secure place and always want to be with me. It seems now it's only half the time he wants to be with me, and it hurts my self-esteem a lot—actually, especially with all the dissing I've received in the past year and all. Well, a lot was my own doing. So I need to be perfect. I have nothing else to *really hold on to right now, and I don't feel rooted at all anywhere. So I want to focus on my grades, work and weight. That's all. And I don't want to be touched anymore. I'm in a lot of pain—rejection to the highest degree, from including myself, I guess.*

I know he is a young man, boy really. I need so much more maturity, but that will come with the years. I don't know.

I just don't know. I hate the future so much. I'm so overwhelmed. I need to sleep now.

Is it so wrong to want to have a family? It's always been such a big dream for me. But my old family life seems to come up now, being alone, abandoned, rejected and neglected. My voice doesn't seem to carry me very far away from things of this sort. It's all such treacherous ground, I suppose. Uncertainty and doubt creep into what I have now, and I have the things I've been through. It has affected my life with people. It's alienated me from simply [sic] honesty, open personality. I wish I could live free not to have to worry about a thing and not long internally for some sort of unity and security by being close to someone. I guess as long as I feel this and have felt this, everyone I know has rejected this and me along with it. So I guess I will still continue to punish myself sometimes for such cravings, and everything will come full circle, everything. So I can see what I have been starved for and what I starve and what starves me— if any of this makes any sense. I'm scared, but I have to tell myself I'll be all right because I've always been by myself, and I need to hold myself and carry myself for a little while.

Goodnight.

6/20

I weigh 139.5

As least that is what I need, and I'm so very glad. But I can't see much right now. It's been only a two pound loss. I feel it a little bit around my tummy. My butt seems to still be big, so what can you do? I think I'm going to take notes on Chapter 32, or maybe not. I hate all this note taking. Well, I have one more examination left.

I still cannot believe all the pettiness of Linda. "She could use a walk," or rather, "She sure looks like she could use a walk," and Gwen said, "You are so terrible." And then I asked Diane if that was a weight comment. She said she was only joking.

Well, it hurt. It hurt a lot. I'm so sensitive about my body beyond belief. I know I used to numb and hide behind my food. Well I guess no more. I would so much love to break 130 lbs even. I wonder what my body would look like. It's been so long since I've weighed that. Well, it feels like an eternity. I realize, aside from food, I have a lot of self-esteem, self-image, and the way I relate to other people is an issue to work out.

I cried like a baby today. Well, not exactly, but I was so pure and free I guess. God, why did she say that? I guess she was very jealous. Well, that's one person out. I do intend to say something to her tomorrow. Am I really that fat? I mean, really? Am I? I'm so sick of these comments. They hurt so much. I want to be proud of my body, not shameful about it. All the things my sister, Jenna, Beth, etc. have said to come back up from where I laid them down. I work so hard not to feel bad about myself. But when this happens, I feel so ripped up, and usually I guess I start eating and dieting (cycle) to get away from it. It is all such madness. Well, I'm willing to be my friend through all of this. I've worked hard on this. I still am not really where I'd like to be. It's just the overeating (binges), the occasional ones. I want to stop. It is such a trigger. But I have to put away these tactics of escape and lay out who I truly am—not just in body, a tiny bit here—but in soul, spirit and mind. I am trying to lose weight. I've always tried. What else could they expect from me. Honestly? What else? But patience is sincerely a virtue, and I wish to hold on to my strong side through frustrations like this. This too shall pass, and I truly believe so. Choice and thought before action are great gifts from God himself. I must admit [that] to have lived that educatedly has been a blessing to my life and will always be so. To let go of other things, or rather let them slip away, while I keep my eyes on what is important and real is the greatest joy and experience ever. It happens. It happens not *partially, but entirely. I hate when I feel shut out or off from life. It's such a dreadful feeling—isolation, alienation. It's sickness, mind-altering and life-altering at times also. If I have to be alone for right now, I want to experience solitude, not alienation, nor isolation. I just have to keep my eyes and heart and words and spirit open and on true and wonderful things in life. Appreciate everything for what it is worth. <u>Nothing lasts forever</u>. But to let oneself dive into the experience of everyday will create a feeling of aspirations and vitality.*

But, on food, I would like to eat a normal, spanned out time, so I don't get hungry at night at all, and when I go to someone's house, I have the right to say no to what I don't want to eat and use my pains as an excuse and be as inoffensive as possible.

Please, dear God, let me get an A on that test today. It would mean so very much to me. It would help lift my spirits higher. It truly would, and please let everything work out wonderfully the rest of the summer and let me accomplish a lot of good things for myself and be healthy and disciplined. Please, dear God, bring some wonderful encouraging, unbiased, loving, respecting people in my life.

I have to be so honest. There are just some things that I am so in need of. And a good number of encouraging friends would help along the way. A group of wonderful people, open, that have good social status, nice people and giving.

Please, dear God, let things pick up in my life beautifully. I want to feel whole inside, instead of being severed in hundreds of little pieces from my own and others' actions. It's all so much, but it's controllable, and I'm the one in charge. No one else is. I'm just going to let that go (stupid comment).

And please, dear God, let Mark come to good grounds with himself, that are solid, and help him find a great job with great people. Please don't let him fall for any other girl.

Please let our relationship become awesome and wholesome and freeing with each other. Let our talks soar and minds and hearts. Let us join our strengths and reflect off each other to make us feel wonderful and become the best that we could be. I know we could be best of friends. Please help me to overcome the challenges that I face every day in my life. Please let me come out on top of everything, and let it put me on sure ground so I won't fall and won't lose anything at all.

Please let me feel an ever encouraging life force in my everyday existence from the time I wake to the time I sleep. Let my voice become strong and defined along with my character—strong, warm, distinct, good, downright real. And let my nurturance be doubled or even tripled when I do what is right and let the times I fall be soft so I can pick myself up on what I worked so hard on and have overcome. And please let Mark call soon, because I want to go to sleep soon and be uninterrupted.

Please let us unleash, and a spiritual and emotional relationship emerge. Now focused. Please help me through this and next week especially; things are so hard right now.

I must write.

Completed two weeks

14 days

P.S. Please make my package get here this week, tomorrow.

[*Katie was found dead on June 29, nine days after this last entry in her diary.*]

PART

Commentaries

CHAPTER 4

Silvia Sara Canetto

Why Did You Kill Yourself, Katie?
Questions and Reflections
on a Young Woman's Suicide

Spleen: 130 grams
Right lung: 290 grams
Left lung: 255 grams
Heart: 225 grams
Brain: 1415 grams

With the other parts, that should come to about 143 pounds. The re-port of your autopsy eerily evoked the rhythm of your diet notes. Re-member, Katie, how you used to keep track of what you ate, and then add up the calories?

Slim fast	120
- - -	200
Milk	110
2 Wheat	180
1 can tuna	210
2 prunes	46
1 cup AS	110
	966 (June 11)

Calories yesterday
600
200
160

960

I guess about 1000   (February 4)

After getting to know your vibrant spirit through your diary, it was
jarring to read about your inanimate body being exposed and dissected
by the medical examiner.[1] That body you felt so insecure about. The body
that had been the battlefield of so many of your efforts to be different,
and in your mind, better: thin, long-haired, pure, free. That body that
had been the theater of so much of your pain.

He measured, weighed, and judged every part of you, one piece at a
time, carefully, systematically, almost obsessively. The texture of your brain
and that of your hair; the size of your heart and your breasts; the condition of your irides and that of your pubic hair. By the middle of it, I started
to question the meaning and purpose of his analysis. Why measure, cut,
weigh, and comment on every body part of a woman who died of hanging? Why palpate her breasts? What is the point of noting that her "pubic
hair" was "well manicured" (p. 2)? What is the purpose of comments
about her physical appearance, such as the statement that she was slim
above the waist but heavier at the hips? As I got more and more uncomfortable about his intrusive, voyeuristic gaze, I also started expecting you
to suddenly raise up, sit up straight, look at him in the eyes, push him
away, and tell him off. I imagined you yelling at him in your best angry
voice, "I am so fucking sick of being manhandled," as you wrote in your
diary on February 20. I imagined hearing your voice roaring to him, "The
fact that I sometimes despise my body does not give YOU the right to treat
it like dead meat. I am not [a] fucking doll[s]" (September 18).

At the end, the medical examiner got all the body parts measured cor-
rectly. But his butcher-like analysis surely did not give a clue of who you
were as a person, and why you killed yourself.

Why did you kill yourself, Katie?

Beside your body on the floor of your room, you left us a diary. Five
books of notes, starting June 8, a couple of months before your 20th
birthday, and ending, a year later, on June 20, a couple of months away
from your 21st birthday, and nine days before your death.

The typed copy of your diary arrived in my university office mailbox in
a large white envelope.[2] A couple of hundred pages, in irregularly typed
format, some double-spaced and some single-spaced; some back-to-back

and some single-sided. It looked like the first draft of a dissertation of a sloppy graduate student. I was given your diary because I am a so-called expert in suicidal behavior. I was asked to analyze it in light of my background in women's studies. I was to offer my insights about your journey to suicide. I was to help unlock the mystery of your suicide.

I took your diary home. It sat on my desk for weeks. It seemed like a big, heavy, and difficult project to tackle. I felt your diary required a long time to read; lots of quiet time, lots of quiet, emotionally available hours. When I finally started reading it, I went through the five books in one day. It is not because it was easy reading. It is not the best of writing. You know, Katie, your diary is rather rambling and repetitious. It reminds me of therapy sessions with long-term, well-defended clients. On the other hand, I realize, Katie, that a personal diary is a personal record. You did not write it for people like me to read as if it were a novel. Anyway, once I started reading your diary, I realized it just was not the kind of text I could leave and pick up again. To understand it, I needed to gulp it all at once. Stay with it to the end. Through your bitter end.

What did I learn about you from your diary? What does my expertise in women's studies offer to an understanding of your psychology, your struggles, your journey, your end? I will start simply. I will first describe the different parts and contents of your diary, like the medical examiner described the parts and contents of your body. As I said earlier, your journal is divided into five books. Each of these books has unique content and themes.

☐ The First Book: The "Summer Journal"

The first book, which Katie called her "Summer Journal" (p. 89), covers the three and a half months between June 8 and August 28. It is by far the longest of the five books: ninety-eight pages of typed single-spaced text.

The first entry reads like a presage of her end. "I am so depressed and suicidal." If this is all it took to predict suicide! In this first entry, one finds some of the main themes of Katie's negative self-dialogue: her discomfort with and antipathy toward her body ("My body feels restless and tired. . . . I really hate my body. . . . I decided to start exercising today"); her feelings of insecurity about her boyfriend Mark ("I love Mark . . . but . . . I don't know if it's true love for him"); her loneliness ("I feel so unbelievable lonely and battered").

This first half of this book is dominated by themes of self-doubt, self-discounting, and self-silencing. For example, she denies her own feelings in order to accommodate to those of others. "I feel I have to sacrifice myself to be close to people or make them love me," she writes. She also starves herself because she thinks Mark wants her to be slimmer ("I would stop eating for him"). During moments of intimacy with Mark she has flashbacks of her father sexually molesting her ("I had flashbacks and Mark held me. I was shaking so badly"; "I feel daddy's sick presence here"; and "I can't take the shaking and flashes"), but she forces herself to have sex with Mark to make him happy ("I really don't like it [sex] but I force myself because this might make him happier"). If she is in pain, her main concern seems to be how her pain may affect others, especially Mark ("It hurts me that my pain hurts someone else"). She also writes about feeling trapped and wanting to start over ("I hate this story. I want to rewrite it. I want a new book not a new chapter"). Her dreams are "to do well in school, broaden my mind and learn, good relationships with good people, good relationship with myself, my mind in control. Spirit, life, strong in my recovery, free."

In the second half of the first book, she becomes more self-aware and more trusting of her perspective and wishes. She begins to recognize that she is "making [herself] do things that [she does not] want," and writes about wanting to be true to herself and her feelings. She wants to change her relationship with Mark to make it more responsive to her needs. "I think we have just spent too much time together, and we need to take a break. It's all too much. I'm going to fucking explode. Something needs to be confronted. I think cutting sex out will be a big factor in calming the storm"; and "I really don't feel like being touched for a very long time. I need to honor that in myself." She also promises herself to try to keep safe: "I promise not to kill myself and do stupid things to myself." "This is a book to establish my freedom," she says of her diary.

During this time she painfully recovers more memories of childhood physical and sexual abuse. "I hate these damn memories," she writes; and "Daddy, why did you do all those bad things?" She expresses her anger about being a victim at the hands of people who should have protected her. "I never deserved this! Never! You bastard. You were supposed to protect little children," she writes; and "I want to scratch out my father's eyes while he's looking at me." At the same time, she also starts articulating the elements of an affirmative identity beyond that of being a victim. She writes: "[Some people] see an abused orphan. That's not me. I'm separate. My identity is not what I lived through. . . . The past is just history. . . . I survived all this. That makes me strong in character and mind. It makes me a hero."

In sum, this period is marked by both negative, regressive and positive, progressive themes. On the one hand, Katie is shaken by memories of sexual abuse and often feels lonely, depressed, insecure about her body, and entangled in her relationship with Mark. One the other hand, she is also beginning to listen to and to trust her feelings. This is also a period when she is connected with a number of people. She lives with a room-mate. She spends time with her boyfriend, though not always in a way that is meaningful and satisfying to her. She attends support meetings like Overeaters Anonymous, as part of a "recovery" that she says started three years before. She also mentions a "recovery" sponsor, Ken, who offers her affirming feedback—though she cannot always accept it ("I spoke to Ken, my sponsor. It was nice but, when he says nice things about me, I don't take it seriously at all because I don't feel he really knows me").

☐ The Second Book: Rage and Dreams of a Better Life

The second book begins on August 31, after Katie's twentieth birthday and ends on December 2. It covers three months and sixty single-spaced pages.

During these three months the emotional temperature of the diary increases. Anger is a frequently reported mood. This anger is often directed at herself and particularly at her body. She is constantly planning a new drastic way to lose weight. She engages in self-cutting and in life-threatening behaviors ("I ran in front of a car so it would hit me").

There is also rage against others, particularly her boyfriend. Katie writes about "huge" and "horrid fights" with Mark. She says she feels "like such a savage . . . with all the rage [she] feel[s]." One source of her anger seems to be the realization of how dependent she is on Mark and how she often tries to makes herself small to please him ("I'm sick of making myself less so I can make other people feel more"). She continues to express a desire to take a break from Mark so that she can find out who she is and can set her own goals. She even talks about going to England for a while, to get some perspective ("I want to go so I can get some perspective on my life. If I can't get perspective where I am now—maybe, just maybe—I can get it somewhere else—another country for a few weeks. I think that it will open up a whole new world for me. I don't think I would be as dependent on Mark").

She also feels bogged down about her poor school performance ("Got my two exams back. Got a 64 on one and a 46 on the other. . . . I'm so upset. I really feel bogged down"; and "I can't afford to fail these classes. Even if I get all D's. I honestly just want to pass") and has concerns about her education and her employment prospects ("I don't know what I'll major in anymore—theatre is so much easier—but if I major in psychology I'll have a job right out of school. I really want to go on to schooling—for a good-paying job in the medical field. . . . Maybe I'll become a RN after all"). This uncertainty makes her feel anxious, stuck, and out of control ("What the hell am I going to do? I'm too young to be stuck. I hate being stuck"; and "I feel like I have no control of absolutely anything. It drives me crazy"). As some areas (e.g., future employment) do not appear amenable to control, she tries to exert control over her body and gets busy developing diet and exercise regimens ("I really need to get some control in my life. Losing some extra weight would be absolutely wonderful"). But she maintains hope in a better future: "I want to feel like I've got my foot in the door of having a better life."

☐ The Third Book: Hate, Hurt, and Longing for Psychological Space

The third book begins on December 14 and ends on January 11, one month in eleven single-spaced pages. It is a period of deep hate and hurt, as she notes in her entry from December 31: "I hate so deeply and hurt so deeply." During this time she has serious concerns about money and school performance. She is in debt. She is concerned about her future because she did poorly in her courses the previous semester: "I've got two F's and two D's. God, my academic career sucks"; and "I've got to get on top of my grades." She also feels socially isolated and totally dependent on Mark: "It seems to me my whole world revolves with being with Mark. I hate it."

She writes about wanting to stop trying to fit into other people's life, especially Mark's. She is tired of making herself what she is not. For example, she wants to stop repressing the fun part of herself in order to conform to the straitjacket of femininity. "I don't feel free to be crazy around him and hate it. I love being off the wall. However, I feel like I have to be so feminine. Fuck it. I have so much fun when I let myself go." And she wants space from Mark: "We really needed time away from each other. It is highly important to have space. I fear so much of our relationship will only become sexual."

☐ The Fourth Book: Dreams under Threat

The fourth book begins on January 15 and ends on April 6: four months in seventeenth single-spaced pages. During this period she is growing more isolated ("I don't seem to have girls I really hang out with at all"), and more exclusively emotionally dependent on Mark ("He's a great boyfriend, but I need not everything from him, just some things"). At the same time, she is struggling to develop an identity and a life ("I want to live life my way") separate from Mark. What keeps her going are "strong dreams . . . of a good life." For example, she dreams of getting a "master's in psychology." But these dreams are under threat. She is experiencing school problems. "I'm really scared this semester about school. I've missed so many classes," and she is anticipating even greater school challenges ("This week I thought of dropping out of school and going to the community college"). As she feels she is losing grip over "what is really important in life" ("Everything seems much out of my control"), and despairs of reaching her life goals (e.g., "doing well in school, making money"), she falls back onto trying to control her appearance: growing her hair ("my hair will be so much longer"); changing her way of speaking ("I need to change some. My way of speaking and what I speak about"); and, of course, dropping some weight ("I still weigh 147 lbs. I'm so mad. . . . I feel so trapped in my body"; and "Goal: 115 lbs. He would love me").

☐ The Fifth Book: Some Dreams Are Fulfilled but She Is Isolated

The fifth book covers only one month, from May 15 to June 20. It is twelve single-spaced pages long. Her death is recorded as May 29, nine days after her last entry.

In this last month, Katie struggles with some of the same issues she has been dealing with for the past year. She wants to find herself, and she wants to gain some sense of control over her life. As always, much of her focus is her body ("What I really hate is my body and I've decided to change it"), but she argues that her slimming regimen is not suicidal ("I've just freaked out because I don't have any control whatsoever in my life at all. It's absolutely terrifying. I have to just say for the record that I'm not going to try to kill myself by doing this—only perhaps the old Katie, so a new isolated individual one could rise up and emerge"). She says she wants be born as a new person. In reality, much of her dieting ideation sounds suicidal ("I wish could just melt away right now"). There are times when she is aware of the self-silencing and self-destructive tendencies behind her dieting plans. "I may have once again lost my identity in something. It might be dieting, Mark, wanting to meet up to the image in my head of myself." She writes about wanting to achieve self-acceptance and peace ("Be happy, laugh and be free Katie. I give you permission; to be a distinct individual; don't mesh and just live; and do what you can to do what is right and smart").

In some ways, this is a positive time for Katie. She has been able to achieve many of her goals. She is staying away from Mark; she gets good grades in her classes—in fact she makes Honors; she has a job; she has even lost weight, too much weight actually (fourteen pounds). She feels she is growing psychologically. "I believe my spirit and inner person is growing back rapidly. I need to focus on and to do things to nurture this growth process." She writes that she feels wise, strong, and in control. "I am wise now. . . . I do have control over my fate now." "Nothing is hopeless, absolutely nothing," she concludes.

At the same time she has become quite isolated. She does not see Mark much, and she does not see her friends either. She says she misses "real and good friends, really bad"; she wishes she could be around "encouraging" people that are "nice . . . and giving." She also writes about being "scared of losing everything and everyone [she] love[s]." Perhaps due to this isolation, she feels vulnerable and unsteady. "I have nothing else to really hold on to right now, and I don't feel rooted at all anywhere." She feels her diary has become her only friend. "I intend to make this book my best friend and only confidante." And in her diary now she dialogues with God. It is to God she now turns for help for all of her needs—from becoming whole to making friends to getting a package delivered on time. "Please, dear God, bring some wonderful encouraging, unbiased, loving, respecting people in my life. . . . Dear God, let things pick up in my life beautifully. I want to feel whole. . . . Please let me feel an ever encouraging life force in my everyday existence from the time I wake to the time I sleep. Let my voice become strong and defined along with my character—strong, warm, distinct, good, downright real. . . . Please help me through this and next week, especially things are so hard right now. . . . P.S. Please make my package get here this week, tomorrow." These are the last words in her diary.

☐ Questions and Reflections

I cannot believe you killed yourself, Katie.

I know I always knew that you did. I knew you were dead before I ever read your diary. That was how I came to read your diary. Remember, I am a so-called expert in women and suicidal behavior.

When I started reading your diary and came across that first statement in your first entry ("I am so depressed and suicidal"), I said to myself: Here it is. It is all laid out. You have explicitly told us you are suicidal. There are no mysteries here. Your case is simple and unambiguous. However, once I proceeded through the five books, your story became complex, and a suicidal decision did not seem inevitable to me anymore.

At the beginning, you came across as an insecure, vulnerable, and confused young woman. But along the way, you seemed to grow stronger, more aware of your needs and boundaries and more willing to stand up for them. Along the way, the rage you used to turn against yourself started being directed outside of you. You had "huge fights" with your boyfriend. You rebelled against the crazy social rules about female body shape and femininity that made you feel constantly inadequate. Based on clinical theory (Jack, 1991), one could read these behaviors as good signs, as indications you were moving away from depression and suicidal behavior. In the last book of your diary, which you entitled "Book of Reflection and Self-Healing Action and Growth," you seemed to be coming into yourself. You made important positive changes in your life: you distanced yourself sexually and emotionally from your boyfriend; you achieved a 3.6 GPA and made honors; you got a job; you even achieved a significant weight loss. You wrote that you were starting to feel strong and independent. You seemed to be surging and soaring after years of self-doubt, self-invalidation, self-restraint, and self-punishment. I was surging and soaring with you.

I knew Katie had killed herself. But things were going relatively well for you in the June of your final year. So, up to the last page of your diary I expected a setback or a crisis. You were surely quite isolated. You were also very demanding of yourself in terms of goals and schedules, and thus vulnerable to disappointment. I was expecting that you would run into some obstacles eventually (perhaps a health crisis, given your dangerous dieting behavior; perhaps an academic disappointment; maybe a work difficulty; possibly an issue with Mark; conceivably, a psychological problem, like a relapse into a panic episode) and find yourself deep in suicidal depression, what on June 18 you called the "dark waters . . . ice waters, ice sky." I thought you might have been hospitalized before your suicide.

When I did not find such a crisis, even on the penultimate page of your diary, I thought—I really wished—I was coming up to a surprise, a positive ending to your story. Katie may have killed herself. But you, the real you whose name I do not know, actually lived on. You graduated and went to England for the summer, as you said you always wanted to do (on October 17). There, in a new environment and away from the ghosts of the past, I imagined you getting stronger and healthier every day.

Why did you kill yourself, Katie? And why did you stop writing in your diary nine days before your death? You kept such a detailed record of your psychological experience over such a long period of time and yet you did not leave us any direct, explicit clue to your suicide. Not even a suicide note. I have to confess I was surprised that you did not write a suicide letter. During a previous episode of suicidal ideation, you had written in your diary: "I have to write my suicide letter" (August 31). "So what?" you could say. "People are not consistent. Why should I be?" I know, Katie, but I so much wanted to hear from you, to know what you went through. I wonder if perhaps you did not write in your diary because all of your energy went into surviving first, and then into the suicide. Or perhaps you felt ashamed about recording a major downfall in the same pages where your had written about your beautiful recovery, your positive resolve and your future dreams.

You stopped writing in your diary nine days before your death. What happened in those nine days? You wrote you felt "scared inside about everything." You added, "I'm slipping away without choice—or everything else is slipping away." You even said you were afraid someone would come and kill you. "Things are so hard right now," you said in your last entry. What was so hard? How did things become perhaps even harder?

Whatever it is that happened in those nine days, why did you respond with suicide? I am aware you talked about suicide all the time. Your diary is full of references to suicide. Thinking and talking about killing yourself was almost ordinary for you. Perhaps too ordinary. How many different ways did you talk about killing yourself? Here are some: I do not care about my life that much anymore; I want to kill myself. Bullet through the heart; I want to kill myself on my birthday. I have to; I was so devastated that I wanted to kill myself; I really want to cut myself off from the world permanently; I did so fucking terrible with my food today. It was horrible. I want to kill myself today; I would stop eating for him; I feel so suicidal; My life's in danger by a stranger—myself; I wanted to die. I partially still want to; I want to hurt myself so badly; I want to die. I feel like I'm dying or that I'm basically already dead. I wanted to kill myself so badly last night but I thought of the people who loved me—love me. I feel so alone. I want to die; I cried over hurting myself today; I hate myself. I want to die! What I do isn't good enough; I told him that, if I get pregnant, I'm gong to kill myself first and then the baby. . . . I have to write my suicide letter later; I would give my life to be thin; I will diet till I die; I have to give in to starving myself. It's no big deal; If she [my sister] ever died I'll kill myself; I feel so horrible for my mother. It makes me want to slash my wrists and cut up my body. It makes me all so angry; I want to die so badly. I hurt so much inside over everything; If I could slender myself, disappear, angelic form, model ideal, beauty. . . . I want to disappear, I want to fade away; I wish I could just melt away right now. (You even invented a story that your mother had killed herself.)

Perhaps this easy suicide talk was one of your major vulnerabilities. Suicide was not enough of a taboo for you. Suicide came up easily and quickly for you as an idea, a solution, an escape, a refuge, a punishment. At some point you had written that death was "a hug or a place where I can be tortured and close to my parents." Soon or later you were going to get trapped into actually acting on that idea. But why then, on June 29, and not earlier, when things in your life seemed more negative and out of control?

Also, why did you kill yourself in your room? Why hanging, why hanging by the door-closing mechanism located at the top of your door, and why with a cloth belt? When you wrote about suicide, you had talked about putting a "bullet through [your] heart." In your previous suicidal episodes, you had used a knife to cut yourself. You had purposely run in front of a car. But you never wrote about hanging yourself. How did you come up with that suicide method? Why take your breath, your voice, your spirit away?

I am a suicidologist, a clinical psychologist, and a women's studies scholar. I can easily come up with elegant, persuasive, and empirically cogent explanations for your suicide, based on theory and research.

To start, your psychosocial profile fits that of young persons at risk for suicide. Low self-esteem, low academic achievement, peer difficulties, and social isolation have all been identified as factors in suicidal behavior for people your age (Canetto, 2001; King, 1997; Lewinsohn, Rohde, & Seeley, 1996).

I could point to your experience of sexual abuse by your father and to your history of emotional and physical abuse by your mother. Research indicates that a disproportionate number of individuals who are suicidal have experienced abuse (e.g., Fondacaro & Butler, 1995).

One could blame your death on your traumatic family experiences— your father's alcoholism, his abuse of your mother, your mother's psychiatric hospitalization, your experience in foster homes. Studies have suggested that a history of instability in key relationships is a risk factor for suicidal ideation and behavior (Jacobs, Brewer, & Klein-Benheim, 1999; King, 1997; Lewinsohn, Rohde, & Seeley, 1996).

It could be argued that your suicide makes sense in light of the invalidating environment you experienced in your relationships. According to Linehan (1993), invalidating relationships leave individuals unable to trust their judgment and to understand and regulate their emotions.

Explanations for your suicide could also be drawn from clinical cognitive theory (Weishaar, 2000). According to clinical cognitive theory, suicidal ideation and behavior are associated with a unique way of thinking, including cognitive distortions (such as overgeneralization) and dichotomous thinking. Problem-solving deficits as well as so-called irrational beliefs and dysfunctional attitudes (such as perfectionist attitudes and social oversensitivity) have also been suggested as typical of the suicidal individual's cognitive style. One could certainly find examples of how your thinking pattern resembled that of suicidal persons. You certainly had a perfectionist streak. Remember when you wrote you were "having a hard time becoming perfect"? One could view your absorption with your body weight as a cognitive distortion as well. Considering women's socialization, and your particular experience in relationships, one would be hard pressed to treat many of your beliefs as idiosyncratic distortions. Society teaches women to hate their normal bodies. As a woman, you were socialized to define yourself in terms of appearance and to value thinness. As a result, your weight obsession could really be seen as conventional, perhaps overconventional thinking and behavior, not as an aberration. Also, you were often aware of, and rebelled against, the tyranny of our cultural obsession with female thinness. "I look at all these model perfect women and clothes and they all sicken me because where is the natural beauty of a woman with all their imperfections. We're not fucking dolls. We don't have to act like fucking model perfect mannequins"; and "This is the myth that kills women," you wrote in your diary. "I struggle with wanting to be thin, but I know what's really important in life."

Those steeped in personality disorder theory may read in your diary the signs of a borderline personality (Davis, Gunderson, & Myers, 1999). They will point as evidence to your insecurities about your identity, your vacillations between idealizing and despising those to whom you were attached, your anxiety, your anger, your self-harmful behaviors. Other personality clinicians may diagnose you as having a dependent or hysterical personality (see Canetto, 1995, for a review). Within a conventional personality disorder theory, your suicidal behavior would be conceptualized as "manipulative" (Davis et al., 1999, p. 318), as a "posture of helplessness" or as a form of "clinging" (Birtchnell, 1983, p. 29). Your death could be even dismissed as a "miscalculated manipulation" (Davis et al., 1999, p. 321).

Some may point to your history of mental disorders, and particularly your depression and eating disorder, as key explanations for suicidal behavior. An eating disorder is a particularly important risk factor for women (Canetto & Lester, 1995). Suffering from more than one mental disorder also increases the probability of suicidal behavior. (Canetto & Lester, 1995; Jacobs et al., 1999; Lewinsohn et al., 1996). Others may emphasize a combination of depression, anxiety, hopelessness, impulsivity/aggression, and self-consciousness/disengagement, all of which you suffered from (Conner, Duberstein, Seidlitz, & Caine, 2001).

Another "obvious" red flag is your chronic suicidal ideation and past history of suicidal behavior. A past history of suicidal behavior is considered the best predictor of future suicidal behavior (Canetto & Lester, 1995; Jacobs et al., 1999; King, 1997).

The list of post hoc explanations for your suicide could go on and on. None of them, however, really contributes to understanding the specific circumstances and reasons for your suicide, its timing, and the manner in which you did it. Information about general risk factors does not help fill the gap in information in your diary from June 20 to the day of your death. Also, the literature indicates that women, especially women your age, tend to respond to the various risk factors with nonfatal suicidal behavior, what many authors called "failed suicide attempts" or "suicide gestures." Women in the United States do not typically die of suicide. Women in this country are not usually "successful" at suicide. Women your age also commonly use so-called nonviolent methods, such as poisoning (Canetto, 1997).

You went counter to most predictions. You used a method that is considered violent, and you did not survive your suicidal act. Some clinicians would perhaps insinuate that your death was a "miscalculated manipulation" (Davis et al., 1999, p. 312). Consider the irony in the language of suicide. The fact that you killed yourself makes you successful at suicide, according to conventional terminology. Still, since as a woman you are expected to attempt and fail at suicide, your death may still be coded as an accident, as a failure. It seems there is no way to be successful at suicide as a woman (Canetto, 1997).

Without access to your thoughts in those last nine days, I cannot say I would have necessarily predicted your suicide. There surely were many negative signs in your diary: your isolation and the feeling of being rootless; the bouts of endless anxiety and turmoil; the emotional brittleness and vulnerability; the feeling of "being severed in hundred of little pieces." There were, however, enough positive signs so that one could have expected continued positive growth: your recent scholastic and work achievements; your growing insight into the reasons for your insecurities; your developing self-affirming attitudes; your resolution to "be happy, laugh and be free . . . and to do what is right and smart"; and your intent "to keep [your] eyes and heart and words and spirit open and on true and wonderful things in life."

If I had to identify one risk factor in the months before your suicide, I would say it was your isolation. You were no longer living with a roommate, however much you disliked your last roommate. You had moved away from Mark, but you had not made new close friends. You did not seem in contact with your sponsor anymore. I wonder if perhaps the ghosts of the past became louder in the silence of your single room. Maybe they also got more vicious as you had become a more formidable contender for them. I think those ghosts may have been quite surprised at how awesome you had become.

☐ Epilogue

Katie, I said I would not have necessarily have predicted your suicide based on your diary. I do not think anybody actually could. But I feel I did connect with you by listening to the narration of the last year of your life. I think I understand your experience; I appreciate your sensibilities; and I empathize with your feelings and reflections. So now you are alive in my memory. With the voice I have come to know through your diary, through the range of its tones and moods, not just in what you called your "abused orphan" mode and identity. I tell you because I know this would have been important to you.

Notes

1. The contributors were given the medical examiner's report and the report of the police investigation in addition to a typed copy of the diary.
2. The diary was typed by the editor of this book.

References

Birtchnell, J. (1983). Pscyhotherapeutic considerations in the management of the suicidal patient. *American Journal of Psychotherapy, 37,* 24–36.

Canetto, S. S. (1995). Suicidal women: Intervention and prevention strategies. In S. S. Canetto & D. Lester (Eds.), *Women and suicidal behavior* (pp. 237–255). New York: Springer.

Canetto, S. S. (1997). Gender and suicidal behavior: Theories and evidence. In R. W. Maris, M. M. Silverman, & S. S. Canetto (Eds.), *Review of suicidology* (pp. 138–167). New York: Guilford.

Canetto, S. S. (2001). Girls and suicidal behavior. In M. Forman-Brunell (Ed.), *Girlhood in America: An Encyclopedia,* Vol. 2 (pp. 616–621). Santa Barbara, CA: ABC-CLIO.

Canetto, S. S., & Lester, D. (1995). The epidemiology of women's suicidal behavior. In S. S. Canetto & D. Lester (Eds.), *Women and suicidal behavior* (pp. 35–57). New York: Springer.

Conner, K. R., Duberstein, P. R., Seidlitz, L, & Caine, E. D. (2001). Psychological vulnerability to completed suicide: A review of empirical studies. *Suicide and Life-Threatening Behavior, 31,* 367–385.

Davis, T., Gunderson, J. G., & Myers, M. (1999). Borderline personality disorder. In D. G. Jacobs (Ed.), *The Harvard Medical School guide to suicide assessment and intervention* (pp. 311–331). San Francisco: Jossey-Bass.

Fondacaro, K. M., & Butler, W. M. (1995). Suicidality in female survivors of child sexual abuse. In S. S. Canetto & D. Lester (Eds.), *Women and suicidal behavior* (pp. 192–204). New York: Springer.

Jacobs. D. G., Brewer, M., & Klein-Benheim, M (1999). Suicide assessment: An overview and recommended protocol. In D. G. Jacobs (Ed.), *The Harvard Medical School guide to suicide assessment and intervention* (pp. 3–39). San Francisco: Jossey-Bass.

Jack, D. C (1991). *Silencing the self: Women and depression.* New York: Harper Perennial.

King, C. A. (1997). Suicidal behavior in adolescence. In R. W. Maris, M. M. Silverman, & S. S. Canetto (Eds.), *Review of suicidology* (pp. 61–95). New York: Guilford.

Lewinsohn, P. M., Rohde, P., & Seeley. J. R. (1996). Adolescent suicidal ideation and attempts: Prevalence, risk factors, and clinical implications. *Clinical Psychology: Science and Practice 3* (1), 25–46.

Linehan, M. M. (1993). *Cognitive-behavioral treatment of borderline personality disorder.* New York: Guilford.

Weishaar, M. E. (2000). Cognitive risk factors in suicide. In R. W. Maris, S. S. Canetto, J. McIntosh, & M. M. Silverman (Eds.). (2000). *Review of suicidology: 2000.* (pp. 112–139). New York: Guilford.

CHAPTER **5**

James W. Pennebaker
Lori D. Stone

What Was She Trying to Say?
A Linguistic Analysis
of Katie's Diaries[1]

Although we have many ways to communicate our thoughts and feelings, words provide the primary way we make our thoughts known, both to ourselves and to others. The specific words we select, the way we frame our thoughts, the ideas we choose to convey (and those we choose not to disclose) are obviously important elements of communicating a message. However, the less noticeable aspects of language can reveal a great deal about us beyond the specifics of what we express, including information about our gender or age, our level of dominance within a relationship, the likelihood that we will or will not successfully recover from a traumatic experience, and whether we are depressed or suicidal. While this information is sometimes conveyed directly, it is also communicated in a nearly transparent fashion, through the small and apparently insignificant words we use in our sentences to hold the nouns and verbs together.

For decades, psychological research that included an examination of language relied heavily on content or qualitative analyses. Trained judges read and coded bodies of text along relevant dimensions, a time-consuming process that could be difficult when judges failed to reach agreement. This technique typically focused on the content of what was being said, along with the context in which the language was occurring. The little words that carry no meaning on their own (such as articles, prepositions, pronouns, etc.) were scarcely noticed at best, and were more typically ignored. Research on natural language use has recently uncovered dramatic and surprising findings, suggesting that some of the psychological power of words lies in those nearly invisible ones. How we say things—our linguistic style—reveals our level of understanding of our relationship to the world and to others. We are learning that the obvious and seemingly interesting linguistic elements (nouns, verbs, and adjectives) frequently take a psychological backseat to the more subtle elements (e.g., articles, pronouns). Our linguistic analysis of Katie's words revealed much more than a careful reading of her diary might suggest, and, in fact, this is an important strength of linguistic analyses. The patterns of language she used across time were consistent with a growing body of research linking linguistic style with psychological state and experience. In this chapter we will first describe recent research on language use, followed by our analysis of Katie's diary entries.

☐ A Text Analysis Approach and Findings

Several years ago, Pennebaker and Francis developed a text analysis program called LIWC (Linguistic Inquiry and Word Count; Pennebaker & Francis, 1996; Pennebaker, Francis, & Booth, 2001). Relying on a built-in dictionary of more than 2,300 words and word stems, LIWC counts words in text files and sorts them into categories, such as linguistic dimensions (e.g., word count, articles, prepositions, pronouns), psychological processes (e.g., positive and negative emotions, cognitive processes, social processes), relativity (e.g., time, space, and motion), and current concerns (e.g., work, leisure, physical states, metaphysical). Words occurring in a text can be assigned to multiple categories. For example, the word "cried" is an element of four word categories: sadness, negative emotion, overall affect, and a past tense verb.

The lists of words that define each category were created over a period of several years and multiple steps. After an initial set of categories was created, three to six judges met to devise broad lists of words for each category. A complex rating scheme was devised, and the words were rated over several samples of the same participants, resulting in 93% to 100% agreement among judges. These 72 categories of words were further validated by judges who rated text files, which were then compared with the LIWC analyses. The result of a LIWC analysis is percentages of total words that occur in each category (i.e., the percentage of total words that are negative emotions, positive emotions, insight words, future tense words, etc.). While context is not considered when analyzing text with LIWC, a great deal of personal and psychological information can nevertheless be gained, particularly when these language markers are correlated with physical and psychological outcomes. Consider the conclusions one might draw on reading an essay about coming to college that contained an ex-traordinary number of swear words, or an interview in which the speaker continued to use filler words, such as "um" or "like." Word count can be quite informative.

Linguistic Profiles

Specific linguistic profiles have been uncovered through LIWC analyses. For example, relative to men, women use more pronouns, including self-references and references to others, more social words, more references to home, and more negations. They also use fewer big words, articles, prepositions, spatial words, occupation, and money words. This is a ro-bust and reliable profile of gendered language. However, after participat-ing in a writing intervention in which men and women write a number of times (typically three) about their deepest thoughts and feelings sur-rounding a traumatic or upsetting event from their own lives, men show a slight increase and women a slight decrease in their use of first personal plural pronouns—"we," "us," and "our"—following the intervention, re-flecting a subtle shift in emphasis on social relationships.

Another profile has been discovered of reliable age-related develop-ments in the use of language. As people age, they use increasing numbers of positive emotion words, large words, cognitive processing words, exclus-ive words (e.g., "but," "except," "without"), and future tense words, while using declining percentages of first-person singular pronouns, references to the past, and time-related words (Pennebaker, 2002). These robust findings are counter to the unpleasant stereotype some hold about older people living in the past and possibly using more negative emotion words. An interesting aspect of these linguistic profiles is that they are reliable discriminators among groups of people, suggesting that language may be a valuable measure of individual differences (Pennebaker & King, 1999).

Of the language categories, pronouns in particular have been found to be potent correlates of both social structure and psychological health. By their very nature, pronouns are the linguistic link to social relationships and reveal a great deal about those relationships. To whom does a speaker refer when she says "we" or "they"? In which relationships will a speaker firmly place herself by using "I" rather than focusing on the listener, "you?" In an unpublished study, Pennebaker, Davis, Rentfrow, and Mehl (2002) explored linguistic evidence of relationship dominance by analyzing e-mail correspondence. Participants in the study chose ten people to whom they had sent and received at least ten e-mails, and rated each e-mail partner in terms of relationship dominance. Intriguingly, dominance was starkly displayed in the use of personal pronouns. When an e-mail writer was in the subordinate position within a relationship (e.g., a professor writing to the department chair), the writer used a large percentage of first-person singular pronouns such as "I" and "my." When that same writer was in a dominant position, however (e.g., the same professor writing to an undergraduate student), he or she used very few first-person singular pronouns, instead relying more heavily on second-person pronouns such as "you" and "your."

Pronoun usage reveals much more than social structure, however. In a number of studies over the past two years, pronouns have been found to be intricately linked to physical and mental health in a number of ways. At the most general level, research by Campbell and Pennebaker (2003) has explored flexibility in pronoun use. Analyzing the language of different groups of people, from college students to prison inmates, these researchers applied a new approach called Latent Semantic Analysis (LSA) to examine the ways in which writers used language across writing sessions. Using a technique somewhat akin to factor analysis, LSA analyzes the interrelationships between words to establish a measure of similarity. Campbell and Pennebaker found that those who told their stories in the same ways each time, using the same types of pronouns, did not show health improvements. Only those writers who exhibited flexibility in their use of pronouns (particularly between first-person singular and first-person plural) exhibited health improvements after the writing intervention. In other words, the research participants who were able to take a variety of perspectives on their own upsetting experiences were better able to gain health benefits as a consequence of exploring their troubling experience. It is doubtful that any of the writers explicitly recognized that they were changing their pronouns from writing session to writing session—the power of pronouns seems to be in their transparent depiction of the social self. Investigations are currently underway (Stone & Pennebaker, 2002) exploring the possibility of pronoun manipulation in a writing intervention to determine whether directed flexibility can produce the same physical health benefits that were gained by participants who naturally took differing perspectives.

Psychological distress has also been found to be associated with pronoun use, specifically, first-person singular pronouns. In an analysis of suicide notes, Henken (1976) reported an unusually high incidence of first-person singular pronouns, concluding that suicidal people are extraordinarily preoccupied with themselves. As researchers attempted to uncover the direction of causality in this relationship, they discovered that when people are induced to sad moods, they develop an increase in self-focus and use an increased number of first-person pronouns (Salovey, 1992; Wood, Saltzberg, & Goldsamt, 1990). While promising, these studies were focused on sad mood rather than depression.

Two more recent projects are of particular relevance to this chapter.

First, Stirman and Pennebaker (2001) conducted an analysis of word use in the poems of suicidal and closely matched nonsuicidal poets. A comparison of the first-person pronouns among the two groups of poets was quite remarkable. Poets such as Sylvia Plath and Anne Sexton placed themselves—through the first-person pronouns—quite intimately in their work. For example, in a poem discussing a broken relationship, Plath writes, ". . . I fancied you'd return the way you said, / But **I** grow old and **I** forget your name. / (**I** think **I** made you up inside **my** head.) . . ." The poet matched most closely with Plath in this study was Denise Levertov. While she also writes of broken love, the remove she displays is evident by a striking absence of first-person pronouns: ". . . The ache of marriage: / thigh and tongue, beloved, / are heavy with it, / it throbs in the teeth / We look for communion / and are turned away, beloved, / each and each. . . ." This pattern of pronoun use was consistent across the analysis, with suicidal poets using "I" at a much greater rate than nonsuicidal poets. This study provided evidence in support of a social integration model of suicide. The preoccupation with self and relative absence of references to others suggests the social detachment of the suicidal individual.

Another relevant experiment focusing on the relationship between first-person pronouns and depression was conducted by Rude, Gortner, and Pennebaker (2002). The participants in that study were college freshmen who were currently depressed, formerly depressed, or never depressed. The task for these students was to write their deepest thoughts and feelings about coming to college, and the researchers explored the pattern of pronoun use throughout. Not surprisingly in light of the growing evidence of this relationship, they found that currently depressed students used significantly greater numbers of first-person pronouns in their essays when compared with never-depressed students. An unexpected finding arose in the language of the formerly depressed students. Although they began by using fewer first-person pronouns than the never-depressed students, by the end of their essays they used higher levels than the currently depressed students.

These studies offer converging evidence of a reliable association between particular patterns of pronoun usage and psychological state. This linguistic evidence supports early theory and empirical evidence depicting an intense self-focus among depressed and suicidal individuals, and suggests that additional research may allow us to develop a reliable index of depressed or suicidal language.

☐ Katie's Diary

The generous sharing of Katie's diaries allowed us a unique opportunity to look for naturally occurring evidence of the linguistic markers of depression and suicide that we have uncovered in the laboratory and in historical literary analyses. We also had a chance to follow one individual across a length of time that is somewhat uncommon in a psychological laboratory, allowing us to map the ebb and flow of Katie's psychological state onto her language. Because we have a large corpus of texts in which college students wrote about traumatic experiences, who they are, their plans for the day, or simply in a stream-of-consciousness manner, we were able to place Katie's diary in a context of other students similar in age and developmental stage.

Analytic Strategy

In order to process the diary entries with LIWC, each entry was first converted to an individual text file. There were 152 unique diary entries, beginning June 8, year 1 and ending June 20, year 2 (the following year), and there was no regular frequency with which Katie made a diary entry. Most of the entries were made one per day (77.6%) or two per day (17.8%), but occasionally she made up to four entries in one day. Katie turned to her diary with great irregularity across the 13 months of entries we have available for analysis. As shown in Figure 5.1, the frequency of diary entries per month ranges from 2 (in April, year 2) to 24 (in July,

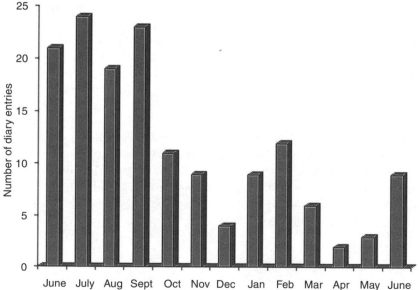

FIGURE 5.1. Frequency of diary entries, from June year 1 through June year 2

year 1). It is clear that she wrote in her diary much less frequently in the last few months of her life.

We organized Katie's diary into five groups based roughly on the academic school year:

Grouping	Dates	Number of entries	Mean number of words per entry	Life issues
Summer	6/8–8/31	64	761	Intense focus on family history; very little mention of body; extreme sorrow and pain
Fall semester	9/1–12/31	47	586	Anger and self-abuse; body and dieting; breakup with Mark; visiting sister and mother
Jan-Feb	1/1–2/28	21	415	Feeling strong and in control
Mar-May	3/5–5/30	11	350	Lack of control; disconnecting from people; anger at self
June	6/1–6/20	9	639	Loss; pain

The spring semester (year 2) was subdivided to allow a finer-grained analysis of the last months of Katie's life. We particularly wanted to examine the June entries in close detail in an effort to uncover linguistic hints of her emotional state.

We examined three broad categories in our analysis of Katie's diaries. First, we considered Katie's self-relevant and social language in order to understand how she was talking about herself and the people she knew. Because of their relevance for psychological distress and social connection or alienation, we analyzed Katie's use of pronouns over time. We focused primarily on first-person pronouns because of their established role as markers of depression and suicidality. To explore her social integration, we also analyzed first-person plural pronouns ("we," "us," "our") and social words (e.g., "friend," "family," "party").

Second, we examined Katie's emotional and cognitive language. The analysis of depressed college students (Rude, Gortner, & Pennebaker, 2002) revealed that depressed people use more negative emotion words and fewer positive emotion words. In addition, because of the well-established link between different aspects of cognitive style and depression (e.g., Beck, 1976; Beck, Lester, & Albert, 1973), we examined cognitive words (e.g., "cause," "think," "realize") and the LIWC categories that have been associated with cognitive complexity (Pennebaker & King, 1999).

Finally, we explored specific content categories that had unique relevance for Katie's life. The analysis of words related to the physical aspects of life—eating and sex—was important because of their relevance for Katie's struggles with her physical appearance and weight and her current and past sexual relationships. We also examined her word usage in the religion and death categories. Because both areas were frequently mentioned in Katie's diaries, we wanted to test for significant patterns that might provide insight into her state of mind.

Comparison Group

In order to determine whether Katie's language use was typical of college students similar in age, we compared her diary entries to essays written by college students in our emotional disclosure paradigm. Within the paradigm, students are asked to write their deepest thoughts, feelings, and emotions about the most upsetting experience of their lives for 15 to 20 minutes a day for three to four consecutive days. Students generally write about a wide range of traumatic events, from the loss of a family pet to relationship problems to childhood sexual or physical abuse. We have also used a variety of other topics with this writing technique, including stream-of-consciousness writing, plans for the day, and deepest thoughts and feelings about who they really are—a kind of self-exploration. These essay topics were chosen as a comparison group because of their similarity (when combined) to diary entries. Katie did indeed write about traumatic experiences, plans for her day, her thoughts and feelings about who she was, and often in a stream-of-consciousness style. Our comparison group for this project therefore comprised 764 essays written on these various topics, and we used the mean value across all groups for each category in one-sample t-tests to determine whether Katie's language was statistically unusual. The mean scores for the primary linguistic categories, by writing group, are presented in Table 5.1. Correlations among these variables are shown in Table 5.2.

☐ Results

The writing themes that we are best able to analyze can be broken down into three broad categories: issues of self and social integration, emotional

TABLE 5.1. Mean scores of linguistic categories for comparison group and Katie

Linguistic category	Comparison group				Katie
	Traumatic experience	Self	Plans for the day	Stream of consciousness	
I/me/my	7.58	13.87	10.62	11.23	12.23
We/us/our	1.43	0.22	1.03	0.67	0.32
Positive emotion	2.00	4.14	1.51	3.39	3.21
Negative emotion	2.79	1.74	0.61	1.58	3.80
Question marks	3.19	3.78	0.79	3.10	1.42
Eating	0.11	0.01	1.49	0.37	0.58
Sex	0.23	0.51	0.04	0.21	0.80
Death	0.41	0.06	0.02	0.06	0.20
Religion	0.25	0.56	0.10	0.11	0.44
No. of texts	284	81	294	105	152

Note: For the analyses, a total mean score was calculated for each linguistic category by calculating the average of the four comparison groups.

and cognitive processes, and specific writing topics. Each is discussed separately.

Self and Social Integration

The ways individuals think about themselves vis-à-vis their social network can be analyzed in multiple ways. As noted above, a tremendous

TABLE 5.2. Overall correlations among linguistic categories

	I/me/my	We/us/our	Question marks	Positive emotion	Negative emotion	Religion	Death	Sex
I/me/my	—							
We/us/our	−.15	—						
Question marks	.24**	−.12	—					
Positive emotion	−.18*	.16	.07	—				
Negative emotion	.41**	−.07	.01	−.26**	—			
Religion	.04	.23**	.13	.17*	.05	—		
Death	.10	−.14	.03	.03	.19*	.39**	—	
Sexual	.08	.06	.17*	.32**	−.02	−.02	.20*	—
Eating	−.19*	−.12	−.06	−.26**	.06	−.08	−.08	−.17*

* Correlation is significant at the 0.05 level (2-tailed).
** Correlation is significant at the 0.01 level (2-tailed).
N = 152

amount of information can be gleaned from the ways people use pronouns and, more broadly, how they make reference to other individuals.

Because of the accumulating evidence of the relationship between first-person pronouns and depression, our first analysis focused on these pronouns. During the summer of year 1, the more frequently Katie was using "I," "me," or "my," the more she used present tense verbs, cognitively complex language, and more optimism and sad words. This pattern of language use suggests that Katie was exploring her thoughts and feelings about herself in the present. The fall semester was characterized by a continued focus on the present, and a strong association with affect in general, negative emotions (particularly anger), and body-relevant language. The correlates for this period suggest that Katie was not writing about herself in a cognitively complex way: she used shorter sentences, and common (and small) words, and the linguistic categories that represent cognitive mechanisms were no longer significantly related to first-person pronouns. During January and February of year 2, she returned to her cognitive orientation. The pronoun correlates during this period also indicated that Katie wrote about herself and other people, and that her self-relevant entries were characterized by strong associations with negative emotions and swear words.

As the semester continued, March through May, Katie began to write more often about the past as well as the present, using insight language (e.g., "understand," "because," "believe," "know," "accept," "wonder"). Indicating a withdrawal into herself, the more she used first-person pronouns during this period, the less she used language referring to other people. By the last month of her life, relationships between these pronouns and other linguistic categories were mostly negative. The more Katie referred to herself, the less she used future tense verbs, positive emotions including optimism, and anger words. The only two positive correlates during the June of year 2 were sadness words and discrepancy words (e.g., "not," "except"). Perhaps tellingly, this was also the only period in which Katie's use of first-person pronouns was not correlated with present tense verbs. The linguistic character of her last month of entries, as portrayed by first-person pronoun usage, is one of emotional and physical distancing, sadness, and an orientation toward the past.

Because frequent usage of these pronouns, particularly the first-person singular "I," has been associated with depression and suicide, we expected to see elevated frequencies of these pronouns. Indeed, as seen in Figure 5.2, Katie's writings were characterized by high levels of these pronouns relative to our control group. Two-tailed t-tests comparing the mean scores for each period against the mean value for first-person pronouns from our comparison group revealed that this difference was significant at every period (all $ps < .02$). Recall that our comparison group comprised students writing in a focused and relatively brief way about self-relevant

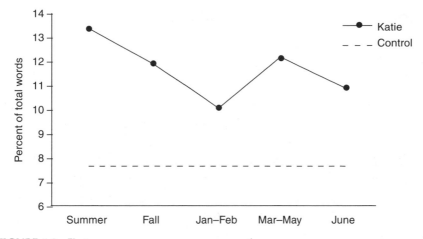

FIGURE 5.2. First-person pronoun usage across time

and often traumatic experiences in their lives. The fact that Katie's language contained higher levels of these pronouns suggests that she was maintaining an unusual amount of self-focus for a very long period of time.

Although the LIWC analysis can provide us with a quantitative picture of Katie's language, it is helpful to turn to her diary entries for a snapshot of her experience as it relates to our analysis.

*8/22: **I** refuse to eat anymore. **I** refuse to take care of **myself** anymore. **I**'m sick of it—all of the fucking heaviness on **my** heart. **I**'m FUCKING SICK OF ALL OF IT. **I** WANT TO GO AWAY! **I** WANT EVERYBODY TO GO AWAY. **I** WANT TO BE LEFT ALONE. **I** DON'T WANT TO BE TOUCHED—NOT **my** body, nor **my** heart! It hurts. It always hurts. It's no different this time. **I** feel like **I**'m being shut out for who **I** am. **I**'m so sick OF **MY** WRITING IN THIS JOURNAL. **I** HATE IT. **I** SOUND SO DAMN PATHETIC! **I** HATE **MYSELF**. **I** WANT TO DIE! WHAT **I** DO ISN'T GOOD ENOUGH!!*

*11/28: It killed **me** how much **I** hurt Mark. **I** want so badly to make him happy and make it up to him. Maybe we got the kinks out. Maybe it's better now. All **I** know, **I** hate to argue. **I** hate it. . . . **I** never want to hurt him again. **I** will do much better now than **I** did before. **I**'ll relax and work on being **me**. **I** have had a difficult time with **my** food. **I** struggle with wanting to be thin, but **I** know what's really important in life. If **I** become a strict* *vegetarian,* **I**'*ll be ok.* **I**'*ll lose weight easily. Like* **my** *Mom did.* **I** *don't want to eat barely any fat.* **I** *know* **I**'*m obsessing today—understandable. A lot of things are going on inside of* **me**. *I'm different than* **my** *family.* **I** *know a lot more,* **I** *think.* **I** *think* **I** *can make it—somewhere good in life.*

2/8: **I** *love Mark. He told* **me** *that he feels trapped. How could* **I** *tell him that* **I** *was reading his diary?* **I** *feel so awful.* **I** *had to know what his intentions were with* **me**. **I** *can't believe* **I** *told him all about Chris.* **I** *hope he never talks about it again.*

I *feel awful that* **I** *hurt him yesterday. So* **I** *made* **myself** *eat an incredible amount.* **I** *wonder if* **I** *spoiled his birthday.* **I** *didn't mean to, if* **I** *did. It's all so awful.* **I** *wish he would come here soon so* **I** *could make love to him.* **I** *do anything and everything for him because he truly deserves it. He has put up with so much crap from* **me**.

Katie's pronoun usage is consistent with a growing body of empirical evidence associating depression-related self-focus with high frequencies of first-person pronouns. The excerpted passages provide evidence of another important factor: the relative absence of pronouns other than first-person. Except for using "him" and "his" as she writes about Mark, there is a dearth of any other pronouns such as "we," "they," etc. A closer examination of these few male pronouns reveals that they occur in a totally self-focused context. Katie may have been talking about "him," but the focus of her thoughts and words remained on herself and what she did or did not do with Mark. The healthy flexibility in pronoun usage reported by Campbell and Pennebaker (2003) seems to be absent in Katie's writing. The linguistic correlates further suggest a chilling picture of a young woman's emotional struggles with herself and her world. Finally, the saturation of her language with first-person pronouns indicates a psychologically unhealthy focus on her own experience.

The Social World

Pronouns provide a linguistic reflection of social experience. It is impossible to talk about oneself in a social setting without using first-person plurals like "we" or "us." In addition, the LIWC category of social words (e.g., "friend," "children," "meeting," "girls," "party") fleshes out other aspects of social relationships and participation. Fitting in and relating to her peers was somewhat difficult for Katie, and she frequently wrote about feeling socially isolated and alone. The conclusion to her entry on September 1, year 1, "Alienation and isolation are my dearest friends" echoes a common theme in her journal:

> *I hate people. I don't need anyone—or anything anymore. They treat me like I'm a fucking disease or something . . . I hate them all. I know factually that it is harder for me to reach out than for them because I don't have anyone who loves me. No one has proven to me that they love me—only that they'll put up with me. (8/12)*
>
> *. . . Is it so wrong to want to have a family? It's always been such a big dream for me. But my old family life seems to come up now, being alone, abandoned, rejected and neglected. . . . It has affected my life with people. It's alienated me from simply [sic] honesty, open personality. . . . I'm scared, but I have to tell myself I'll be all right because I've always been by myself . . . . (6/18)*

Linguistic evidence of Katie's detachment from social relationships was found in an analysis of words from the social category. Katie used significantly fewer words from this category across all but one of the periods of diary entries, relative to our comparison group. As illustrated in the top panel of Figure 5.3, the final month of entries was characterized by the fewest social words. An indication of social integration can be suggested by use of the pronoun "we." The bottom panel of Figure 5.3 depicts Katie's use of this pronoun. One-sample t-tests comparing Katie's language with that of our comparison group indicated that she used significantly lower levels of this pronoun across all periods. Together, these two categories provide a picture of a young woman who was detached from a cohesive social structure.

Emotional and Cognitive Factors

1. Positive and Negative Emotions

Depression is typically associated with high levels of negative emotion (Wood et al., 1990b) and a consistent inverse relationship with positive emotion (Watson & Kendall, 1989). Our work has provided mixed evidence for these relationships in language. Among college students who were either currently, formerly, or never depressed, high negative and

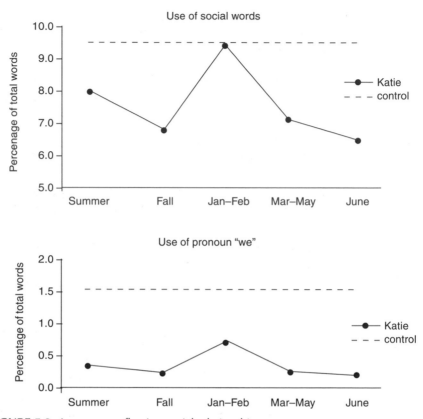

FIGURE 5.3. Language reflecting social relationships

low positive emotion word usage was associated with depression (Rude, Gortner, & Pennebaker, 2002). However, no such pattern was detected in the comparison of suicidal and nonsuicidal poets (Stirman & Pennebaker, 2001).

As Figure 5.4 illustrates, Katie's language in her diary did not fit the expected pattern typically reported for depression. In every period, two-tailed t-tests revealed that she used significantly more positive emotion words (e.g., "love," "care," "nice") than are typically used by college students writing about emotional topics (all $ps < .04$). Her use of negative emotion words also strayed from the expected pattern, for the most part. T-tests indicated that she did use significantly more negative emotion language in the summer and fall periods in year 1 ($ps < .01$), but the remainder of her diary entries displayed average levels of these words ($ps > .3$). These patterns are particularly interesting because the stereotype of depression and suicide-proneness is the use of emotion word patterns more

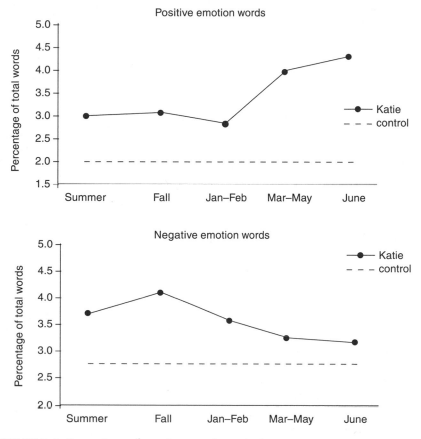

FIGURE 5.4. Percentage of emotion words across time

than anything else. In Katie's case (as in previous research), emotion words were not particularly diagnostic.

2. Cognitive Language

There are several linguistic markers of cognitive processes, including exclusive words (e.g., "although," "however," "than") and negations (e.g., "aren't," "can't," "don't") (Pennebaker & King, 1999). Frequent use of words from another cognitively oriented word category, certainty (e.g., "always," "never"), is indicative of severe depression (Teasdale et al., 2001) and reflects the development of rigid, black-and-white thinking. Katie's use of exclusive and negation words was not different from that of her peers, nor were there significant changes over time in her use of these words. The certainty category did show change over time, with Katie using

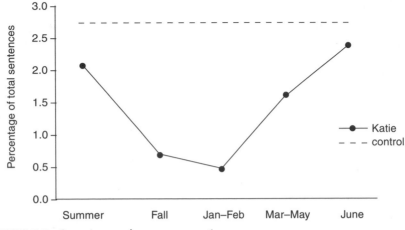

FIGURE 5.5. Question mark usage across time

very high levels of certainty words in the January to February period in year 2. All other periods were not different from our comparison group.

Post hoc analyses revealed one other intriguing finding. In Katie's last months of diary entries, her use of question marks rose significantly, as seen in Figure 5.5. Although the frequency of use in the final month was not significantly different from the comparison group, in the preceding months it had been much lower than normal. The interesting finding is that she demonstrated a significant rise in question mark usage from January to June in year 2 ($F[4,147] = 4.15$, $p < .01$). This certainly suggests a shift in perspective, and—if not due to chance—provides insight into a potential linguistic indicator of depression and/or suicide.

☐ Specific Issues

Within the broader category of words related to physical states and functions, the subcategories of eating and sex were directly relevant to Katie's experience. Her struggles with her weight and her often obsessive focus on food suggested that this category of words could tell a part of Katie's story. The sex category was assumed to be important because of the nature of her relationship with her boyfriend and her self-reported history of sexual abuse. Both of these categories of words are also relevant for depression, because depression can have a variety of consequences for appetite and sexual desire. They have also been found to be linguistic indicators of depression.

Eating

Katie wrote frequently about food and eating, whether she was denigrating herself for having eaten, voicing a desire to eat normally, or planning an often-severe dietary regimen. As shown in Figure 5.6, Katie did use significantly higher frequencies of words related to eating (e.g., "diet," "eat," "fat," "meal," "skinny"). The difference between her use of these words and that of our comparison group was significant at every period (all $p < .02$), demonstrating Katie's intense focus on issues surrounding food. The last two periods showed a decline in physical words in general, and eating words in particular, suggesting that Katie had begun to distance herself from her physical experience. Linguistic categories correlated with eating words suggest a change in the way Katie was writing about issues surrounding food. From the summer in year 1 to the March-to-May period in year 2, eating words were correlated positively with anger, sports (e.g., exercise), and numbers (reflecting calories or pounds), and negatively correlated with references to others. The June period in year 2, however, was characterized by a very different set of correlates. In her final month, the more Katie wrote about eating, the more she wrote about being sad, about her body, and about sleeping.

Sex

An unexpected finding in the suicidal poets project was that they used significantly greater percentages of sexual words across their careers than did nonsuicidal poets (Stirman & Pennebaker, 2001). This finding had

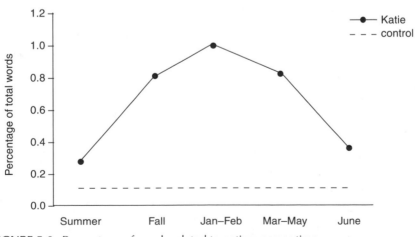

FIGURE 5.6. Percentage of words related to eating, across time

not been predicted, and the authors acknowledged that it may have been due to chance. However, similar patterns emerged with these words in Katie's diaries, suggesting that this relationship should be explored further. A related issue concerns the association between sexual abuse and suicide. In a recent review of studies exploring this relationship, all 21 studies found a significant relationship between abuse and suicidal ideation or successful suicide (Santa Mina & Gallop, 1998). The combination of these two findings suggests that the category of sexual words could be an important addition to the developing linguistic profile of depression and suicide.

Intimate relationships were quite complicated for Katie, and sex was often a potent source of that complexity. While it often provided a great deal of happiness and closeness with her boyfriend, just as often it was a source of pain, anger, and loneliness. Her references to childhood sexual abuse were also complex, sometimes engendering anger and other times sorrow. Figure 5.7 illustrates the time course of Katie's use of words relating to sex, and a similar pattern emerges here as with the other physical words, that is, a marked decline in the last period of diary entries. In fact, Katie used a significantly elevated percentage of sexual words until the last two periods (March to May, and June, year 2), when she dropped to more typical levels.

Religion

Quite often Katie addressed God in her diary entries, particularly during periods of upset. Figure 5.8 illustrates her use of these words across time,

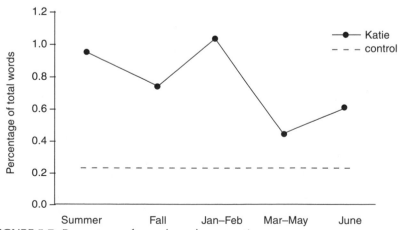

FIGURE 5.7. Percentage of sexual words, across time

in comparison to the average use of words in this category by college students. The rise in religious words (such as "God," "heaven," "church") is particularly noteworthy during the last period. In fact, her final diary entry was written as a prayer, or a series of pleas to God:

*Please, dear **God**, let me get an A on that test today. It would mean so very much to me. It would help lift my **spirits** higher. It truly would, and please let everything work out wonderfully the rest of the summer and let me accomplish a lot of good things for myself and be healthy and disciplined. Please, dear **God**, bring some wonderful encouraging, unbiased, loving, respecting people in my life....Please, dear **God**, let things pick up in my life beautifully. I want to feel whole inside, instead of being severed in hundreds of little pieces from my own and others' actions. . . . Please help me through this and next week, especially things are so hard right now.*

Death

Because Katie made references to death in some of her diary entries, we examined the frequency with which she used words in LIWC's death category. Surprisingly, Katie used significantly fewer death-relevant words than are typically used by people writing in an emotional context, across all periods of analysis. A comparison of the graphs in Figure 5.8 reveals an intriguing pattern. The sharp rise in religion words seen during the final period is accompanied by the lowest frequency of death words in all periods.

Although the frequency of death words during the final period represented the lowest value across all periods of analysis, the character of death words in that final period had a somber and personal quality, as shown in this portion of an entry:

6/15
*It **kills** me inside—not a friend in the world. I feel no connection with anyone, and it scares me so much. The world seems so cold, dark and scary. No matter what Mrs. W says, I'm alone, alone and left to myself. . . . I want to **kill** myself. **Bullet** though my heart—the only way I'll ever stop caring about people. . . . I did try reaching out again for the last time. People are so mean and selfish. I want to **kill** myself on my birthday. I have to.*

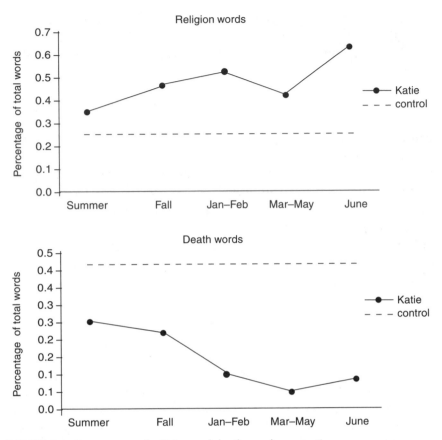

FIGURE 5.8. Percentage of religion and death words across time

Despite the intuitive assumption that death words would increase as an individual becomes despairing enough to contemplate and commit suicide, this pattern was not evident in Katie's diaries. However, the correlates of death words in June, year 2 were very evocative: the more she wrote about death, the more she talked about the past ($r = .71$, $p = .03$), anxiety ($r = .68$, $p = .04$), and sleep ($r = .77$, $p = .02$). The only other significant correlates of death words occurred in fall of year 1 and January–February year 2, and these were religion and swear words.

☐ Discussion

Supported by excerpts from her diary, our linguistic analysis of Katie's language provided clear snapshots of this young woman and her struggles with life. An overall picture of intense self-focus emerged, painted by her extraordinary use of first-person pronouns. Especially evocative were the correlates uncovered in the last month: the more Katie referred to herself, the more she used sadness and discrepancy words such as "but," "could," "if," and "wish." It may be especially important that during this month, the more she referred to herself, the less she used future tense verbs. Her comment on June 2, year 2, "I always had the answer for everything. What happened to me?" is startling as she refers to herself in the past tense. This negative correlation with future tense verbs provides insight to her statement "I just don't know. I hate the future so much. I'm so overwhelmed. I need to sleep now" (June 18). Katie was not writing about herself in the future during this period.

Another important pronoun-relevant issue is the lack of variability in her pronoun usage. Because flexibility in pronoun usage has been shown to be an important factor in healthy recovery from traumatic experiences (Campbell & Pennebaker, 2003), Katie's overreliance on first-person pronouns may be an important and telling issue. It is not simply the use of other pronouns that is believed to be important; Katie did use male and female pronouns at normal rates. The important relevance for pronoun flexibility appears to be associated with the ability to take on more than one perspective. This was not evident in Katie's language. When she used pronouns other than first-person, she frequently remained self-focused. For example, on December 1, year 1, Katie wrote:

> *I am so upset, so I'm going off on her. What am I going to do if Mark doesn't have his car. How am I going to see him at all next semester. . . . I know I could take the bus down to see him. . . . I love him so much. I don't want to lose him. I know things are hard for him. I feel everything he feels. . . .*

Although she uses nearly as many third-person pronouns in this brief passage (eight) as first-person pronouns (ten), she does not lose her ruminative self-focus.

The findings related to positive and negative emotion language were surprising in light of the literature on emotions and depression. Although we expected to find high levels of negative emotion words and low levels of positive emotion words, Katie used exceptionally high levels of positive emotion words and, for the most part, normal levels of negative emotion words. One potential explanation for these unexpected findings is that findings in the literature are typically based on brief, if intense, samples of college undergraduates' writings (e.g., Rude, Gortner, & Pennebaker, 2002). While these samples are quite informative concerning the relationship between emotional language and mood, they may not adequately address the language of true depression or suicide. Recall that the analysis of the poems of suicidal and nonsuicidal poets failed to find differences in emotional language between the two groups (Stirman & Pennebaker, 2001). That study, in combination with the current analysis, suggests that there may be a qualitative difference in the language of suicidal individuals that may make simple detection of suicidal despair difficult to detect on a cursory reading. The occurrence of normal levels of positive emotion words may not necessarily mean that the writer is safe from self-harm.

While Katie had sustained a higher than normal focus on the physical aspects of life throughout her diary, including frequent references to her body, eating, and sex, these diminished during the last four months of her life. This shift away from the physical experience of life, particularly for someone who had been so intensely focused on these elements, could indicate either a positive shift away from the obsessive focus on her physical appearance, or could provide further evidence of withdrawal from life. The latter suggestion is supported by the fact that all physical references during the last month were associated with an increased number of sad words and decreased references to achievement, other people, and her social life. Her use of religious words also displayed a marked increase in the last month. This combination hints at a change in focus for Katie away from the unhappiness of her life.

Finally, linguistic profiles associated with social integration (i.e., social words and "we") revealed a disconnected and isolated young woman. While she explicitly talks about her loneliness and separation from a social community, the casual reader of her diaries might mistake her constant discussion of particular individuals for a kind of social connection. Overall, Katie used significantly lower levels of this kind of language than are typically used by people her age. The precipitous drop in social words from January–February to June is particularly suggestive of a young woman detaching herself from others. The combination of this pattern with linguistic detachment from the physical aspects of life may be an important indicator of a dangerous psychological state. An interesting and unpredicted finding was the sharp rise in question marks, which accompanied the decline in social and physical words. While this may be poignant in its suggestion of questioning detachment, additional research is needed to uncover evidence of a reliable association. Of course, this is difficult because researchers and clinicians seldom have access to an adequate sample of writings from a suicidal individual. If this finding was not due to chance, it may provide a quick linguistic flag indicating trouble ahead.

Prediction and Intervention

An important goal of research into depression and suicide is identification of predictors and opportunities for intervention. Could Katie's diaries have offered such an opportunity to anyone reading them? She often wrote about others reading her diary; if she had given it to someone, could they have identified periods of strength or concern? One problem for Katie's diaries, in particular, is the inconsistency of her thoughts, often from sentence to sentence. After writing a sentence about hating Mark and wanting to punish him, the next sentence often spoke of her deep and abiding love for him. These shifts occur at the sentence level and the diary entry level, making it difficult to get a concrete sense of her state of mind. Statements of intent to kill herself are sprinkled throughout the entire diary. Focusing explicitly on the content of what Katie wrote gives the reader an ever-shifting and difficult to grasp image.

Linguistic analyses paint a different picture. For example, there was an unmistakable change in Katie's language during the January–February period of year 2. Examination of nearly every figure reveals a marked difference in that period, relative to all others. She wrote more diary entries and in them made fewer self-references and more social references. This period was characterized by the highest levels of eating and sexual words and the fewest question marks. While it is difficult to characterize any period of her diary entries as belonging to a neat categoriy, the tone of this set of entries suggests that Katie was generally doing quite well at this time. She wrote about feeling whole, in control of herself and her life, and living her life the way she wanted to live it. For example, on January 29 she wrote, "I really feel whole or pretty close to it inside my heart. I think I'll be ok now . . . I know I'm ok now, and I need to live the know-how in my actions. I want to live life my way." There is a stab at self-worth when she wrote on February 5, "She wanted me to be real with her. Fuck her. She had to earn it. Both of them." Of course, there are also references to a desire to commit suicide, and painful or sorrowful entries during this period. At the linguistic level, however, it is immediately obvious that Katie's language during this two-month period was most like that of a psychologically healthy individual, and it stands in marked contrast to all other periods. The shifts in her language after this period might have provided some suggestion that her psychological state was becoming worse, and the continued trend toward psychologically unhealthy language could have served as a flag, identifying her as a young woman in trouble.

It is important to recognize that the immediate content of Katie's diary entries was often misleading. For example, in her final entry, she wrote of events in the future: the arrival of a package, hopes for her relationship with Mark, and hopes for herself. A reader focusing on the content of this entry might not recognize the dangers that were revealed by a linguistic analysis. We believe that our approach can provide great insight into a writer's state of mind, offering signposts of trouble and of hope.

☐ Conclusion

Katie's diaries allowed us to expand our exploration of linguistic correlates of depression and suicide. Because of the unfortunate prevalence of both depression and suicide, any contribution to our understanding of indicators or predictors is invaluable. In this case, we found additional support for the relationship between depression and first-person pronouns and physical words. The patterns of emotional language exhibited by Katie, in combination with the suicidal poets study (Stirman & Pennebaker, 2001), suggest a new avenue of exploration in the hunt for markers of severe depression and suicide. Following changes in language across a relatively long period of time in the life of a depressed individual provided insight into the relationships among these variables as Katie's psychological health waxed and waned, and as her depression took hold of her one last time. The casual reader of these diaries would undoubtedly be struck by the experiences Katie wrote about—the nouns and verbs—but would probably not detect the more subtle changes in the important smaller words across the entries. We believe there is great potential for linguistic analyses to continue to flesh out both the experience of depression and also to provide a linguistic fingerprint of this terrible disorder.

☐ Notes

1. This research was funded, in part, by a grant from the National Institutes of Health (MH52391) and a National Science Foundation Graduate Research Fellowship (LDS). We are indebted to Christina Garcia for her excellent and conscientious help in preparing the diary entries for analysis.

☐ References

Beck, A. T. (1976). *Cognitive therapy and the emotional disorders*. New York: International Universities Press.
Beck, A. T., Lester, D., & Albert, N. (1973). Suicidal wishes and symptoms of depression. *Psychological Reports, 33,* 770.

Campbell, R. S., & Pennebaker, J. W. (2003). The secret life of pronouns: Flexibility in writing style and physical health. *Psychological Science, 14,* 60–65.

Henken, V. J. (1976). Banality reinvestigated: A computer-based content analysis of suicidal and forced-death documents. *Suicide and Life-Threatening Behavior, 6,* 36–43.

Pennebaker, J. W. (2002). Words of wisdom: Analysis of word use across the lifespan. Manuscript submitted for publication.

Pennebaker, J. W., & Francis, M. E. (1996). Cognitive, emotional, and language processes in disclosure. *Cognition and Emotion, 10,* 601–626.

Pennebaker, J. W., Francis, M. E., & Booth, R. J. (2001). *Linguistic Inquiry and Word Count (LIWC 2001): A computerized text analysis program.* Mahwah, NJ: Erlbaum.

Pennebaker, J. W., & King, L. A. (1999). Linguistic styles: Language use as an individual difference. *Journal of Personality and Social Psychology, 77,* 1296–1312.

Rude, S. S., Gortner, E. M., & Pennebaker, J. W. (2002). Language use of depressed and depression-vulnerable college students. Manuscript in preparation.

Salovey, P. (1992). Mood-induced self-focused attention. *Journal of Personality and Social Psychology, 62,* 699–707l.

Santa Mina, E. E., & Gallop, R. M. (1998). Childhood sexual and physical abuse and adult self-harm and suicidal behaviour: A literature review. *Canadian Journal of Psychiatry, 43,* 793–800.

Stirman, S. W., & Pennebaker, J. W. (2001). Word use in the poetry of suicidal and non-suicidal poets. *Psychosomatic Medicine, 63,* 517–522.

Stone, L. D., & Pennebaker, J. W. (2002). Facing the terrorist attacks of 9/11: The surprising consequences of emotional writing. Manuscript in preparation.

Teasdale, J. D., Scott, J., Moore, R. G., Hayhurst, H., Pope, M., & Paykel, E. S. (2001). How does cognitive therapy prevent relapse in residual depression? Evidence from a controlled trial. *Journal of Consulting and Clinical Psychology, 69,* 347–357.

Watson, D., & Kendall, P. C. (1989). Common and differentiating features of anxiety and depression: Current findings and future directions. In P. C. Kendall & D. Watson (Eds.), *Anxiety and depression: Distinctive and overlapping features* (pp. 493–508). San Diego, CA: Academic Press.

Wood, J. V., Saltzberg, J. A., & Goldsamt, L. A. (1990). Does affect induce self-focused attention? *Journal of Personality and Social Psychology, 58,* 899–908.

Wood, J. V., Saltzberg, J. A., Neale, J. M., Stone, A. A., & Rachmiel, T. C. (1990). Self-focused attention, coping responses, and distressed mood in everyday life. *Journal of Personality and Social Psychology, 58,* 1027–1036.

CHAPTER Thomas E. Ellis

Thoughts of Katie:
A Cognitive Perspective

> The human understanding, once it has adopted an opinion . . . draws all things else to support and agree with it. And although there may be a greater number and weight of instances to be found on the other side, yet these it either neglects or despises . . . in order that its former conclusions may remain inviolate. —Francis Bacon

What was she *thinking*? This simple yet essential question surely must have perplexed those who cared about Katie, not only after her death, but during her troubled life as well. Moreover, the question is of crucial significance to clinicians and scholars who would seek to understand her life and death and to prevent the premature deaths of others like her. We will begin with an overview of the empirical literature on cognition and suicide, illustrated with excerpts from Katie's diary, and then proceed to a synthesis in the form of a cognitive case conceptualization. We will conclude with an examination of Katie's failed attempts at self-improvement vis-à-vis the cognitive model.

☐ Cognition and Suicide

Cognitive-behavior therapy (CBT) views thinking processes as a critical aspect of psychopathology and therapeutic intervention. In this context, "cognition" is viewed, not only as *what* the individual is thinking, but also *how* she is thinking. In the content arena are such constructs as irrational beliefs and dysfunctional attitudes; in the "how" arena are such processes as cognitive distortions, problem solving, schema activation, and explanatory style. Large bodies of research have established these constructs and others as key in the genesis, maintenance, and resolution of psychopathological conditions (e.g., Clark and Fairburn, 1997).

Although cognitive therapy's rise to prominence in the treatment of depression and other conditions began in the 1960s (e.g., Beck, 1967; Ellis, 1962), the application of concepts specifically to suicidal states and processes is relatively new (Ellis, 1986). A key question is "How does the thinking of the suicidal individual differ from that of other, even severely depressed but nonsuicidal, individuals?" In other words, is it safe to assume (1) that the suicidal person sees the world differently from the individual who may be troubled but has no urge to die, and (2) that helping suicidal individuals to change the way they view things would decrease the likelihood of their ending their own lives?

The current state of the science indicates that the first of these is, in fact, a safe assumption. An analysis of the empirical evidence is beyond the scope of this chapter, but reviews can be found in Ellis (1986) and Rudd, Joiner, and Rajab (2001). Conclusions regarding the second assumption is awaiting further study, but preliminary findings are promising (e.g., Linehan, 1993; Rudd, Joiner, & Rajab, 2001; Townsend et al., 2001).

Let us consider briefly some of the more prominent findings in the cognition and suicide literature. Most of these are evident in Katie's diary, and I will illustrate them with specific passages where possible.

Dichotomous Thinking

In some of the first research into the relationship between cognition and suicidality, Neuringer (1961) found that suicidal subjects evaluated various concepts, including life and death, more *extremely* than comparison subjects. This was first observed in 1885 by Wescott, who referred to it as "polarization" (Hughes and Neimeyer, 1990). "Black-and-white thinking" has since become a prominent focus in CBT with suicidal individuals (e.g., Ellis and Newman, 1996).

Polarization describes Katie's world better perhaps than any other single characteristic. Her life is a virtual roller coaster ride, as her emotions follow day-to-day (sometimes hour-to-hour) reversals in her thinking. A consistent theme, for example, is her difficulty in finding a middle ground between dependent involvement with others and the safety (and sadness) of social isolation; she is constantly swinging from one extreme to the other. Indeed, she understands this to some extent: "I need to be open to certain people. I seem so extremist in some ways. All or nothing. I can't live an empowering balance this way" (June 23). Later entries show her inability to find this balance, such as when she admonishes herself, "Great going, Katie. You're managing to throw and push some-one else away" (August 5), and then, one week later, "I hate people. I don't need anyone or anything anymore. They treat me like I'm a fucking disease. I hate all of them." The very next day, she writes, "I went out with Carl last night. It was so nice. . . . I really love him. He has always been so incredibly good to me."

Regardless of the subject—her weight, her friends, her boyfriend's love, or the general state of the world—it is impossible to predict from one day to the next how Katie will feel about things. One day she resolves to "eat healthy," the next day she is on a starvation diet. On several occasions, she describes enjoyable sexual encounters with Mark, only to resolve soon thereafter to abstain from sex entirely because she feels used. It is no wonder that Katie experiences her happiness as beyond her control (see below).

Cognitive Rigidity

Commonly observed by clinicians and confirmed empirically by Neuringer (1964) as well as several later researchers, cognitive rigidity is thought to impede effective problem-solving by interfering with the generation of creative alternatives. Origins of this rigidity are not well understood. How-ever, it is a central focus in problem-solving training programs, and there is some evidence that it can be modified (e.g., Clum & Lerner, 1990; Rudd et al., 2001). This characteristic will be addressed further as we explore possible reasons why Katie's persistent efforts at self-betterment were unsuccessful.

Hopelessness

Conceptualized by Beck (Beck et al., 1979) as a *cognitive* process rather than an emotion, hopelessness is viewed as a compelling set of negative expectations for the future leading to an affective state of despair. Studies utilizing the Beck Hopelessness Scale have shown that hopelessness plays a crucial mediating role between depression and suicidality (Minkoff, Bergman, Beck, & Beck, 1973).

Katie's hopelessness follows a waxing and waning course. She shows considerable optimism on many occasions, as when she reflects, "The past is just history. . . . I survived all this. That makes me strong in character and mind. It makes me a hero for and of myself. . . . It happened. I won't deny such a thing, and it happened to my family. This is like a book that sits on the shelf . . . .but it's only a book" (July 5). However, in the weeks leading up to her death, her entries take on a distinctly and consistently more pessimistic tone:

I can't stand myself and my life anymore. The very things I believe in are starting to disappear. I'm really hurting, but I can't talk about it because there is nothing left to talk about. . . . I've just freaked out because I don't have any control whatsoever in my life at all. It's absolutely terrifying. (May 30)

Deficient Problem Solving

A relationship between interpersonal problem-solving ability (or appraisal) and suicidality is perhaps the most consistent finding in the research literature on cognition and suicide (see Rudd, Joiner, & Rajab [2001] for a recent review). Problem-solving difficulties may be one of the main contributors to the development of hopelessness (Dyer & Kreitman, 1984), and training in problem-solving skills shows considerable promise in the treatment of suicidal patients (Townsend et al., 2001).

Katie is constantly aware of her interpersonal difficulties (a perception that is validated in the police report following her suicide, which notes that Mark had stated that Katie "did not really have any friends that she hung out with"). Often, her attempted solution to interpersonal problems involves high emotionality and confrontation:

I can't afford to let anyone close to me again to hurt me. My sincere love for my friends brings the most pain once it's been taunted. I have to tell Joyce off for my own self. . . . I'm going to call up Joyce and tell her what a complete asshole she is and that I think it's best we don't see each other anymore. . . . Joyce is just going to get it when she least expects it. She's so ruthless and cruel. She's got nothing on top of me, to destroy me with. I hate her so much that she's going to just get it. (May 30)

Perfectionism

Various authors have discussed perfectionism as a vulnerability factor for suicide (e.g., Maltsberger, 1986). Hewitt, Flett, and Weber (1994) found that perfectionism discriminated between suicidal and nonsuicidal individuals and played a mediating role between life stress and suicide ideation.

Perfectionism is the vulnerability into which Katie seems to have the least insight. Her ruminations on her weight, appearance, and achievements have a monotonous and ruminative quality. Although she concedes, "I know I can't be perfect" and sometimes goes on at length about the disadvantages and unfairness of perfectionism ("It makes me miserable"), her behavior consistently shows that her perfectionistic ideals endure. Her lack of resolution on this issue is particularly evident in the following passage:

I'm just so sick of all this crap. If I could lose 30 lbs, I definitely would stay perfectly *healthy. I wish I was so skinny and beautiful already. I know I'm exceptionally beautiful. However, it's as if I'm still the sweet girl next door. I don't stand out very much like I know I would if I got much thinner. I am so used to this abusive cycle. If I had a plan to follow, I would follow it* perfectly. *I refuse to lose my health and my concentration. I finally feel like I'm getting it back. I never cared really if people thought I was beautiful or not because everyone knew I was smart, artistic and strong. But overall, I'm sick of it. I'm twenty and really want to be noticed by everyone. I think if everyone considered me gorgeous, Mark would see how lucky he is to have me by his side. Then, in his mind, no girl would or could compare to me because I reached utter* perfection—*not just physical but also mental—I would not be sloppy with my words and actions. Everything would be in a complete balance. I would never need to get jealous anymore. (December 6, emphasis added)*

Dysfunctional Attitudes

A key focus in CBT, dysfunctional attitudes (such as "I must gain everyone's approval" or "If I do not achieve highly, then I am a failure") have been studied extensively with respect to depression but relatively little with respect to suicidal individuals. Ellis and Ratliff (1986) found that, even when compared with equally depressed counterparts, suicidal patients exhibited dysfunctional attitudes to a greater extent regarding acceptance, achievement, and emotional control. Katie clearly struggled with all of these, none more so than the belief that her negative emotions are caused by other people (rather than the way she views things). This typically takes the form of her sense of being "hurt" by other people:

> *I know Mark would rather live with his guy friends. That really hurt my feelings. (December 14)*
>
> *I asked Mark if I could stay here for the summer. I saw that he didn't really want me around. It all hurt my feelings. Oh well. What do I expect? (December 26)*
>
> *It hurts so much to see that he still does things for her. (January 9)*
>
> *I do it to please him and keep him satisfied, but all he does is get tired of me and not want to put much effort into holding me. That hurts. It* <u>makes me feel</u> *so empty inside. (January 15, emphasis added)*

It is clear that Katie believes that she is responsible for others' feelings as well:

> *I don't like hurting people or their feelings at all. It irks me, especially when I get stupid with Mark. I see it hurt[s] him and vice versa. (January 18)*
>
> *I want to put my focus on building him up inside. . . . I know I'm very good with people this way. (June 2)*
>
> *I always spent so much time trying to figure out what would* <u>make him happier</u>, *help him, why he acts the way he does. (June 28, year 1, emphasis added)*

☐ Process Issues

As previously observed, Katie's emotional life is highly unstable. How does cognitive therapy explain the fact that Katie seems to think and feel something one day and something very different the next? The answer lies in the concept of "schema activation" (Beck, Rush, Shaw, & Emery, 1979). A schema can be thought of as a deeply entrenched set of beliefs about the self and the world that is learned through early experience. The schema filters information and predisposes the individual toward certain types of emotional and behavioral responses. For example, an individual with a schema characterized by distrust might be slow to disclose personal information, hypersensitive to signs of threat, and quick to become defensive about perceived slights. Many schemas are thought to lie dormant until activated by relevant stimuli. When this occurs, the person is said to enter a "mode," a state comprising congruent thoughts, feelings, behaviors, and physical reactions (Beck, 1996). Modes can be benign (e.g., "school mode"), clinically significant (e.g., the "primal mode" seen in a panic attack), or potentially lethal (e.g., the "suicidal mode," recently proposed by Rudd [2000]).

In Katie's case, the schema of greatest salience clearly has to do with her own worth and lovability, and the "relevant stimuli" are events experienced by Katie as interpersonal criticism or rejection. It is impossible from diary material to gauge accurately the extent to which Katie is actually mistreated by her peers; but it is an almost daily issue, and one senses an exquisite sensitivity on her part to the slightest hint that a friend or acquaintance dislikes her or looks down on her. Most importantly, regardless of whether her mistreatment is real or perceived, her reaction is not disappointment or annoyance, but rage and despair and she quickly and easily slips into suicidal mode. Here is one of many examples:

I feel so suicidal. People still don't understand me—thought a few did. Well obviously, not really. I want to die. My heart hurts. Everything I ever wrote about marriage and relationships are true. Everything bad I've ever saw and learned as a child is true. I'm so hurt. Mark still doesn't understand me. I feel like time is running out for me. He told me his Mom has been acting all prissy. I suppose she's right. I won't be the one Mark will love that much to want to marry. Why do I dare to dream when all is truly here—my reality. Nobody would ever want to keep me. (June 27)

Although we cannot be certain, it appears that Mark's mother had said something negative about Katie. Yet, rather than disappointment, annoyance, or concern, what we see is activation of Katie's defectiveness schema, with the result that she feels depressed, views the future as hopeless, and feels the urge to end her life. However, by the end of this entry, she seems to have regained some equanimity. After describing a recent argument with Mark, she says,

Thank God we got back together. I knew it is so stupid to let my insecurities play such a huge part in my life and relationships. How else do I intend to get over them—by going against my fears—insecurities.

It is important to note that her sense of relief is not due to a change in her beliefs about her worth or the necessity of being loved my Mark, but because she feels reassured that their relationship will continue; consequently, she remains highly vulnerable to future rejection experiences.

☐ Synthesis: The Cognitive Case Formulation

Let us now synthesize this collection of cognitive distortions, dysfunctional attitudes and beliefs, and schema processes into a coherent picture of a person. For this we turn to Judith Beck's (1995) cognitive conceptualization method. As shown in Figure 6.1, core beliefs, shaped by early life experiences, are thought to give rise to derivative assumptions and beliefs, which then determine what automatic thoughts are triggered by events. These automatic thoughts are associated with characteristic emotional and behavioral reactions to these events.

To illustrate, let us consider Katie's frequent upset about Mark's noticing other girls. Here is a representative entry:

Well, tonight went to see this comedian with Mark. He looked at these two Latino girls a lot and a redhead. I'm sick of it—trying to accept myself the way I am. I have to give in to starving myself. It's no big deal. I fought so hard all year because I wanted to be healthy for Mark & for love. I won't get sick, I just won't eat again. It is so damn easy . . . I'm so angry. I'm sick of being not prettiest or the smartest. I used to be. I will be again I won't stand in my own way. (November 11)

Here we see a rapid progression from irritation with Mark to self-loathing and self-injurious behavior. One imagines a dramatically different reaction in an individual with a core belief of self-acceptance and a basic sense of worth. Core beliefs for a given individual are numerous and can be classified as beliefs about the self, beliefs about others, and beliefs about the world. Table 6.1 lists some of Katie's more salient beliefs and diary passages that reflect them.

Equally significant as beliefs and attitudes are the behaviors that are shaped by them. Known as "compensatory strategies" (Beck, 1996), these behaviors are the means by which an individual attempts to lessen the distress created by negative core beliefs. They often lead to as many problems as they solve, and are a major focus in cognitive therapy. Thus, because her extreme sense of defectiveness causes self-loathing and fear of abandonment, Katie tries desperately to lose weight and make good grades,

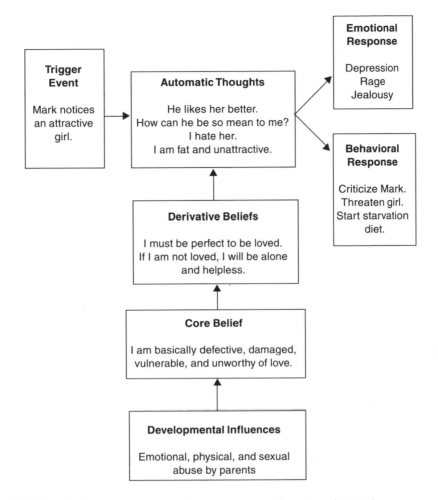

FIGURE 6.1. Cognitive conceptualization (Adapted from J. Beck, 1995)

and even attempts to gain acceptance by falsely telling others that her mother is dead. Unfortunately, even these extreme efforts to gain acceptance are not sufficient; for as soon as she begins to receive the closeness she craves, schemas based on past mistreatment are activated and she must change strategies and seek distance to lessen her fear of being rejected, betrayed, or abused. She is caught in a classic double bind: "If I am not loved, I will be helpless and alone; if I am loved, I will be abused and eventually rejected."

Eventual abandonment is an inevitable outcome of her belief system, no matter what or how hard she tries. This bind is reflected in numerous journal entries:

TABLE 6.1. Core beliefs, derivative beliefs, and representative passages

Core Beliefs	Representative Passage
Self: I am basically defective, vulnerable, and unworthy of love.	*I have to accept and appreciate what affection, little or a lot, they are willing to give. I feel like I'm some sort of bum begging for scraps. . . . I've been scarred in so many ways. . . . I feel like a wounded animal. (6/24)*
Others: People are undependable and will always hurt me and leave me.	*I just don't feel safe! I try and try and try, but I just don't. I am always looking out, or getting ready for someone to hurt me. (6/24)*
The world: The world is a dangerous and uncaring place, where vulnerable people can't survive.	*I don't feel like I have a friend in the world now—nobody. It kills me inside—not a friend in the world. I feel no connection with anyone, and it scares me so much. The world seems so cold, dark and scary. No matter what Mrs. W says, I'm alone, alone and left to myself. (6/15)*
Derivative beliefs	
I must be above average in every way.	*I don't care that much about being perfect anymore, just great. (10/3)*
I must be perfect to be loved.	*I think if everyone considered me gorgeous, Mark would see how lucky he is to have me by his side. (12/6)*
My body is my worth.	*He seems to respect her. Women like her that are so skinny . . . or who are drop-dead sexy and gorgeous. That all destroys me. Where do I fit in? I'm neither. (12/18)*
If I get too close to someone, I will be rejected.	*I don't want to be shaken and abused or mistreated at all. But I'm so afraid. My trust is not very good. (11/28)*
If I subordinate my needs to others, I will gain the love I need.	*I sacrificed all the good and bad things of this world so I could be with him. (6/22)*
If I can't be loved, my life is not worth living.	*People's love and trust is so elusive—so unreal. I want to die so badly. (2/4)*

I have to get myself together. I have things to hold on to here, people who love me. I suppose a big part of the upset lies in the past. I wonder if Mark really loves me. Does he? I feel that this relationship is stuck. Because of my own periodic emotional (more positive) state, I'll get myself out. (June 8)

I feel so abandoned and unconnected with everyone, everyone. I feel like I'm going to die. Ahhhhhg! Arg! Arrrrrg! Let everyone get a mass suicide. I'm just angry, just angry. I'm angry at all I've taken so far from people and life and fate. No more. In no more lies the freedom. No more! Fuck you all! Who tries to hurt me, control me, fuck with me? Fuck you all! Ahhhhh! (June 14)

I hate this heavy, stuck feeling. I hate it. I always run from situations that give me this feeling. I don't want this stuck, tied-down way I get when people get close to me. I hate it. It's so damn uncomfortable. I don't deal well with this. I feel a PTSD-attack coming on. It's not good. I need to get out, somehow, run away, be free. (June 26)

I can't help but think about people dying that are very close to me. If anything would happen, I don't know what I'd do. I risk so much when I let people get close to me—weak or strong—who gives a fuck—it's a very scary place to be. (June 26)

I cried a lot today. I miss my sister and home, but I just needed to cry, to embrace the present. Cried because I realized Mark really loved me and so do other people. Always yearning for love, but focused on Mommy's love and others who were mean to me. CAN'T GO ON LIKE THIS. DON'T WANT TO DIE LIKE MY FATHER. I AM AN ADDICT. I HAVE TO GET my life in line, order, chaos. (July 4)

Katie occasionally shows insight into the maladaptive nature of her strategies:

I feel I have to sacrifice myself to be close to people or make them love me. That's wrong. I don't owe that to anyone at all. It's wrong, and I won't lower my standards anymore. I can't believe I did. It's wrong—unfitting—and doesn't establish the environment I deserve. No, it doesn't. I refuse to put myself in situations that hurt me or make me feel uncomfortable. (June 24)

In summary, let myself go with people and connecting. I thought not connecting anymore was good. Well, I'm wrong—connecting is salvation. This way, I can accept people for what they are and have deep a connection and relationship I can have with them. THIS IS TRULY FREEDOM. (July 5)

Unfortunately, it is seldom possible for a person simply to decide to change his or her compensatory strategies without changing the beliefs causing the distress in the first place. Such a solution is not available to Katie. Only by seeing that she is, in fact, lovable and that not everyone will turn out to be as untrustworthy as the significant others in her past would she have been able either to seek true intimacy or tolerate being alone. Instead, even when she has experiences contrary to her schemas (and occasionally even rejoices about this), the information ultimately is either not attended to or is distorted to fit into her existing perceptions of others and the world. For example:

> *Wow. Shirley called me back and told me that she will give me rides to the incest survivors meetings, and Diane called back. She said she will give me a ride to Thursday weight meetings. Well, wow. Feel so good when people hear me and answer my needs. (July 17)*

And then, within the same entry:

> *I still feel very alone besides all this. Inside, I feel so stressed and uncared for, like I'm waiting for some vision containing my heart and mind in their own fullness. I feel so trapped right now.*

Indeed this rigid schema structure is one hallmark of a severe personality disorder and the central focus of CBT with such individuals (Beck, Freeman, & Associates, 1990).

☐ Katie's Constant Efforts to Change: Why Didn't She Succeed?

As the opening quote indicates, Francis Bacon (as well as others) recognized long before the birth of psychotherapy that human beings do not easily change deeply held beliefs, nor readily modify ingrained behaviors. Katie, however, seemed to plan a new self-change strategy every few days. On 20 occasions over the course of a year, she makes varying sorts of lists, from innocuous "to-do" lists to multilevel plans for self-improvement like the following:

> *stick to twelve steps*
> *focus: Mark, grades, inner balance, honesty, trueness, realness (not all the time), openness*
> > *realness—be true to heart and mind, voice it to the world*

*be objective—treat oneself and others fairly body will come all
into play naturally, spirit be natural. (July 3)*

Her sense of desperation seems evident in the increasing frequency of such "self-improvement" lists in the last book of her diary. Sadly, even her final entry prior to her suicide contains a feeble attempt at such a list.

With such a focus and seeming dedication to self-improvement, why didn't Katie's "self-help program" help her? While one wishes she had received formal psychotherapy as she became more dysfunctional, she did receive help in some forms through the years. She had been psychiatrically hospitalized, attended Alcoholics Anonymous and Overeaters Anonymous meetings, read self-help material, taken psychology courses, and talked extensively with Mark and others about her difficulties. Indeed, even her expressive writing, recognized as a therapeutic force, failed her, at least to the extent that she used it less and less and ceased writing entirely toward the end.

Moreover, Katie was not without a significant number of psychological strengths. She was clearly bright, verbal, and energetic, and she had high motivation to improve her life. She also sometimes shows striking insight into her weaknesses and how her past relates to her current difficulties. She sometimes seems to have boundless optimism and belief in her ability to make changes to better her life. She also shows many of the qualities of a survivor: remarkable resiliency in the aftermath of a chaotic childhood and terrible abuse at the hands of her parents and perhaps others. These are all valued individual characteristics in choosing psychotherapy candidates and predicting favorable outcomes.

However, Katie also faced a staggering array of liabilities as well. Her likely *biological* vulnerabilities include those described in Linehan's (1993) account of borderline personality disorder and consistent with her parents' psychiatric histories. Also on a biochemical level, Katie (1) abuses alcohol and other substances, (2) apparently does not take antidepressant medications consistently, (3) likely suffers from consistent sleep deprivation (judging by the common notation of journal entries during the early morning hours), and (4) may suffer from malnutrition on occasion due to her starvation diets.

Katie's *psychosocial* vulnerabilities were substantial as well. Her traumatic past resulted in the development of deeply ingrained patterns of thinking and behaving that, while serving survival needs, were ultimately both self-defeating and highly resistant to change. One is reminded of some victims of the Great Depression who, despite gaining affluence during later years, remained excessively frugal because of continuing insecurity feelings about finances. Moreover, like the miser who stores money in his mattress, Katie's security operations were ultimately self-defeating, because they were based on erroneous beliefs: She tried harder and harder to be perfect and lovable because she did not see that she could be loved and respected, by herself and others, imperfections and all. She often voiced "a change of attitude" along these lines, but the words generally rang hollow. As is often said in CBT, saying the right words is one thing; believing them is something else entirely.

☐ Reflections

It is beyond the scope of this chapter to discuss therapeutic intervention in any detail. However, we would be remiss not to mention the relevance of this case to the body of work known as Dialectical Behavior Therapy (DBT; Linehan, 1993). DBT shares many features with conventional cognitive-behavior therapy, but differs significantly in its emphasis on important tensions that are evident in borderline individuals. For example, the borderline patient is commonly seen (by herself and others) as remarkably capable ("apparent competence") while at the same time being exquisitely vulnerable to collapse, dependency, and demandingness under certain types of stress ("active passivity"). Similarly, one commonly sees extreme emotionality ("emotional vulnerability") together with self-invalidation, a pronounced tendency to deny feelings or to condemn oneself for having them (Katie's habit of criticizing herself for her emotions and frailties is prominent throughout her diary). Recognizing these dialectic tensions is thought in DBT to be key to the development and maintenance of an effective working relationship, as well as being a central focus in helping patients to come to terms with their characteristic emotional dysregulation and dichotomous thinking.

Finally, as clinicians, we cannot help but ask a fundamental question: Might Katie have been saved if she had received cognitive-behavioral therapy? It is not only our native optimism, but also empirical evidence, that suggests that the answer is "Quite possibly, yes." A variety of studies shows that suicidal individuals have benefited from cognitive-behavioral therapies, from those narrowly focused on problem-solving training (e.g., Clum & Lerner, 1990) to more wide-ranging programs (e.g., Rudd, Joiner, & Rajab, 2001). Perhaps most compelling has been the work of Linehan (1993; 2000; see also Scheel, 2000), who has shown that by addressing the full range of vulnerabilities, from emotional dysregulation to difficulties in managing interpersonal relationships, even individuals with severe and chronic suicidality and borderline conditions can be helped to stay out of the hospital and reduce the occurrence of self-harm behaviors. This is still a far cry from the "perfect" life that Katie longed for; but if she had been helped to give up the quest for perfection itself, it might very well have been enough.

☐ References

Beck, A. T. (1967). *Depression: clinical, experimental, and theoretical aspects*. New York: Harper & Row.

Beck, A. T. (1996). Beyond belief: A theory of modes, personality, and psychopathology. In Salkovskis, P. (Ed.), *Frontiers of cognitive therapy*, pp. 1–25. New York: Guilford.

Beck, A. T., Freeman, A., & Associates (1990). *Cognitive therapy of personality disorders*. New York: Guilford.

Beck, A. T., Rush, A. J., Shaw, B. F., & Emery, G. (1979). *Cognitive therapy of depression*. New York: Guilford.

Beck, J. S. (1995). *Cognitive therapy: Basics and beyond*. New York: Guilford.

Clark, D. M., & Fairburn, C. G. (Eds.). (1997). *Science and practice of cognitive behavior therapy*. Oxford: Oxford University Press.

Clum, G. A., & Lerner, M. (1990). A problem solving approach to treating individuals at risk for suicide. In D. Lester (Ed.), *Current concepts of suicide* (pp. 194–202). Philadelphia: Charles Press.

Dyer, J. A. T., & Kreitman, N. (1984). Hopelessness, depression and suicide intent in parasuicide. *British Journal of Psychiatry*, 144, 127–133.

Ellis, A. (1962). *Reason and emotion in psychotherapy*. New York: Lyle Stuart.

Ellis, T. E. (1986). Toward a cognitive therapy for suicidal individuals. *Professional Psychology: Research and Practice*, 17, 125–130.

Ellis, T. E., & Newman, C. F. (1996). *Choosing to live: How to defeat suicide through cognitive therapy*. Oakland, CA: New Harbinger.

Ellis, T. E., & Ratliff, K. (1986). Cognitive characteristics of suicidal and nonsuicidal psychiatric inpatients. *Cognitive Therapy and Research*, 10, 625–634.

Hewitt, P. L., Flett, G. L., & Weber, C. (1994). Dimensions of perfectionism and suicide ideation. *Cognitive Therapy and Research*, 18, 439–460.

Hughes, S. L., & Neimeyer, R. A. (1990). A cognitive model of suicidal behavior. In D. Lester (Ed., *Current concepts of suicide* (pp. 1–28). Philadelphia: Charles Press.

Linehan, M. M. (1993). *Cognitive-behavioral treatment of borderline personality disorder*. New York: Guilford.

Linehan, M. M. (2000). Behavioral treatments of suicidal behaviors: Definitional obfuscation and treatment outcomes. In R. W. Maris, S. S. Canetto, J. L. McIntosh, & M. M. Silverman (Eds.), *Review of suicidology, 2000* (pp. 84–111). New York: Guilford.

Maltsberger, J. T. (1986). *Suicide risk*. New York: New York University Press.

Minkoff, K., Bergman, E., Beck, A. T., & Beck, R. (1973). Hopelessness, depression, and attempted suicide. *American Journal of Psychiatry*, 130, 445–449.

Neuringer, C. (1961). Dichotomous evaluations in suicidal individuals. *Journal of Consulting Psychology*, 22, 445–449.

Neuringer, C. (1964). Rigid thinking in suicidal individuals. *Journal of Consulting Psychology*, 28, 54–58.

Rudd, M. D. (2000). The suicidal mode: A cognitive-behavioral model of suicidality. *Suicide and Life-Threatening Behavior*, 30, 18–33.

Rudd, M. D., Joiner, T. E., & Rajab, H. (2001). *Treating suicidal behavior: An effective, time-limited approach*. New York: Guilford.

Scheel, K. R. (2000). The empirical basis of Dialectical Behavior Therapy: Summary, critique, and implications. *Clinical Psychology: Science and Practice, 7,* 68–86.

Townsend, E., Hawton, K., Altman, D. G., Arensman, E., Gunnell, D., Hazell, P., House, A., & Van Heeringen, K. (2001). The efficacy of problem-solving treatments after deliberate self-harm: Meta-analysis of randomized controlled trials with respect to depression, hopelessness, and improvement in problems. *Psychological Medicine, 31,* 979–988.

CHAPTER

Antoon A. Leenaars

Katie: A Protocol Analysis of Her Diary

How can we understand suicide? What data can we legitimately use to understand the suicidal mind? I believe that personal narratives or documents are one of the most valuable sources, sources such as suicidal notes, suicidal poems, and suicide diaries. Shneidman (1980) in *Voices of Death* concluded from over forty years of study that such personal "documents contain special revelations of the human mind and that there is much one can learn from them."

The diary of a suicide is a lengthy, literate document kept over a fairly long period of time, often years; the diarist writes explicitly about suicide, including his or her suicidal thoughts, impulses, reflections, and resistances; and the diarist commits suicide. The suicidal diarist is but one subgroup of people, those who keep a book about their life. Rosenblatt (1983) notes that diaries "allow one to see . . . clearly day-to-day changes, long-term trends, and the effects of specific events." A diary is a document about how life is lived. Most of us are curious about diaries as we are about suicide notes. To cite a diarist, Evelyn Waugh, "the routine of their day properly recorded is always interesting." The personality of its keeper is found richly within a diary—a document not only of events but of the very writer him/herself.

Why do people keep such documents? Mallon (1984) cites Virginia Woolf, who later drowned herself, reflecting on her diary, "I wonder why I do it. . . . Partly I think, from my old sense of the race of time 'Time's winged chariot hurrying near.' Does it stay it?" Both Mallon (1984) and Rosenblatt (1983) point out that diaries are written for various reasons—

all diarists wanting to write "it" down on pages, like the writer of the suicide note. Katie offered this insight, "A journal is the most therapeutic thing for me." Both the diary and the suicide note are rich personal documents left by their writers, something they wanted to communicate to themselves and, almost always, to specific or unknown others. They want their stories to be read.

☐ A Theory of Suicide

Theory is a necessary step for understanding a suicide note or a diary. Theory allows us to sort out the buzzing mess of the writings. Theories begin with definition. Therefore, to begin, let me offer a formal definition of suicide from Shneidman (1985):

> Currently in the Western world, suicide is a conscious act of self-induced annihilation, best understood as a multidimensional malaise in a needful individual who defines an issue for which suicide is perceived as the best solution. (p. 203)

Suicide is *intrapsychic*. It is not simply the stress or even the pain, but rather the person's inability to cope with the pain or life's demands. However, from a psychological view, suicide is not only intrapsychic, it is also *interpersonal*. Individuals are interwoven—suicide occurs *in* a person and *between* people. Metaphorically speaking, suicide is an intrapsychic drama on an interpersonal stage.

Two a priori concepts that have been found to be essential and helpful in understanding suicide, before one can present a theory, are lethality and perturbation (Shneidman, 1985, 1993). Lethality refers to the probability of a person killing him/herself and, on quantification scales, ranges from low to moderate to high. It is a psychological state of mind. Perturbation refers to subjective distress (such as disturbed, agitated, or sane-insane) and can also be rated from low to moderate to high. It is important to note that one can be perturbed and not suicidal. Lethality kills, not perturbation.

Suicide can be theoretically understood from at least the following concepts (Leenaars, 1988, 1995, 1996):

I. Intrapsychic

1. Unbearable Psychological Pain

The common stimulus in suicide is unendurable psychological pain (Shneidman, 1985, 1993). The suicidal person is in a heightened state of perturbation, an intense mental anguish (Styron, 1990). Although, as Menninger (1938) noted, other motives (elements, wishes) are evident, the person primarily wants to flee from pain, experienced as a result of a trauma. The situation is unbearable and the person desperately wants a way out of it. The suicide, as Murray (1967) noted, is functional because it abolishes painful tension for the individual. It provides escape from intolerable suffering.

2. Cognitive Constriction

The common cognitive state in suicide is mental constriction (Shneidman, 1985)—rigidity in thinking, narrowing of focus, tunnel vision, and concreteness. The suicidal person exhibits at the moment before his/her death only permutations and combinations of these constricted thoughts about the trauma (e.g., business failure, political scandal, poor health, or rejection by girl/boyfriend). In the face of the painful trauma, a possible solution becomes *the* solution. This constriction is one of the most dangerous aspects of the suicidal mind.

3. Indirect Expressions

Ambivalence, complications, redirected aggression, unconscious implications, and related indirect expressions (or phenomena) are often evident in suicide. The suicidal person is ambivalent. There are complications, concomitant contradictory feelings, attitudes, or thrusts, often toward another person and even toward life itself. What the person is conscious of is only a fragment of the suicidal mind (Freud, 1917/1974). There are more reasons to the act than the suicidal person is consciously aware of when making the final decision (Freud, 1917/1974; Leenaars, 1988, 1993).

4. Inability to Adjust

People with all types of problems and pain are at risk for suicide. Psychological autopsy studies suggest that as many as 90 percent of the people who kill themselves have some symptoms of psychopathology or problems in adjustment (Hawton & van Heeringen, 2000; Wasserman, 2001). Up to sixty percent appear to have mood disorders although other emotional or mental disorders have been identified, such as anxiety disorders, schizophrenic disorders (especially paranoid type), panic disorders, borderline disorders, and antisocial disorders (Sullivan, 1964; Fawcett, 1997). Yet from psychological autopsy data, it has been learned that as many as 10 percent may have, in fact, no disorder identifiable in *DSM-IV* (or some other classification scheme).

Suicidal people see themselves as unable to adjust. Having the belief that they are too weak to overcome difficulties, these people reject everything except death—they do not survive life's difficulties.

5. Ego

The ego with its enormous complexity is an essential factor in the suicidal scenario. Ego strength is a protective factor against suicide. Suicidal people frequently exhibit a relative weakness in their capacity to develop constructive tendencies and to overcome their personal difficulties (Zilboorg, 1936). The person's ego has likely been weakened by a steady toll of traumatic life events (e.g., loss, rejection, abuse, or failure). This implies that a history of traumatic disruptions has placed the person at risk for suicide. It has handicapped the person's ability to develop mechanisms (or ego functions) to cope mentally or emotionally.

II. Interpersonal

6. Interpersonal Relations

The suicidal person has problems in establishing or maintaining relationships (object relations) (Leenaars, 1988). There is frequently a disturbed, unbearable interpersonal situation. A positive development in those same disturbed relationships may have been seen as the only possible way to go on living, but such a development was seen as not forthcoming. Suicide appears to be related to an unsatisfied or frustrated attachment need, although other needs, often more intrapsychic, may be equally evident (such as achievement, autonomy, dominance, or honor).

7. Rejection-Aggression

The rejection-aggression hypothesis was first documented by Stekel in the famous 1910 meeting of the Psychoanalytic Society in Freud's home in Vienna (Friedman, 1910/1967). Adler, Jung, Freud, Sullivan, and Zilboorg have all expounded variations of this hypothesis. Loss is central to suicide. It is, in fact, often a rejection that is experienced as an abandonment. It is an unbearable narcissistic injury, which leads to pain and, in some, self-directed aggression. In the first controlled study of suicide notes, Shneidman and Farberow (1957) reported, for example, that both hate directed toward others and self-blame are evident in the notes. The suicidal person is deeply ambivalent, and, within the context of this ambivalence, suicide may become the turning back upon oneself of murderous impulses (wishes or needs) that had previously been directed against a traumatic event, most frequently someone who had rejected that individual. Suicide may be veiled aggression—it may be murder in the 180th degree (Shneidman, 1985).

8. Identification-Egression

Freud (1917/1974, 1920/1974, 1921/1974) hypothesized, in order to understand the suicide, the analyst needs to understand the suicide's identification with a lost or rejecting person. To this Zilboorg (1936) added the need to understand an identification with any lost ideal (e.g., health, youth, employment, or freedom). Identification is defined as an attachment (bond) based upon an important emotional tie with another person (object) (Freud, 1920/1974) or any ideal. If this emotional need is not met, the suicidal person experiences a deep pain (discomfort). There is an intense desperation, and the person wants to egress, to escape. Something must be done to stop the anguish. The suicidal person wants to leave, exit, get out, get away, be gone, be elsewhere, not be, be dead. Suicide becomes the only solution, and the person plunges into the abyss.

In conclusion, the schema outlined is only one point of view. Yet the elements, I believe, have utility in understanding suicide. These elements highlight that suicide is not simply due to external "stress" or pain or even unattachment. The common consistency in suicide is, in fact, in lifelong adjustment patterns (Shneidman, 1985). Suicidal people have experienced a steady succession of life events (such as threat, stress, failure, losses, or challenges) that have undermined their ability to adjust. They do not cope, but rather perceive suicide as the only solution.

☐ Katie's Diary

Katie's diary was assessed for the themes discussed above that occur most frequently in the suicidal mind. Her narrative illustrates common suicidal protocols (Leenaars, 1988, 1996). One does not, in fact, have to read far— she says it almost all in the very first entry.

Katie writes:

I am so depressed and suicidal. My body feels restless and tired. I don't know who to turn to for help. I don't want to bother anyone with my battle. I've been acting out in all sorts of ways. I just feel like crying. I presume that all has to do with the fact that I love Mark so deeply. I think he cares for me but, however, I

don't know if it's true love for him. It definitely is for me. I really
want to marry him so badly. I don't care if he reads my journal
at all. I am just so stressed out. I haven't done any of my work. I
have a hard time getting along with people. I really hate my
body. I really hate my life where it is, with everything I am. I
decided to start exercising today. I need to do it every day. I
leave all my life's frustrations there out on the track.

God give me strength. Help me today. I feel so unbelievably
lonely and battered. (June 8, year 1)

Katie is clearly suicidal on June 8. All the writings after the opening
words are permutations and combinations of the same theme. What
Murray (1938) called the "unity thema" is already written. She is already
ready to jump in the abyss.

Intrapsychic

1. Unbearable psychological pain: Katie's mind, based on her own
words, was permeated with pain. She felt "so depressed" and "stressed."
She felt "so unbelievably lonely and battered." Katie needed to adapt, but
was so frustrated. She wanted to escape; she wanted relief from her anguish, restlessness, and tiredness. She was "suicidal."

2. Cognitive constriction: Katie's mind was a constricted mind. She was
focused only on her "battles"—with Mark, people, her body and life. She
writes, "I really hate my life."

3. Indirect expression: There is so much Katie says in these first few
lines, but there is also so much Katie does not say. What battered her so?
Why does she ask whether it is true love for him (Mark)? What does she
fear? There are so many questions. Katie, I believe, was overwhelmingly
angry, a common emotion in suicide. Why the submission? Why does
God need to give her strength?

4. Inability to adjust: Katie could not cope; she saw herself as too weak
to adjust ("I just feel like crying"). She was, in fact, so emotional in her
story. Indeed, her state of mind was indicative of a mental disorder. Katie
likely suffered from, at the very least, a mood disorder.

5. Ego: Katie's ego was weakened. She lacked constructive tendencies.
She writes, "I have a hard time getting along with people."

Interpersonal

6. Interpersonal relations: Katie was weakened and defeated. Not only
was there a current trauma (Mark's love), but there was a history. Her

needs were frustrated. A positive development ("I really want to marry him so badly") was seen as the only possible way to go on living, but even this was deeply questioned. She was strained and "battered."

7. Rejection-aggression: Katie was hurt. She was, in fact, singly preoccupied with her "battle" ("I love Mark so deeply, I think he cares for me but, however, I don't know if it's true love for him"). Yet the "battle" is deeper, well beyond Mark. She had a "hard time" getting along with people. We learn later from the diary that the people are her peers but, in the past, included her father and her mother.

8. Identification–egression: Katie needed to be attached to someone, but she lacked such bonds. She was even unattached to her body ("I really hate my body"). She dissociates from her pain, body, and life. She wanted to escape. She says that she is "suicidal."

Yet Katie does not say, "I am going to kill myself." She wants help; yet she writes, "I don't know who to turn to for help." She feels hopeless, not only helpless, but she asks God, "Help me today." In her diary, we learn that help never comes. She kills herself.

Katie's opening paragraph, which reads like a suicide note, is most revealing.[1] Yet it lacks some decisive elements or protocols. She states that she is "suicidal," but what is lacking is the stark ambivalence that we often see in the suicidal mind. There is also no definitive statement like "I'm going to kill myself." The common statement in last farewell stories is that of "This [suicide] is the only way." Katie does not say it; not yet, anyway.

In suicide, a person has an intent to end the pain, the "battle," by a self-destructive act. He or she intends to be dead. Death is yearned for. Katie does not say that in her first words. However, later in the diary she does give evidence of both egression and ambivalence. Let me explore in more detail these themes in Katie's diary.

People can both love and hate. We can think both A and not-A, what Shneidman (1985) called being of two minds. The suicidal person is strikingly ambivalent. He or she wants both to live and to die. This is the common internal attitude in suicide: to want to be rescued and to want to be dead. This ambivalent attitude is lacking in Katie's first paragraph, but it appears a few pages later.

In the next entry, she vents about Mark, whether he loves her or not. She states, "I wonder if Mark really loves me. Does he?" On that first day, June 8, she later writes, "I don't care about my life that much anymore" and "My life must go on." There is some ambivalence there from the first push of the pen, even if lacking in the first words.

The egression is equally there on the first day. She writes, "It kills me inside. . . . It really kills me" on June 8. Then, on June 15, we read, "I want to kill myself. Bullet through my heart," adding, "I want to kill myself on my birthday. I have to."

All the elements of the suicidal mind are written in the diary by this point. Katie was highly suicidal; she herself says so in the first sentence ("suicidal").

☐ Speculations on the Unconscious

There is much more to suicide (or any behavior) than what a person writes or says. Narratives, like all data, have limitations. There is, for example, more than what informants, as in psychological autopsies, say. We need the concept of the unconscious. Suicidology, in fact, would be overly barren without the concept.

Suicide is inevitably interpersonal. I have suggested, in fact, that *unconscious* processes in suicide are primarily related to the interpersonal aspect (Leenaars, 1986). Freud (1920/1974) speculated on the latent interpretation of what leads someone to kill oneself, in the following well-known statement:

> Probably no one finds the mental energy required to kill himself unless, in the first place, in doing so he is at the same time killing an object with whom he had identified himself and, in the second place, is turning against himself a death wish which had been directed against someone else. (p. 162)

The person had developed a strong identification with a person (or, as Zilboorg [1936] has shown, some other ideal). Attachment, based upon an important emotional tie with another person, was for Freud (1921/1974) his early meaning of identification. Later Freud used the concept of identification as a mechanism of structuralization, the superego. I adhere to the earlier view; attachments are identifications.

A person (or other ideal) does not only exist in the external world (the stage), but it becomes introjected in one's own intrapsychic life. Attachments are introjected into one's own personality. The attachments are deep within one's conscious and unconscious. As Litman (1967) noted, our "ego is made up in large part of identifications." These identifications are associated especially with our earliest attachments (e.g., parents) and significant people (e.g., spouse and siblings). With loss and rejection, the energy (libido) in an attachment is withdrawn, but the person continues to exhibit an overly painful attachment. As Fenichel (1954) noted, "the loss is so complete that there is no hope of regaining it. One is hopeless . . . and helpless." It is the attachment that is the basic unconscious process in suicide, not the death wish. Although aggressive wishes, whether inwardly or outwardly directed, occur in many suicides, it is primarily identification (attachment) that is the key in most suicides. Suicide is more an outcome of frustrated attachment needs (wishes) than of aggressive wishes (or other dynamics). The loss of the attachment, often experienced as abandonment, at both the more obvious manifest level and the deeper latent level fuels the pain that becomes unbearable. For many suicidal people: No love, no life.

The dynamics in suicide, I believe, are therefore related to a key significant other person or other people, especially the father and mother. One's needs are frustrated or blocked interpersonally. This was that case for Katie.

Freud himself had associated suicide and love (Jones, 1953–1957). Karl Menninger, when asked (Jacobs & Brown, 1989) if he would change any aspect of his triad of motives in suicide (to kill, to be killed, and to die), stated: "I think there is one more unconscious motive to add to the triad. I think some love gets into suicide motivation" (p. 484). It is likely that a group of suicidal individuals are quite pathological in their love. In his analysis of Freud's speculation on suicide, Litman (1967) wrote: ". . . Freud often referred to certain dangerous ways of loving, in which the ego is 'overwhelmed' by the object. Typically, the psychic representations of the self and other are fused and the other is experienced as essential for survival" (p. 340). We term such attachments "symbiotic," and it is likely that "symbiotic love is a potential precursor of suicide" (Litman, 1967). Some suicide notes and suicide diaries exhibit such unhealthy love, and this was true for Katie.

Suicide occurs in a needful individual.

> It is difficult to conceptualize an individual committing suicide apart from that individual seeking to satisfy certain inner felt needs. . . . there can never be a needless suicide. . . . it focally involves the attempt to fulfil some urgently felt psychological needs. Operationally, these heightened unmet needs make up, in a large part, what the suicidal person feels (and *reports*) . . . " (Shneidman, 1985, pp. 208–209, italics mine)

If we let the unconscious speak in the suicidal person's own report, like Katie's diary, we learn that the suicidal person is loving, needing, wanting, liking, accepting. In the suicidal person, love and sacrifice are closely intertwined. A person sacrifices everything for love. Love may well be a driving (conscious and unconscious) force in many suicides as it was for Katie. Let me here allow Katie to speak for herself with a sample of statements from her diary which illustrate her strong emotions felt toward her parents and their impact on her relationship with Mark.

I miss my Mom. I really wish she was better. Oh, how I wish she was my Mom. I need her to love me—so deeply. (June 17, year 1)

I hope my father feels it! I don't want his spirit to be free to come and visit me. (June 24, year 1)

My mother is alive! Screaming viciously, Jekyll and Hyde. Mommy Dearest, dearest. (June 25, year 1)

My dad. When neighbors would call police on him, when he was beating my Mom. I was so scared all the time. (June 26, year 1)

. . . the darkness was evil—the night was evil—for the night held my Daddy's hands—hands he caressed me with—a scream I choked on—flutters inside me now—like a bird swallowed by a cat. (July 24, year 1)

Mommy, your sickness did control you, even though you tried fighting for us. Oh, how my heart always fought to get your attention by being good and even being bad, to pull you away from your sickness, your sadness to the world around you. But I could never connect. I felt like my heart was dying. (August 22)

I want it so much to be different with Mark. But it seems that anything, everything I've ever loved or wanted has been taken away from me. I don't know anyone who tried more than me to be such a good and loving person and friend. These pure qualities seemed to be lost now. I struggle with rage, anger and hate. I hate these traits—remind me of my father and my mother's sickness. I am so terrified right now. (December 1)

☐ Conclusion

Suicide notes, suicide diaries, suicide poems, and other narratives, written or oral, are open to analysis. They allow us to read about the person him/herself. Narratives can be windows to the suicidal person. This is true for Katie's words. There are qualitative and quantitative possible methods of study (Leenaars, Lester, & Goldney, 2002). Procedures developed to study suicide notes can be easily extended to a diary written by a suicide (Leenaars, 1988, 1996; Shneidman & Farberow, 1957). Katie's diary is an illuminating example. Katie's diary is not only a window, but many windows. Unity thema, such as unbearable pain, can be found in both notes and diaries, but in the diary it is much more *richly* elaborated. Katie's pain lies in the detail of her narrative on her life, her diary. Suicide diaries, to somewhat quote Virginia Woolf again, "Say it." Katie does!

On a final note, the study of Katie has implications and applications for treatment, such as psychotherapy or counseling. The best way to treat a suicidal person is to understand him or her. If Katie had, for example, been in long-term psychotherapy, the themes identified are those that need to be addressed, discussed, and resolved (or, at least, the pain should be reduced and, therefore, the lethality). Suicide diaries, suicide notes, and suicide narratives give us clues for this psychotherapy.

☐ Note

1. The actual protocols are 1, 2, 3, 5, 6, 7, 8, 9, 11, 12, 13, 14, 15f, 16, 17, 19, 20, 21, 22, 23, 24, 25, 26, 27, 33. See Leenaars (1996).

☐ References

Fawcett, J. (1997). The detection and consequences of anxiety in clinical depression. *Journal of Clinical Psychiatry*, 58 (suppl. 8), 35–40.

Fenichel, O. (1954). *The psychoanalytic theory of neurosis*. New York: W. W. Norton.

Freud, S. (1974). Mourning and melancholia. In J. Strachey (Ed. & Trans.), *The standard edition of the complete psychological work of Sigmund Freud, Vol. XIV* (pp. 239–260). London: Hogarth. (Originally published in 1917)

Freud, S. (1974). A case of homosexuality in a woman. In J. Strachey (Ed. & Trans.), *The standard edition of the complete psychological works of Sigmund Freud, Vol. XVIII* (pp. 147–172). London: Hogarth Press. (Originally published in 1920)

Freud, S. (1974). Group psychology and the analysis of the ego. In J. Strachey (Ed. & Trans.), *The standard edition of the complete psychological works of Sigmund Freud, Vol. XVIII* (pp. 67–147). London: Hogarth Press. (Originally published in 1921).

Friedman, P. (Ed.) (1967). *On suicide*. New York: International Universities Press. (Originally published in 1910).

Hawton, K., & van Heeringen, C. (Eds.). (2000). *The international handbook of suicide and attempted suicide*. London: Wiley.

Jacobs, D., & Brown, H. (Eds.). (1989). *Suicide: Understanding and responding*. Madison, CT: International Universities Press.

Jones, E. (1953–1957). *The life and work of Sigmund Freud*. New York: Basic Books.

Leenaars, A. (1986). A brief note on the latent content in suicide notes. *Psychological Reports*, 59, 640–642.

Leenaars, A. (1988). *Suicide notes*. New York: Human Sciences Press.

Leenaars, A. (1993). Unconscious processes. In A. Leenaars (Ed.), *Suicidology: Essays in honor of Edwin Shneidman* (pp. 127–147). Northvale, NJ: Jason Aronson.

Leenaars, A. (1995). Clinical evaluation of suicide risk. *Psychiatry and Clinical Neurosciences*, 49 (suppl. 1), 561–568.

Leenaars, A. (1996). Suicide: A multidimensional malaise. *Suicide and Life–Threatening Behavior, 26,* 221–236.

Leenaars, A., Lester, D., & Goldney, R. (Eds.) (2002). Qualitative and quantitative studies in suicidology. *Archives of Suicide Research, 6,* 1–73.

Litman, R. (1967). Sigmund Freud on suicide. In E. Shneidman (Ed.), *Essays in self-destruction* (pp. 324–344). New York: Science House.

Mallon, T. (1984). *A book of one's own: People and their diaries.* New York: Ticknor & Fields.

Menninger, K. (1938). *Man against himself.* New York: Harcourt, Brace & World.

Murray, H. (1938). *Explorations in personality.* New York: Oxford University Press.

Murray, H. (1967). Death to the world: The passions of Herman Melville. In E. Shneidman (Ed.), *Essays in self-destruction* (pp. 3–29). New York: Science House.

Rosenblatt, P. (1983). *Bitter, bitter tears.* Minneapolis: University of Minnesota Press.

Shneidman, E. (1980). *Voices of death.* New York: Harper & Row.

Shneidman, E. (1985). *Definition of suicide.* New York: Wiley.

Shneidman, E. (1993). *Suicide as psychache.* Northvale, NJ: Jason Aronson.

Shneidman, E., & Farberow, N. (Eds.). (1957). *Clues to suicide.* New York: McGraw-Hill.

Styron, W. (1990). *Darkness visible.* New York: Random House.

Sullivan, H. (1964). *The fusion of psychiatry and social sciences.* New York: W. W. Norton.

Wasserman, D. (Ed.). (2001). *Suicide: An unnecessary death.* London: Martin Dunitz.

Zilboorg, G. (1936). Suicide among civilized and primitive races. *American Journal of Psychiatry, 92,* 1347–1369.

CHAPTER 8

David Lester

The Ophelia Complex[1]

When down her weedy trophies and herself
Fell in the weeping brook. Her clothes spread wide,
And mermaid-like awhile they bore her up,
Which time she chanted snatches of old lauds,
As one incapable of her own distress,
Or like a creature native and indued
Unto that element. But long it could not be
Till that her garments, heavy with their drink,
Pulled the poor wretch from her melodious lay
To muddy death.[2]

In Shakespeare's *Hamlet*, Ophelia seems to have no mother. Hamlet woos the motherless girl, but her father warns her not to trust Hamlet at all. Obediently, Ophelia repels all Hamlet's advances. As Hamlet's personal troubles develop, he admits to Ophelia that he loved her once but that he no longer does. He gets angry at her and tells her to go join a nunnery. Later in the play Hamlet inadvertently murders her father (who is hiding behind a curtain in the bedroom of Hamlet's mother).

Ophelia goes mad[3] after the loss of her father. As she wanders around the castle and its grounds, it is her father's death that is on her mind. At one point, she climbs on to a tree, and she falls into the river when a branch breaks. She makes no effort to save herself, but floats downstream until her wet clothes drag her under. She commits suicide.

Tompkins noted that Ophelia is a "creature" designed by men. In her first appearance in the play, she is questioned by her brother, Laertes, about Hamlet's intention and urged not to have intimate relations with Hamlet. Later, after Laertes has left for Paris, Ophelia's father asks her about Hamlet's intentions and tells her to avoid Hamlet. Ophelia tells her father that she will obey.

Her next appearance is merely to confirm Hamlet's apparent madness to her father. As Jardine (1983) observed, Ophelia is under the total control of both her father and the king, Claudius. For example, they order her to return Hamlet's gifts to her so that they may observe his reaction, and she obeys. She is used as bait to catch Hamlet's emotions.

And Hamlet is no better. He uses Ophelia merely to further his plans to expose his uncle as a murderer. If Hamlet really loves her, then she is chaste; but if he does not love her, then she is lewd and lascivious for accepting his gifts. Either way, she should go to a "nunnery" (which could mean a convent or a brothel). Jardine also noted that if Hamlet married and had heirs, then they would inherit the throne. On the other hand, if Hamlet remained unmarried and without heirs, then Claudius and his offspring are the heirs to the throne. Thus, it is in Claudius's interests to have Hamlet break off his engagement to Ophelia. Female sexuality, therefore, represents "woman's intolerable interference with inheritance . . . " (Jardine, 1983, p. 92).

No one in the play cares about Ophelia—what she wants, what she feels, or what she thinks.

McGee (1987) has pointed out that Ophelia is presented by Shakespeare in a way that would not endear her to Elizabethan audiences. There are clues that she is a Roman Catholic, and England then had its own Church of England. Furthermore, the innuendo in the play is that Ophelia is also a whore. (Ophelia is described as mermaid-like as she drowns in the river, and "mermaid" was a slang term for prostitute.) Ophelia's madness is connected with the Devil, for she has displayed sexual feelings and so is evil. Had she lived in Elizabethan England, she might have been labeled a witch and subjected to an exorcism or killed. In one conversation with Ophelia, Hamlet says

> I have heard of your paintings too, well enough. God hath given you one face, and you make yourselves another. You jig, you amble, and you lisp; you nickname God's creatures and make your wantonness your ignorance. Go to. I'll no more on't; it hath made me mad.

Painting is a metaphor to suggest prostitution. Whores painted their faces to cover the ravages of smallpox and the venereal diseases that caused disfigurement.

Ophelia, then, has suffered the loss of her mother and has become an obedient daughter, but the loss of both her father and Hamlet's love leaves her ungrounded and unable to continue to live. (Had she not killed herself, she would also have experienced the loss of her brother in a short time since he dies in the fight with Hamlet.) Furthermore, no one is concerned for her well-being, but rather they manipulate her to serve their own well-being.

It was not I, but rather Mary Pipher (1994), in her book *Reviving Ophelia,* who suggested the relevance of Ophelia for understanding adolescent girls. Pipher presented cases of adolescent girls she had counseled who were depressed, suicidal, and self-mutilating, anorexic and bulimic, abusing drugs and alcohol, sexually promiscuous, and victims of sexual harassment and rape.

Pipher argued that Ophelia committed suicide because she was not able to grow. She became the object of other people's lives and lost her sense of self, if she had ever had it. Her development was thwarted, and her potential truncated.

Pipher noted that girls between the ages of seven and eleven rarely come to psychotherapy, not because these years are "latent" in the psychoanalytic sense, but rather because girls this age are interested in the world. They can be and do anything they want without worrying what others are thinking about them or how others are judging them. They can be their natural selves.

But once adolescence arrives, along with puberty, the girls lose their resiliency and optimism. They are no longer curious, and they begin to avoid risks. Their assertiveness leaves them, their energy declines, and they become more deferential, self-critical, and depressed. Pipher notes, too, that menstruation occurs at an earlier age today than it used to, and so the stress of adolescence begins at an earlier age. In addition, daughters stay at home longer, often until they finish college at the age of twenty-two, and so adolescence ends at a later age.

Ophelia in *Hamlet* followed this path. After she fell in love with Hamlet, she became dependent upon his approval. Lacking inner direction, she tried to meet the demands of Hamlet and her father, Polonius, and the struggle to win the approval of both tore her apart. When Hamlet rejects her because she obeys her father, she drowns herself. Ophelia epitomizes the plight of adolescent girls today.

Adolescent girls encounter a world that demands that they subjugate their real selves and conform to the ways required of them in the society. But the lifestyle demanded of them is full of contradictions, contradictions so great that all cannot be met.

This split between the real self and the façade self, as I have called it (Lester, 1995), begins early in life when the parents demand that the child suppress particular desires and introject those of the parent instead. "Finish your food," "Be polite," "Do well in school," and all of the other demands made by the parents as they socialize their child create this split between the real self and the façade self. Almost all Western theorists of personality have described this phenomenon, although they use different terms to describe it: introjected desires forming the superego in psycho-analytic theory, conditions of worth by Carl Rogers, and the pattern of vicarious living by Andras Angyal, to name a few (Lester, 1995).

Pipher has pointed out that present-day culture now extends this. In the past, to be sure, parents continued to socialize their daughters well into adulthood, but girls typically had a large extended family nearby, sometimes living in the same house, who provided support and praise for them as they really were. They were, nonetheless, monitored closely and shaped to be "feminine" in the traditional sense of the word so that they would be found attractive by a young man and become fine wives and mothers.

However, today, this continued socialization, with its accompanying suppression of the real selves of the girls, is taken over by the peer subcul-ture and reinforced by the media. An extended family living nearby is rare, and the parents often both work and provide less support for their daughters.

This is made worse by the high frequency of divorce, which removes some of the parental influences and introduces even more chaos when the parents remarry and redivorce. Drugs are much more freely available today than they were fifty years ago, adolescents engage in sexual inter-course at a much earlier age than in the past,[4] and girls are encouraged by the media to focus on their bodies and their looks and to minimize their intellect. Pornography is everywhere, in videos and in song lyrics, and the media reinforces the thin, anorexic look, all the while running ar-ticles on the dangers of eating disorders.

If adolescent girls remain true to their selves, then their female peers ostracize them, and the boys ridicule them. On the other hand, if they conform to the sexy stereotype that the peer culture and media reinforce, then they run the risk of joining subcultures that use alcohol and drugs and encourage early sexual intercourse. In the course of this, they may be raped and then ostracized for being a "slut." Adolescent girls have to play dumb, be cute and pretty, and act sexy, yet resist the overtures of the boys who are "turned on" by this image.

Adolescent girls diet when they are hungry and should eat; they spend time with the "in-crowd" rather than the friends they prefer; they act dumb when they could excel academically. Interestingly, now parents tend to fight for their daughters real selves, but they lose out to the cul-tural and peer pressures.

And our culture remains sexist and misogynist. Pipher browsed through magazines in the 1990s available for young girls, and they all had articles on makeup, weight loss, and fashion. Attracting boys was the sole goal in life, for the magazines had no articles on hobbies, careers, politics, or academic pursuits. Pipher noted four ways of adapting to these pressures: conform, withdraw, become depressed, or get angry.

Thus, the difficulties of adolescence, including extreme and changeable emotions and irrational thinking (which, of course, persists into adulthood, as cognitive therapists assure us), are made more difficult for adolescent girls.

All parents must love their daughters and give them affection. Pipher suggests that girls who make the best adjustment have parents who are not laissez-faire. Laissez-faire parents leave their daughters to make decisions that they are not capable of making wisely, and these girls often adjust worst. Parents who are very strict and controlling have daughters who traverse adolescence with the least trouble but who, as adults, have little sense of their real selves. A lot of affection and moderate control enable daughters to go through adolescence with some stress but with the chance to explore their selves and gain a sense of who they really are and what they really want. They function better when adult. "I love you, but I have high expectations for you" is the message parents should give. "We want you to explore and have fun, but we are setting limits too."

☐ Katie as Ophelia

Katie had an alcoholic and abusive father. In her diary she makes it clear that he molested her sexually, although she is not explicit about the details. (Perhaps she still has difficulty remembering the abuse?) It is likely that he raped her since, in one memory, he is described as replacing his clothes:

June 8: People did such bad things to me when I had no clothes on.

June 24: I felt so misused already, like a piece of meat, like I was when my parents did things to me.

July 22: I remembered my father making me go on the bed naked with him.

July 24: . . . hands he caressed with . . . rubbing my rape away.

July 19: . . . his hands on my body again. . . . I saw him put his shirt on after he was done with me.

August 28: . . . pillow over my face—hands and mouth on my breasts.

September 3: I think something happened in my father's car—I really don't know.

January 1: . . . I remembered something with hay, (bloody) old barn. . . . Daddy at the dresser, don't tell Mommy—me in bed, played with her lingerie. Maybe he dressed me up in it.

In such families, not only does the girl lose her father (since he wants her as a lover, not as a daughter), but she often also loses her mother. The mother may have (consciously or unconsciously) opted out of the sexual relationship with the father and promoted her daughter as a substitute sexual partner. Or she may deny the sexual relationship between the daughter and the father. The daughter, therefore, can turn to no one for help. She becomes, as it were, an orphan.

Katie's mother had been physically and sexually abusive toward Katie also:

June 14: I don't need my mother in my life anymore. I never needed someone who was so sick and raped me—my mind, my heart, soul.

August 28: I'd beat her with the leather strap until she bleeds. The one she beat me with, and I'd kick her till she falls down and has the wind knocked out of her and kick her in the stomach like she did to me. I'd degrade her and make her take off her underwear and hold it into her face and tell her she was a whore and a slut and a bitch like she did to me.

Then, when the father left home (and died), Katie's mother became psychotic.[5] Katie (and her sister Laura) were placed with separate foster families.

Katie had several boyfriends, but her relationship with Mark was the most intense, and he was her first lover. The sexual molestation caused tremendous conflicts in her sexual relationship with Mark.

June 8: I also have had such a problem with sex. I really don't like it that much. I really never want to do it.

June 17: Mark and I made love this morning. It was nice.

June 24: We made love. It was really beautiful.

June 28: I like it when he gets rough with me.

July 4: We made love for 2 hours. It was really nice.

July 5: I can't have sex with him anymore. It is too much for me emotionally.

Then Mark is unfaithful to Katie by having sex with an ex-girlfriend, Claudia, an act that further impairs Katie's trust in him.

July 4: . . . he told me he didn't love me as much as Claudia. Well, they were both sick and fucked in their relationship.

She can no longer be sure that Mark will remain faithful to her. Indeed, it is interesting to wonder whether Katie might have been better able to cope with life if she had not become involved with Mark. He stayed with her and professed his love for her all year. But he was unfaithful early in their relationship, was jealous of her male friends, occasionally hit her, and behaved impulsively at times (for example, slashing his wrists). He broke up with her continually, although they always got back together. With her history of sexual abuse, Katie may not have been ready to handle sexual intimacy yet. But she also says:

October 17: I don't know where my heart would be if I never met him. I honestly think I would've killed myself by now for some reason.

Katie's situation, then, is very similar to Ophelia's. She has lost both her father and mother, and she cannot be sure of Mark's faithfulness and love for her. And like Pipher's adolescent girls, Katie is depressed, has an eating disorder and mutilates herself.

July 3: Weekend, drugs, alcohol, food binge.
July 4: I abuse myself now—mutilate, destroy, manipulate, lie, control (sickens).
July 5: I missed class today. . . . No more alcohol, pot, binges, lying.
July 17: I want to slash up my whole fucking body right now.
July 25: I wish I studied for algebra this weekend.
July 28: I had to withdraw from college algebra again.
August 17: Stealing sometimes is a must for me.
September 11: I ran in front of a car so it would hit me. . . . I got up and said you're right and cut my wrist. Then he ran over to stop me and then he started screaming—saying he was sober—and started cutting himself. I fought him physically to make him stop and get the knife away. I tried every tactic I knew to make him stop. He cut himself, so the only way I made him stop was I started cutting myself. I cut my breast and my shoulder.

November 1: I cut my wrist like a complete idiot. I stopped and thought, but did it anyway.

November 22: I'm not going to eat all day.

November 28: I talked, screamed and banged my head so hard yesterday.

☐ Women, Depression, and Rumination

In discussing Alfred Adler's theory of personality, Mosak and Maniacci (1999) noted that some individuals who develop psychological disturbance "cling" to their trauma. Many of us experience trauma during our lives, but we manage to recover from the shock and continue with a relatively normal life. Others do not. "They 'nurse it, rehearse it,' go over it again in their minds again and again, and ruminate about it, as if they were enslaved by the thought. By clinging to the shock effect, they create an excuse for not moving on with life" (Mosak & Maniacci, 1999, p. 123). The question becomes, therefore, why do some people cling while others let go.

One possibility has been suggested by Nolen-Hoeksema (1987) who suggested that women are, in general, more often depressed than are men because they have a ruminative response style that amplifies and prolongs their depressive symptoms. Rumination involves focusing on the symptoms of distress ("I am so tired") and on the meaning and the consequences of this distress ("What's wrong with my life?" and "Why me?"), trying to figure out why you are depressed, crying to relieve tension, and talking to friends about the depression. Rumination interferes with taking action and effective problem solving, and individuals who ruminate tend to recall relatively more negative events from their lives that make them more pessimistic about the future and help perpetuate the depression. Individuals who get into this state also are more likely to lose social support because their behaviors alienate their friends, relatives, and significant others.

In contrast, Nolen-Hoeksema argued that men are more likely to get involved in distracting activities when they are depressed, activities such as going to movies or playing sports.

Nolen-Hoeksema thought that the ruminative response style in women is a result of the particular ways in which girls are socialized in the society and because women have lower status and power than men (Nolen-Hoeksema, Larson, & Grayson, 1999). As a result of this lower status, women experience more negative events in their lives than do men, and they have less control over their lives, both at work and at home in their families. For example, even though some women work full-time, they are still expected to perform the majority of the child-care and domestic work in their families. This lack of control over their lives leads women to be more likely to develop a generalized expectation that they are unable to control their lives and never will be able to do so. This makes the depression deeper and more chronic.

The role of rumination in depression is supported by research. For example, Nolen-Hoeksema and her colleagues (1987) studied a sample of residents in the San Francisco area and found that measures of chronic stressful events, depression, rumination, and feelings of mastery over events were all interrelated and predicted depression a year later. Sakamoto (1998) in a sample of Japanese students found that self-preoccupation (the tendency to focus on the self), especially when measured for both its degree and duration, predicted the level of depression of the students.

☐ Resentment and Dependency in the Suicidal Individual

Many years ago, as part of my dissertation research, I administered the Situational Resources Repertory Test (RES Test) to suicidal and nonsuicidal individuals. The RES Test was devised by George Kelly (1955). The respondent is asked to think of 22 examples of specific crises in his or her life and then asked to which of 21 significant others he or she could have turned to for help. Kelly was interested in how people distribute their dependencies, and he thought it was healthier if we spread our dependencies around more people. On the RES Test, this would mean that the person could call on more people for each crisis.

I wrote the names of the 21 significant others on cards and had the subjects sort them into seven piles of three each, from the three they liked most to the three they liked least. After completing a questionnaire, I then asked each subject to sort the 21 significant others into seven piles of three each, from the three they resented most to the three they resented least.

The results were obvious to me before I carried out the statistical analysis. When I asked the nonsuicidal subjects to sort the significant others for resentment, most told me just to reverse the sorting they had done earlier for liking. (I made them sort by resentment anyway.) Hardly any of the suicidal subjects made this objection. They sorted by resentment without any quibbling, and the people they liked most were often the people they resented most!

When I did the statistical analysis, I confirmed this observation (Lester, 1969). The suicidal subjects resented those they liked and also those they depended on. On the other hand, the nonsuicidal subjects did not resent those whom they liked, nor those they depended on. Furthermore, the suicidal subjects had a smaller dispersion of dependencies; that is, there were fewer people to turn to for help in crises. The result was that the suicidal individuals more often were dependent upon a small group of people toward whom they felt much resentment. Thus, in times of crisis, it is likely that the suicidal individuals would be less able and willing to turn to others for help because of these feelings of resentment.

Katie displays a great deal of resentment toward Mark and her friends. Her diary is full of ambivalence about the people in her life. About her boy friend Mark, she states that she loves him and that she hates him, sometimes in entries for the same day. June 8: I love Mark. June 15: It's all a façade with Mark. June 24: . . . even though I've been angry at Mark and said I hated him, I never meant it.

The presence of conflicting feelings is also striking.

(1) June 14: *I don't need my mother in my life anymore.* June 17: *I miss my Mom.* June 24: *You selfish cunt. I need a Mommy. . . . I've never loved anyone except my Mom like this.*

She plans to spend time with a friend, Carl. But:

(2) June 22: *I really almost hate Carl. . . . [Carl] is a total jerk actually.*
(3) June 24: *I can't wait to be alone in the house, doing my work. I love it.* [later] June 24: *I'm so alone.*
(4) June 24: *I feel very beautiful and strong right now.* July 1: *My body is against me.*

In fact, it hard to find a person or an issue about which Katie does not express ambivalence. There are only two examples. Katie says only nice things about her sister, mostly about how much she misses her; and she says only harsh things about her father.

This ambivalence reminds me of George Kelly's theory of personal constructs. Personal constructs include those we use to evaluate other people. Is this person trustworthy or untrustworthy, intelligent or stupid, and so on? Kelly postulated that constructs were bipolar; that is, each time we evaluate a person, she is either intelligent or stupid, never somewhere in between. Constructs are dichotomous judgments: either-or. I have always wondered whether this was in fact the case, but Katie's diary convinces me that, at least for Katie, her constructs were dichotomous and bipolar.

Her judgments of people and experiences switch from one extreme to the other.

Shneidman and Farberow (1957) proposed that suicidal individuals were prone to dichotomous thinking, and Charles Neuringer published a number of research studies that documented this (see Neuringer, 1988). He found that suicidal individuals more often thought dichotomously than did nonsuicidal subjects and that they quickly switched judgments about people from one pole to the other. In particular, Neuringer and Lettieri (1982) showed that this was true for suicidal women, and Neuringer conclude that

> It augurs poorly for the futures of these women. Dichotomous thinking imposes inflexibility and polarized thinking on suicidal individuals. It may be that the inflexibility and polarization associated with dichotomous thinking are what perpetuates and maintains for long periods of time a high level of crisis. If the above is true, highly suicidal women are caught in a web that appears to be seamless and never-ending. . . . If the cognitive style does indeed constantly keep the "emotional pot" boiling, it may explain why suicidal individuals feel so hopeless and why they have such difficulties envisioning a future in which they will feel better. (Neuringer, 1988, p. 51).

☐   Positive Disintegration

Many years ago, Dabrowski (1964) introduced the notion of *positive disintegration.*

> In relating disintegration to the field of disorder and mental disease, the author feels that the functional mental disorders are in many cases positive phenomena. This, is, they contribute to personality, to social, and, very often, to biological development. The present prevalent view that all mental disturbance are pathological is based on too exclusive a concern of many psychiatrists with psychopathological phenomena and an automatic transfer of this to all patients with whom they have contact. (p. 13)

Dabrowksi noted that the recovery of some patients results not only in the recovery of their health, but also the attainment of a higher level of mental functioning. There is here, then, the recognition that some crises and some disintegrations of the personality can have a positive growth effect. The person may be unable to grow, perhaps, if disintegration is prevented.

Gut (1989) has touched on the same theme in her book *Productive and Unproductive Depression.* She argues that depression can serve an adaptive purpose for the individual. The withdrawal and lowered mood that accompanies depression allows the person to dwell on their conscious and unconscious processes and perhaps resolve deadlocks in their functioning.

What makes depression unproductive rather than productive? Gut suggested that a person who has been overtaxed in the past will be more likely to have unproductive depressions. This can be caused by early trauma and by family functioning that prevented understanding and resolving these trauma. There may be no one to whom the individual can communicate the depression and despair and with whom the feelings and accompanying thoughts can be discussed. There may also be genetic predispositions and social and cultural factors that make productive resolution of depression difficult.

It is clear that the early trauma experienced by Katie, particularly the sexual abuse by her father, which was then followed by the schizophrenic breakdown of her mother, were the kinds of experiences that would have made a productive resolution of her depressions difficult, if not impossible.

Gut felt that finding a good listener was critical in resolving depressions productively. While writing a diary helps some depressed people (or writing letters, praying, or meditating), a live listener is much better. It is interesting that, despite the large number of people referred to by Katie in her diary, none of them appear to be good friends, that is, the kind of person with whom one can sit down and talk exhaustively about a problem of concern. Katie's only confidant is her boyfriend Mark, and she is too dependent upon (and conflicted about) that relationship for Mark to be the ideal confidant. (We might note also that we have no evidence to evaluate whether Mark himself is capable of being a good confidant for someone who is depressed or in distress.)

☐ Discussion

Many years ago, Binswanger (1958) treated a woman, Ellen West. At the time that he treated Ellen, psychiatrists did not understand the disorder that we now refer to as anorexia, an eating disorder. Ellen was diagnosed as schizophrenic at the time, but the misdiagnosis did not matter that much since there were so few treatments available, if any. Psychotherapy was primitive, and medications unavailable.

Eventually, Ellen committed suicide. Binswanger, an existentialist wrote:

> ... I exist authentically when I decisively resolve the situation in acting. ... In contrast to the "affect"-laden short circuit reactions of her earlier suicide attempts, this suicide was premeditated, "resolved upon mature consideration." In this resolve, Ellen West did not "grow beyond

herself," but rather, only in her decision for death did she find herself and choose. (Binswanger, 1958, p. 299)

. . . the existence in the case of Ellen West had become ripe for its death in other words, that the death, this death, was the necessary fulfillment of life-meaning of this existence. (p. 295)

. . . only in her decision for death did she find herself and choose herself. The festival of death was the festival of the birth of her existence. (p. 298)

Thus, Binswanger concluded that suicide was the correct and necessary path for Ellen West to take. I must confess that, as I read Katie's diary, I sometimes had a similar reaction.

But, like Carl Rogers (1961), I have also criticized Binswanger for his handling of the case (Lester, 1971), accusing him of psychic homicide (Meerloo, 1962), that is, killing a difficult and incurable patient by propelling her to kill herself or putting her in a situation where the likelihood of suicide was great. Binswanger treated Ellen West as an object, and he failed to respond to her in a genuine and empathic way.

Katie needed an intervention. By herself, despite her strengths, she was unable to change her life-path. She reached out to others, both friends and a lover. She went to groups for incest survivors and for those with eating disorders. She went to college and planned a career, perhaps in nursing (helping others). She wrote her diary. But all of this was not enough.

Katie needed a psychotherapist to guide her through this period in her life, perhaps a cognitive therapist like Thomas Ellis (see chapter 10), a Jungian analyst like James Hollis (see chapter 9), a voice therapist (like Lisa Firestone (see chapter 12), or a more spiritually oriented therapist like Robert Fournier (see chapter 6).

But for many distressed individuals, a psychotherapist is not possible for reasons of accessibility and cost. And the fine therapists that I invited to contribute to this book are few and far between. Had Katie found a therapist, perhaps at the college counseling center, if in fact her college had such a center, she might not have "connected" with her or perhaps might have been restricted to brief short-term counseling which might have been insufficient. It is, however, regrettable that Katie was unable, for whatever reason, to find a psychotherapist to help her discover an alternative life-path, one that did not lead to suicide.

☐ Notes

1. This discussion of Shakespeare's Ophelia owes a great deal to the written commentary provided to me by Kenneth Tompkins, my colleague at the Richard Stockton College of New Jersey.

2. The quotes are from Shakespeare (1969).
3. R. D. Laing (1960) considered her madness to be schizophrenia.
4. Indeed, sexual intercourse was not a choice for adolescents fifty years ago.
5. She remains in a psychiatric hospital today.

☐ References

Binswanger, L. (1958). The case of Ellen West. In R. May, E. Angel, & H. F. Ellenberger (Eds.), *Existence* (pp. 237–364). New York: Basic Books.

Dabrowski, K. (1964). *Positive disintegration*. Boston: Little, Brown.

Gut, E. (1989). *Productive and unproductive depression*. New York: Basic Books.

Jardine, L. (1983). *Still harping on daughters*. Totowa, NJ: Barnes & Noble.

Kelly, G. A. (1955). *The psychology of personal constructs*. New York: Norton.

Laing, R. D. (1960). *The divided self*. London: Tavistock.

Lester, D. (1969). Resentment and dependency in the suicidal individual. *Journal of General Psychology*, 81, 137–145.

Lester, D. (1971). Ellen West's suicide as a case of psychic homicide. *Psychoanalytic Review*, 58, 251–263.

Lester, D. (1995). *Theories of personality*. Philadelphia: Taylor & Francis.

McGee, A. (1987). *The Elizabethan Hamlet*. New Haven: Yale University Press.

Meerloo, J. A. M. (1962). *Suicide and mass suicide*. New York: Grune & Stratton.

Mosak, H., & Maniacci, M. (1999). *A primer of Adlerian psychology*. Philadelphia: Brunner-Routledge.

Neuringer, C. (1988). The thinking processes in suicidal women. In D. Lester (Ed.), *Why women kill themselves* (pp. 43–52). Springfield, IL: Charles Thomas.

Neuringer, C., & Lettieri, D. J. (1982). *Suicidal women*. New York: Gardner.

Nolen-Hoeksema, S. (1987). Sex differences in unipolar depression. *Psychological Bulletin*, 101, 259–282.

Nolen-Hoeksema, S., Larson, J., & Grayson, C. (1999). Explaining the gender difference in depressive symptoms. *Journal of Personality & Social Psychology*, 77, 1061–1072.

Pipher, M. (1994). *Reviving Ophelia*. New York: G. P. Putnam.

Rogers, C. R. (1961). The loneliness of contemporary man as seen in the case of Ellen West. *Annals of Psychotherapy*, 2, 94–101.

Sakamoto, S. (1998). The preoccupation scale. *Journal of Clinical Psychology*, 54, 645–654.

Shakespeare, W. (1969). *William Shakespeare: The complete works*. Ed. by A. Harbage. London: Penguin.

Shneidman, E. S., & Farberow, N. L. (1957). The logic of suicide. In E. S. Shneidman & N. L. Farberow (Eds.), *Clues to suicide* (pp. 31–40). New York: McGraw-Hill.

CHAPTER **9** Robert R. Fournier

A Psychospiritual Approach for Understanding Heart and Soul: Katie's Yearning for Well-Being Amidst Chaos and Confusion

> Originality is like a unique mark each man receives at birth. It is a latent ability to be himself in his own way. . . . the atmosphere in which original-ity thrives is not the atmosphere which modern man is accustomed to breathe daily. (Van Kaam, 1972, pp. 1, 132)

When David Lester asked me to participate in this project, he invited me to consider the potential value of my interest in spirituality and suicide to writing about Katie. As serendipity may have it, a third area of interest emerged in my lifework during the past decade which also affects my contribution to this project—that is, my work with post-traumatic stress. "Spirituality" and "post-traumatic stress," it is argued, are two frequently ignored or de-emphasized factors which affect well-being and suicidality. Katie's personal struggle in life presents one significant example of how these two factors influence decisions of life and death and how we may view an alternative for healthy transformation in life. It is my hope that this contribution will help others achieve well-being, assist in the valu-able work of suicide prevention, and serve as a significant memorial to Katie for her friends and loved ones.

Diaries present a distinct glimpse into a person's life, wherein "the per-sonality of its keeper is richly found" (Leenaars, 1988, p. 37). Katie's diary

123

portrays the struggle of a young woman who desired well-being passionately, yet was unable to transform her life adequately after her traumatic experiences to achieve this goal. Frustrated, embittered, exhausted, and desperate, she succumbed to the attractiveness of a premature death by suicide as *the* solution. Katie's religious faith appears as both substantial and symbolic in her attempt to achieve well-being; that is, on the one hand, as a genuine, substantial expression of her faith and hope that salvation was possible now, and, on the other hand, as a symbol of modern society's departure from life's ideals, our present "spiritual vacuum," that is, our "hunger for community, for meaning, for a sense of the transcendent . . ." (Myers, 2000, p. 262).

Suicidality and post-traumatic stress have a significant impact on the human condition, simultaneously and paradoxically threatening our survival and inviting transformation in life (Fournier, 1987; Levine, 1997). Katie's words during the last year of her life appear to demonstrate her valiant, yet unsuccessful attempt to survive and to transform herself amidst suffering and pain. As one reads her journal entries, one may wonder how such an apparently beautiful young lady may have become so distressed as to see no way other than suicide to solve her problems. As I read her entries, I felt an increasing desire to rescue her, to save her and help activate her potential for expressing her uniqueness in life and with others. Again and again the question returned to mind: Why, Katie, why? Perhaps a closer look to Katie's words will provide us with some insight.

□ The Deformative Power of Post-traumatic Stress: A Two-Faced "Beast"

The Source of Katie's Suffering

"Power is the birthright of every human being . . . essential for all living things," the source of self-esteem and the means for expressing our sense of significance and creativity (May, 1972). Conversely, powerlessness is the expression of a yearning for and a struggle to achieve a healthy sense of power, one that, if unsatisfied, leads to its ultimate expression—violence. The violent expression of powerlessness manifested itself in the lives of Katie's parents and herself, showing itself as a hurt directed toward self and others—an uncontrollable, destructive, "deformative" force in life. What was the source of Katie's powerlessness, the reason why she became unhealthy and, ultimately, committed suicide?

I long ago abandoned the search for *one* cause or "reason why" for a suicide, realizing the impossibility of this venture and its consequential oversimplification and nearsightedness for discovering truth (Shneidman, 1993). Katie describes what appears as one major contributor to her distress in life and her "movement" toward suicide (Fournier, 1987), that is, the experience of living with and being raised by parents who significantly abused and neglected her. This experience led to a belief of worthlessness, feelings of inferiority and self-blame, and a deep sense of disconnection from the world. Katie lived in a seemingly perpetual, fear-filled state of being, suffering as if terrorized by a predatory beast who had attacked her and who continued to stalk her. "I feel so bound up inside and trapped in the feelings of my childhood, not able to move" (June 14, year 1).

The word *beast* is defined as "something formidably difficult to control or deal with" (Merriam-Webster, 1998), a good descriptor for both the *source* of Katie's traumatic stress, her past traumatic experiences, and the anguish or *trauma*" experienced by her in its aftermath, including suicidality. Katie's journal entries speak repeatedly about the daily challenge of living with this two-faced beast.

*I anger with my beast (June 25, year 1) alone (June 15, year 1)
. . . in such pain and disarray (June 15, year 1) . . . a raging
whore (June 24, year 1) . . . madness (July 16) . . . the monsters
are here with me (July 17) . . . the black clouds with the demons
rage around me—sometimes on top of me (August 28)*

The source of traumatic stress is defined as an extraordinary stressful or traumatizing life event or series of events that contributes to a "loss of faith that there is order and continuity in life," and that leads to a human response of fear, powerlessness, helplessness, loss of safety, and loss of control (van der Kolk, 1987, p. 31). In her journal, Katie describes the parental mistreatment that she believed was a source of her traumatic experiences, one of the two aspects of the two-faced beast that troubled her.

*felt so misused . . . like a piece of meat (June 24, year 1)
. . . people did such bad things to me when I had no clothes on
(June 14, year 1) . . . my mother made me feel so
horrible . . . yelling at me . . . calling me a slut . . . mommy
dearest . . . Jekyll and Hyde (June 24, year 1) . . . the anti-Christ
(July 1) . . . the belt I was whipped with (July 17) . . . the leather
strap she beat me with (August 28) . . . degrade me . . . [telling
me] no one will ever love you except me (September 28)*

. . . kicked me in the stomach (August 28) . . . kept me in the
house (July 16) [my father] . . . beating my mom . . . neighbors
would call the police (July 26, year 1) . . . remember my father
making me go on the bed with him naked (July 17) . . . his hands
on my body . . . so painful (July 29) . . . you scream (August 28)
. . . don't tell mommy (January 1) . . . I saw him put his shirt on
after he was done with me (July 29)

Katie's "Trauma": Devil Within and Devil Outside

Apart from the traumatic experiences themselves, the other aspect of the
two-faced beast that troubled Katie was the hurt or "trauma" that resulted from it. This trauma constituted a continuous, unresolved tension
with Katie between a private or internal anguish and an external or social
anguish—a devil within and a devil outside. "What is wrong with
me? . . . sickness seems like a concrete wall—holds me in, contains me"
(July 3).

When we experience something threatening or terrible, we wish to get
away from it, toward something pleasant, comfortable, and safe. A child
runs to her or his mother or father when scared. A child also will *remem-*
ber that she or he was scared and that *something or someone*, real or imagined, was the source of that fear. Unless a child learns about the source
and the meaning of the fear, she or he may continue to be scared in other
situations that are perceived as threatening, and will remember with some
anguish the original traumatizing event(s) experienced. Continuous fear
leads to perpetual anguish in body and mind, within and outside the self—
a prolonged and distressful trauma that will continue to evoke its need to
be adapted to or constructively transformed for well-being in life.

The Devil Within

Traumatic events, it is argued, contribute to "bound energy" within us if
we are unable to respond appropriately and express our self at or soon
after the time of the experience (Levine, 1997). The personal anguish
that Katie felt after her traumatic life experiences and the apparent lack
of an outlet for expression (no one there to turn to) presented an ever
present and inescapable burden of hurt bound and held within. Katie
used many words in her journal to describe this "devil within," many of
which echo those expressed by others with similar traumatic life experiences. Katie describes herself as a prisoner, one who was "locked up (June

14, year 1) . . . bound . . . in chains (June 23, year 1) . . . as if locked away, in a tower dungeon (June 22, year 1) . . . cold, scary, dark" (June 14, year 1). She felt "alienated and isolated (August 1) . . . abandoned (February 11) . . . unloved (June 22, year 1) . . . petrified (June 26, year 1) . . . dirty (July 4) . . . left to exist alone" (June 22, year 1).

Katie describes her captors and torturers as the "monsters" of her past (July 17). This "devil within" experience produced a lonely and secretive suffering for Katie, leaving her to shoulder the entire burden of her past hurt, its effects on her life, and her perceived responsibility for subsequent, successful adaptation in life.

How did Katie's "devil within" show itself in her life? No matter how hard we may try to conceal or shield our self, traumatic life events affect us, physically, psychologically, socially, and spiritually (Fournier, 2002). As with many persons who are severely abused, neglected, or otherwise traumatized, Katie displayed her suffering in a complex array of responses, including health problems and changes in personality. Many of Katie responses are associated with features common to a mental health diagnosis of post-traumatic stress disorder or a dissociative disorder. Katie describes flashbacks, nightmares, and other frequently occurring intrusive thoughts, memories, and images associated with traumatic life events. She describes numerous physical health problems, including severe headaches, gastrointestinal distress, dizziness, fatigue, and insomnia. Fear, anxiety, confusion, frustration, depression, shame, and anger were described as frequently experienced emotional responses. Social responses reported included excessive self-consciousness, paranoia, social withdrawal and isolation, overachievement, and jealousy. Personality features described by Katie are among the common features of antisocial and borderline personalities. She describes lying, stealing, substance abuse, fear of abandonment, unstable and intense interpersonal relationships, unstable self-image, impulsivity, self-mutilating and suicidal behavior, difficulty controlling her anger and temper, and apparent dissociative symptoms.

Perhaps more significant than knowing about Katie's response to her traumatic life events is an understanding of what motivated Katie to choose to respond in this apparently peculiar and unhealthy manner. In the aftermath of traumatic events, as throughout our life, we tend to maintain an "illusion of wellness," a belief that all is well. Often, we believe that we can return to a normal and familiar pattern of living, a state of equilibrium, as if unchanged and untouched by life events, without a need to change or to address what happened (Fournier, 2002). After all, we may tell ourselves, it is over with, in the past. Get on with your life! Perhaps this attitude is enhanced in the United States by our American spirit of independence and our competitive drive for personal success: we can do it all, survive, succeed, triumph, overcome adversity. Perhaps it relates to our body chemistry and our inherent, instinctual drive to survive—a part of our normal cognitive and biological processing to sustain life and discourage despair, even if sometimes inclusive of thoughts and ideas that are delusional or invalid. Perhaps, as may be seen in the country's response in the aftermath of September 11, 2001, it relates to our social human need to maintain cohesion or unity and to belong, ensuring safety and protection from hurt, and to empower us to respond and adapt. Also, it does not help that others may knowingly or unknowingly contribute to our distress. Others may be unavailable or inaccessible to us for needed social support, including comfort, reassurance, information, guidance, and material provisions. Others may even discourage us from confronting past traumatic events by emphasizing the disadvantage, inappropriateness, or even danger of doing so, and reinforcing the value and appropriateness of keeping secret and "burying" what happened. Out of sight, out of mind. Or as one grandfather said to his young granddaughter after she was physically abused by her grandmother, "Forget it, because nothing can bother you that you forget. The only thing that can bother you is what you remember."

Katie sought to adapt to her traumatic past as best she could, mostly alone, with the hope and belief that all would be well. Katie's plan for adaptation in life, it seems, was to adjust or compensate for the problems of her past by meeting the demands of the present moment and avoiding reminders of what had happened. If she believed she had become dirty and bad from what happened, then she needed to be cleaned and purified. If she was unloved, then she needed to become more attractive and pleasing to be loved and accepted. If she felt ashamed and damaged by her past hurt, then she needed to perfect herself and conceal the unmentionable details of the past to become worthwhile and fulfilled. As with any plan, constant adjustment to the demands of the changing environment was needed for success.

The Devil Outside

Apart from living with an illusion of wellness, we also tend to experience life with illusions of invulnerability and immortality, believing and behaving as if we are impervious to hurt and will live forever. With confidence, we plan days, weeks, months, or even years ahead for activities we may never experience, or that we may experience differently than anticipated due to unexpected conditions or circumstances. The frustration we encounter in planning events according to the weather forecast is one example of the tension we experience when our illusory and ideal expectations meet the imperfect and uncertain real world. When disappointment, hurt, or threat to life occurs, our illusions about life and living become shaken or shattered. We tend to respond either by reinforcing our illusory living, such as by denial, avoidance, projection of blame, or other means, or by confronting it, facing reality, and, hopefully, developing a more realistic and authentic life perspective (Schwartz, 1966).

As Katie compensated for her past hurt and modified her life away from it, she gradually realized that her efforts fell short of her intended mark of well-being. This led Katie to work harder to compensate and hide the painful past. For example, by telling others that her mother was dead, Katie may have attempted to erase the memory of her mother's presence in life, hoping also to erase past and future pain and suffering and to appear normal. Over time, Katie began to realize that even these "extra" efforts to fit into the world were unsuccessful, and, even more troubling, they were reminiscent of the abusive and neglectful scenarios of her childhood that she sought to avoid: they were "bad." When her efforts failed, she responded with acts of futility, desperation, and self-punishment, including overeating, self-mutilation, alcohol intoxication, verbal or physical outbursts of anger, and suicidality. Ironically, these actions appear to have provided Katie with some relief, stimulating a physiological reaction that calmed her down or deadened the pain and temporarily reduced the intolerable stress to tolerable levels, enabling her to resume her coping efforts (Van der Kolk, 1987). While reinforcing her illusion of wellness, such behavior had a nasty, self-defeating, and self-destructive side effect, that is, the intensification of guilt, shame, self-hatred, and rage toward the perceived source of her anguish—her parents. Katie saw herself as victim and, at times, as perpetrator of abuse of others and herself. She sought belonging, yet felt alienation. The real world demanded a healthy, adaptive response from her, one that required the development of self-esteem, self-mastery, conformity, and responsible behavior, all of which she began to realize she lacked. No matter how hard she tried, unresolved hurt from her past continued to signal its presence and its need to be addressed. Memories, thoughts, and images of what happened in her past persistently haunted her, affecting her mood, attitude and behavior, and seeking discharge (Levine, 1997, p. 176). "I repress so much in order to be coherent. . . . I need to explode. I need to cry. I need to breathe" (July 1). Katie's effort to fit into life produced a "devil outside" existence, that is, a paradoxical and painful struggle between, on the one hand, the crippling anguish of living with an illusory "façade" of acting normal and, on the other hand, the realization that this façade concealed who she actually was and was contradictory and antagonistic to her achievement of well-being. Katie's façade allowed her to interact with others with some protection from her pain, yet at the cost of being inauthentic and being prohibited from well-being: a "bell jar" for suicide (Plath, 1971).

I stand guard to protect what they don't know exists (June 25, year 1) . . . hiding myself (August 22) . . . an outsider (December 31) . . . hate fighting to be honest (September 2) . . . can't pretend that these brain washings don't effect me (September 27) . . . have to put away these tactics of escape and lay out who I truly am (June 20, year 2)

☐ Katie's Search for Love—Her Solution to Suffering

All human action, it is argued, is oriented toward the achievement of two essential life goals: (1) to develop a sense of worth and dignity as a distinct human being—a sense of identity; and (2) to experience one's self as a meaningful and contributory presence in the world—a sense of intimacy with life (May, 1972). These two distinctly human goals of identity and intimacy presented a huge challenge to Katie, one that, with improper and inadequate parenting, she was unprepared to undertake. Nevertheless, Katie sought courageously and ardently to do so, hoping and believing that all would be well.

Identity

Developing a sense of who we are apart from others, "I," is a task that commences early in life, as may be confirmed by any observant parent who tries to feed an infant who has had her or his fill and desires no more. The infant's mouth and jaw tighten, telling us "No." Traumatic life events in early childhood may retard or misdirect this development of self. The child becomes forced to submit to the will of another force, thereby relinquishing her or his own budding significant power (Pelzer, 1995, 1997, 1999). If the force is repetitive and intense, the child overextends her or his human survival response to the perceived threat to life and develops a generalized belief that all is to be feared and all is potentially destructive, all the time. Rather than maturing, this traumatized self insulates to protect what has developed from total annihilation, stagnating, and, if prolonged, slowly decaying and dying. Dependence and helplessness replace self-mastery. Fear and immobility replace trust, exploration, and creative expression. Hypervigilance, dissociation, and compulsivity replace spontaneity and intimacy with others. Agitation, impulsiveness, and rage replace patience, realistic decision-making, and contentment. In short, the traumatized self manifests behavior that indicates a "felt sense" of not being healthy, not esteemed, not I or not worthy of I (Levine, 1997).

The challenge to Katie, to discover her sense of self, was complicated by her perceived need to maintain a façade of who she "had to be," by the haunting anguish of her traumatic past, and by the lack of social support for change. Try as she did, Katie could not escape the fact that she had not been affirmed as significant and worthwhile by those who brought her into the world. She felt essentially incomplete and fragmented as a human being, persistently questioning whether or not she was capable or worthy of change.

Shame

The human emotion of shame has been described as a "cancer of the spirit" that, if left untreated, solidifies within our minds a delusional belief or "fundamental lie" that we are worthless (Bloomfield, 2000). Unlike guilt, shame refers not to what we have *done*, but rather to who we *are*. The developmental experience of guilt and shame is common to all, with varied degree of impact. In early childhood, when we say no and have done something wrong or inappropriate, we are told about it, sometimes scolded. We feel the pain of being at fault, and we gradually become conscious of our self apart from others, a necessary experience for self-awareness and mature development. In later childhood, as our individuality further develops and we learn right from wrong, we experience the necessary pain of delayed gratification of our needs and desires, realizing we cannot have all we want when we want it, and that some things we want we cannot have at all. Through competition, comparison, and ideals, we "start measuring ourself" and receive feedback from peers and others about our self, including criticism, influencing our view of self (Bloomfield, 2000, p. 70). During adolescence, we are bombarded with a comparative analysis of our self with others and society's ideals at a time when our mind and body are undergoing dramatic and uncomfortable changes. Numerous opportunities for shame are present in adolescence, such as in the areas of physical appearance, academic performance, personality, relationship formation, family background, and socioeconomic status. Most of us weather the shames of our childhood and become strengthened from the experience, maturing in self-awareness, strengthened in character and conscience, and compassionate toward others. If burdened with intolerable and unmanageable shame, we develop self-contempt, feel flawed, or defective, worthless, unlovable, hopeless, and undeserving of forgiveness.

Perhaps the most intimate and most damaging pain Katie experienced in her life was a deep-seated sense of shame, the foundation of which she reported came from abusive and neglectful words and actions of her parents. By internalizing or "introjecting" this feeling throughout her childhood, Katie became brainwashed to the self-destructive delusion that she was inherently worthless. She expressed this shame in her diary:

feel dirty (July 4) . . . why do I have this sin of being abused (August 14) . . . unworthy (September 30) . . . fallen angel (February 4) . . . shameful about [my] body (June 20, year 2) . . . scarred (June 24, year 1)

Since the shameful acts of her past were socially unacceptable and, as she believed, her fault, Katie held all secretly within, with self-blame and disgust. As may be attested by those who work with persons severely shamed, this delusional belief may become so overwhelming that, without outside assistance, a person may become incapable of escape and transformation, incapable of discovering a healthy identity. Exiting shame means remembering, "uncovering the origins" of shame, dispelling its lie, and accepting the truth of inherent worth and dignity, often "going against" what was taught by those who we believed expressed truth (Bloomfield, 2000, p. 66). Without successfully transforming shame, attaining a mature identity remained for Katie an illusive and unachievable goal, one that would bother her throughout her life. As a person once told me, "I don't know what's worse, the hell I'm in now or the hell I'll be in if I try to get out of this." I suspect that Katie, too, may have felt the dilemma between remaining with what was familiar, and with which she could cope, albeit shamefully and maladaptively, versus discovering a new and healthier way to cope and escape shame.

Image of God

Human beings, it is argued, naturally seek improvement in life—greater goodness, more beauty, fuller community, or intimacy with others. One perspective for envisioning "God" is as the ultimate object of love, that is, the ultimate motivating force or power for improving human life (Dunne, 1985). Improving our life involves "waking up" or being attentive to the reality of who we are and to the world in which we live through a commitment to wonder, understanding, reflection, deliberation, and responsible action (Dunne, 1985). Improving our life, it is argued, is being in communion with God. Departing from this action, it is argued, leads to a departure from God to the consequential experience of loss, longing, and tension. As we reorient or recommit, we experience joy, peace, and contentment. From this perspective, then, God may be viewed as intrinsically related to the healthy human need for power and the expression of human potential (May, 1972).

In Katie's life, religion may have been not only an expression of her belief in the existence of God, but also of her struggle for self-improvement, including identity formation and authenticity of being. Human beings formulate a particular conception or image of an absolute, ideal power, a "God image," in accordance with their beliefs, religious traditions, needs, hopes, and desires. It may be argued that Katie's God image reflected her need for the love and acceptance that she did not receive adequately in childhood and her need for a successful adaptation in life, including salvation from the suffering of the two-faced beast that tormented her. Katie expresses this essential need in her own words:

my sincere need to be wanted and cared about. . . . There was no friend or person or parent to catch me. No one was there except me, as usual, to pick up the broken pieces (June 22, year 1)

For Katie, God appears to have been her ultimate source of salvation, the comforting, nurturing Parent who listened to her petitions and responded with love. In childhood, Katie mentioned praying to God to fix the hurts that plagued her and her family, "for Mommy to get better" (July 16). To survive like the character Jenny in the movie *Forest Gump*, she prayed in the field and, in her imagination, "had to live in the sky, ride on the clouds with God, with the angels" (July 16), flying above her parents' abuse and neglect. We may hypothesize that, at some point during her childhood, Katie formulated a reliance on religion as a source of protection, solace, and strength for living. One may speculate that her parents' abuse and neglect demonstrated to Katie a lack of caring that left her feeling lonely, powerless, helpless, unloved, and insecure—disconnected from the world in which she lived and in need of connection. As such, the religion to which she was introduced provided an available and accessible "home" in which she could discover an alternate "Provider," God, who could instill "faith in the goodness of [her] strivings and in the kindness of the powers of the universe" (Erikson, 1963, pp. 250–251). Through God, she could feel pure and good, powerful, worthy, and accepted.

Katie also may have sought to receive from her religion the salvation she craved from the beast that tormented her, religion serving as "a community of meaning, empowerment, forgiveness, and hope," a place where she could "explore and experience what God is enabling persons to become" (Wilbanks, 1990, p. 75). With this spiritual resource, Katie could envision herself, not only as worthwhile and dignified, but also as capable of achieving identity and intimacy in life. After all, the Christian God-Man, Jesus, searched for and accepted sinners and demonstrated how sinners could be transformed into saints. This Christian God was a listening, understanding, and loving God who never abuses, never neglects, and always saves. In her journal, Katie called out to this God who knew the truth about her anguish, this God who knew of the goodness that resided beneath her deep-seated shame, this God who could provide her with the power she needed to change.

I cried a lot to God . . . I feel my spirit power, and I need this to help. I NEED TO TRUST AND HELP MYSELF. . . . I HAVE A PURE AND STRONG HEART (July 4)

College Life

Katie's struggle for identity continued in college, with her confusion and frustration becoming most manifested therein. Going away to college involves a move away from the familiar to the promise and expectations of the new, one of the few rites of passage to adulthood available in our society. A teenager leaves the security and comfort of home and enters an environment in which she or he is confronted with one's self, past, present, and future. Katie's entrance into college provided her with a potentially valuable opportunity to search for her authentic identity within an open social system that permitted and reinforced self-expression. At college, Katie could search for a "corrective mirroring about what is real and not real," unlike her childhood experiences wherein an erroneous, shameful egocentric belief was fostered by significant others, reinforcing her view of herself as blameworthy and wrong, even when she was right and good (Bryant, Kessler, & Shirar, 1992, p. 55).

Loss and mourning naturally follow high school graduation and entrance into college, as a teenager seeks self-transformation into adulthood. Learning to mourn and adapt successfully in life is essential for future success, and we are taught to do so through prior success in adapting to stressful life events and through the support and guidance we receive from loving others. "The more incompletely an early loss is mourned, the greater the chance that later loss will result in self-destructive strategies" (Kushner, 1989, p. 163). Katie was ill-prepared for the demands placed on her in college, including mourning the loss of loved ones and home, establishing her identity, confronting her painful past, and becoming intimate with life, including peers who were also in the throes of a life transition. For Katie, this migration to college life meant facing major losses without the "ritual structure that enables people to deal with loss" and with increased vulnerability to crises with any future loss (Kushner, 1989, p. 163). While hoping and praying for a future of health and happiness, Katie entered college "alone and afraid in the promised land" (Kushner, 1989, p. 201).

By the time Katie began college, it appears that her reliance on a supernatural Provider had become an important part of her life, with religious behavior utilized as a real source of strength, guidance, and well-being. Katie's college life challenged her religious belief and behavior through the influence of others' beliefs and the freedom she enjoyed in being able to choose. Enticed by pleasure-seeking behavior and a strong need to belong and be accepted, she put aside some of her upheld moral standards of behavior. Others were "doing it" and apparently succeeding without damaging their integrity or well-being, so why wouldn't she be able to do the same? Others, she believed, were healthy, and if she lived like them and "fit in," especially her close friends, she also would become healthy.

Intimacy

Human life consists of a finite time and space within which to express our self in a meaningful and intimate manner in the world. This lifework reflects the mysterious and paradoxical meaning of love—to love self in order to love others, and to love others in order to love self (Merton, 1983). Katie very much desired this essential intimacy with life, "always yearning for love" (July 4) and wanting her "very own family" (August 22). Katie's desire for intimacy provided her with continuing hope that her life would become wholesome and that her suffering would end. In college, Katie looked to her peers as examples of love and intimacy and, despite jealousy and resentment, sought to model after their belief and behavior, hoping to absorb it within herself, thereby acquiring love and intimacy. This modeling to gain love often meant acting like someone else for-the-moment, so as not to uncover the perceived ugliness within. As time progressed, this "someone else" became more and more difficult to live without and, like a bad habit, the façade took on a life of its own (Gough, 1997). Katie became increasingly frustrated in life as she realized that her behavior not only hid her suffering, but also led her away from love and intimacy with life.

Katie appears to have made a valiant attempt during the last year of her life to become healthy, using numerous healthy coping resources. She writes about using therapy, support groups, medication, peer support, and journal writing. To a significant degree, she became aware of her need to confront her beast in order to understand the meaning of what happened to her and transcend its imprisoning hold on her. She experienced benefit from this healing effort, feeling better.

Well, wow. Feel so good when people hear me and answer my needs . . . (July 16) . . . I'm dealing with my issues, and it feels like my life is really mine (July 17)

As she experienced healing, Katie found herself struggling to stay focused on living a healthier way of life while, simultaneously, meeting the demands of the present moment.

I still feel very alone . . . it hurts . . . I must remember that my words are my freedom—truth out of the darkness, the illusion, the confusion (July 17) . . . It's hard being optimistic about this. . . . I feel like I'm dying, or that I'm basically already dead (July 17) . . . NO ONE SHOULD EVER HAVE TO GO through this. . . . This is such a DISEASE. It sickens and kills me with its symptoms (July 29)

Why did Katie's efforts to heal fail? Perhaps the mental health community could have done more to help. Perhaps the addictive nature of Katie's compensatory behavior to deal with the hurts of the past backfired, misdirecting her to attempt to make the world adjust to her rather than she adjust to the world, gradually weakening her and overpowering her will to seek alternative, healthy behavior (Menninger, 1966, p. 90). Or perhaps Katie's interpretation of life was so distorted that she was unable to see her own healing; that is, she was unable to see progress because she was so intensely focused on her failings and perceived inadequacies. Perhaps her learned helplessness, negativity, and shame-based view of her self led her to become unable to see that some of her suffering was constructive. Seeing only failure blinds us to achievement and success.

hard time getting along with people (June 8, year 1) . . . hard time expressing my true heart and feeling (June 14, year 1) . . . feel I have to sacrifice myself to be close to people . . . to make them love me (June 24, year 1) . . . I get so absorbed in other people (July 7) . . . demand a lot of attention

(June 24, year 1) . . . I'm always looking out, waiting for
someone to hurt me (June 24, year 1) . . . love leaves you
defenceless and makes you vulnerable (August 28)
. . . everything is too intense for me (July 17)

Katie realized the hurtful consequence of her maladaptive relations with others and she sought frequently to seek refuge in isolation: "everybody always leaves me" (August 13), "being alone . . . safe . . . no one can hurt me" (September 18).

Katie's need for intimacy led to her dedicated reliance in college on two idealized others—her boyfriend, Mark, and God: one human, one supernatural; one new to her, one tried and familiar; and one as potential future partner, the other a permanent, guiding, and consulting Parent/ Provider. Both were perceived by Katie as helpful in many ways, serving as sources of power or strength; hope for perseverance; solace, relief, and escape from pain and crises; reflective mirrors of the inherent goodness in life and within her; and trusted shoulders to cry on, to manifest her raw, pain-filled self by expressing the withheld, unimaginable, and intolerable hurt from her past.

Mark

Ostensibly, Katie's relationship with her boyfriend, Mark, appeared as a normal adolescent romance: girl and boy meet, girl and boy fall in love, and girl and boy break up. Beneath its surface, however, this relationship was more complex and of utmost significance for Katie. This was her first true love, wherein she gave her purity of heart and her virginity with the faith and promise of genuine intimacy and self-fulfilment. Mark accepted her as she was, reinforcing her goodness and her ability to achieve genuine intimacy with life, a necessary affirmation for her personal transcendence from the anguish associated with her past. With Mark, she believed she could become healthy and whole. Mark was an ideal image through which she could envision the well-being that she hoped for herself. "Let his sweet heart, mind and body heal here so that, when he rises, he feels whole" (June 24, year 1). Unfortunately, Katie's relationship with Mark also provided Katie with an opportunity to avoid healing and deny or de-emphasize the value of facing the beast that tormented her. Mark replaced her need for therapy and permitted her to envision herself as similar to envied others—accepted, loved, loving, and belonging. Katie, it seems, viewed this relationship with Mark as symbolic of an illusory belief in having already achieved success.

*He makes me feel alive and free. . . . When I'm with him, I forget
that I have problems. I realize I'm a different person (June 24,
year 1) . . . Mark really loves me. I'm ok now, and I'm going to be
ok later (July 22)*

Predictably, this unrealistic view of Mark led to perpetual roadblocks of
frustration as Katie confronted the persistent and inescapable pain from
her past. At times, Katie's preoccupation with the painful past would
markedly intrude into her relationship with Mark, leading to her perception of him as another persecutor or captor who was imprisoning her.

*The aftermath [of sex with Mark] is way too much for me. . . . I
just keep repressing these feelings and have made it worse than
the original flashbacks (July 7) . . . I feel so trapped, bound, tied
up, locked up, like when I was when I was fourteen, thirteen,
twelve, locked up in the house, never allowed to be free . . . felt
trapped in my own body (June 24, year 1) He doesn't love me
truly. He only wanted to use me. . . . He cheapened me and I felt
like such a whore—slut—piece of meat (August 21)*

Deep-seated shame also would lead Katie to blame herself for the failings in her relationship with Mark.

*I feel like I'm some sort of bum begging for scraps. I guess
that's really all I'm allowed to get in life. . . . I've been
scarred . . . damaged (June 24, year 1)*

Katie seemed doomed to not succeed with Mark. Her problems resided
outside of this relationship, and she could not find answers to them within
it. Not established in her identity and not prepared for mature intimacy,
she manifested with Mark the angst of a teenage rebellion to become
authentic, one that would not succeed.

God Revisited

So, with Katie believing so strongly in her God, why didn't God save her
from despair and suicide and enable her to live with the well-being she so
desired and deserved? Human responsibility and choice for life may provide a partial answer to this question. God, one may argue, does not remove human responsibility and choice involved in life experiences,

including adaptation after traumatic life events and the endurance and transcendence of suffering therein. In her last year of life, Katie appeared to have abandoned her mental health work and relied increasingly on Mark and God, two idealized beings that she believed possessed the special potency through which she could change. Katie believed less and less in her own power or ability to adapt in life and, knowingly or unknowingly, viewed herself as less and less significant in life.

Three religious themes may be viewed as helpful for understanding the action of Katie's religion in her life: inspiration, prayer, and forgiveness of sin. These three themes may be viewed as serving naturally as "spiritual resources" to reduce suffering and offer hope and direction for well-being. The means for achieving this well-being, while in accordance with God, occurs not by God, but by a human being, through self-reflection, knowledge, and responsible action (Helminiak, 1987). The underlying hypothesis to this perspective of religion is that "God created the universe (and persons within it) with sufficient wisdom" and a "natural order of things . . . directed toward the good . . ." and that personal empowerment and integration with this universe enables well being or authenticity in life (Helminiak, 1987, p. 134). Human free will permits and directs us toward or away from the good, influencing self, others, and the universe. God invited Katie to know herself and trust in her ability to successfully adapt in life, that is, to effectively use the powers that she had, albeit they were suppressed, neglected, or apart from her awareness. By "knowing herself," Katie would become able to grow and become authentic in life— becoming her real self. As a Catch-22, however, Katie's traumatization and victimization presented a formidable obstacle to knowing herself, necessitating help from others who understood and could help, and fostering the illusion that she was powerless to enact change and achieve well-being.

1. Inspiration

"Religion has tremendous power for inspiring people to live authentically" and move "toward the true and good" (Helminiak, 1987, pp. 125, 130). Belief in a benevolent Supreme Being provides a perfect role model for well-being, the "ever transcendent goal that constantly calls one to purify and renew" (ibid., p. 126). Religious ritual and personal reflection on God enable us to understand our life situations and circumstances as potentially meaningful life events which, with our faithful, hopeful, and loving participation, may enable us to achieve a new level of being, transcending our previous state of being.

Katie's image of God as a nurturing, protective, and rescuing Parent may have led to an unrealistic expectation by her of God's role in her life, that is, as One who answers all desired petitions with gifts given and removes her from life's suffering, similar to the image one may have of Santa Claus or a fairy Godmother (Helminiak, 1987, p. 140). Katie appears to have searched "for magical solutions to life's problems rather than accept them as God-given challenges" to produce change within her own life (Helminiak, 1987, p. 140). As such, Katie's religious faith may have become "a shield from the responsibilities of life," distancing her from awareness and acceptance of her intrinsic power for change, and furthering her dependence on others and her reactivity to life events and circumstances (Helminiak, 1987, p. 140). Rather than move as inspired by God to empower herself, Katie appears to have believed more and more that God would move her by His Power. If she believed and trusted enough in His Power, she may have argued, her religious faith would be rewarded by His enacting positive change to rescue her from her beast.

2. Prayer

Prayer has an effect "by changing us who pray" (Helminiak, 1987, p. 132). Through prayer a person opens herself or himself to The Transcendent, God, Goodness, and Well-Being, the One we seek to be. Communicating with this Being opens us to our responsibility and our fundamental need to "move beyond our narrow selves to the affirmation of all that is true and to the embrace of all that is good, as best we know it"(Helminiak, 1987, p. 132). As we become authentic, we "move in harmony with the will of God as it operates in the universe" and "more freely cooperative with God's creative power" (Helminiak, 1987, pp. 133–134). By listening to our self in communication with God we may identify and formulate the thoughts, ideas, and images that lead to effective action.

Katie used her communication with God as an opportunity to speak and listen to herself about her needs and her life struggle. "God, how I need time away from absolutely everyone close" (August 10). In the last year of her life, as she believed less and less in her own ability to change, Katie's communication with God became more demanding, desperate, and self-centered. Katie's prayers not only included hopeful petitions for courage to bear her suffering ["give me strength" (June 8, year 1)], but also grandiose wishes for whatever she thought might represent an instant cure to her life predicament ["help me become a millionaire" (June 15, year 1)]. Katie's prayers reflected her furthering movement away from her real self to a desperate need for Divine Intervention. She became less and less attuned to the "dynamic human spirit" within her that could lead her toward well-being (Helminiak, 1987, p. 101).

3. Forgiveness of Sin

To believe in the need for forgiveness of sin implies an awareness of the natural imperfection of being human and of the "intrinsic human demand for responsible living" (Helminiak, 1987, p. 135). Sin may be described as a lack of authenticity in life, including human mistakes and failings. Forgiveness of sin may be viewed religiously as the "ever available expression of God's constant love for humankind" that is "built into the design of the universe"(Helminiak, 1987, p. 139). As humans, we are necessary agents of change, free to choose to cooperate or not with the structures of our being and our universe. "We make ourselves be what we will be as a function of every decision of every day" (Helminiak, 1987, p. 137). Beneficial or deleterious behavior is determined not by God, but by the action of human beings. Purging shame and affirming worth and dignity after traumatic life experiences is one method for gaining forgiveness of sin, that is, by accepting responsibility for imperfections (not synonymous with being "at fault" for them or their "cause") and taking corrective action, a person gains harmony with self, universe, and God. Such action leads to a virtuous and contented way of life, to well-being.

Katie's traumatization and deep-seated shame not only contributed to her powerlessness in life, but also led her to believe that forgiveness of sin was possible only through an external agent of change that was good and worthy, such as God. Katie perceived that her power for goodness was taken away from her through her and her parents' behavior, leaving behind, as residue, badness or evil. It was only the redemptive power of God that could remove and forgive this sinfulness, and it was this redemptive action that Katie awaited impatiently until her life's end.

☐ Suicidality: Invitation to Transformation in Life or Premature Death

Hell

As once was told me by a priest who ministered to a man who committed suicide, "I believe only a very few people will not go to heaven," implying that many suffer hell on earth. Indeed, Katie's suffering may be described as such, a "fierce imprisonment in the self," wherein she experienced overwhelming pain and inescapable frustrations (Lewis, 1962, p. 152). This anguish has been described in suicidology as a "psychache," an intolerable pain created and fueled by frustrated psychological needs, leading to an active response for "cessation" or the elimination of this pain (Shneidman, 1993); that is, suicide is seen not as wanting to die, but rather as wanting to become pain-free. Katie wrote in her journal about the deepening, seemingly endless and inescapable anguish from her mounting frustrations:

my old family life seems to come up now, being alone, . . .abandoned, rejected, and neglected . . . my voice doesn't seem to carry me very far away from things of this sort (June 18, year 2) . . . feel all the lies I've told people to keep them away from me have suffocated me (March 5) . . . I don't feel rooted at all anywhere (June 18, year 2) . . . I don't care about my past anymore (June 11, year 2) . . . I always had the answer for everything. What happened to me? (Juen 2, year 2) . . . I've become negative. There does not seem to be a route back to optimism at all (June 2, year 2)

As her frustrations mounted, reaching a peak, Katie perceived herself as having fewer and fewer constructive resources for problem solving. Pain and suffering clouded her thinking, disabling her ability to perceive herself and her situation realistically. Old familiar patterns of viewing herself as shameful and viewing life with negativity influenced her mind, mood, and behavior. A "stoic . . . warrior spirit" emerged to respond to a world that appeared increasingly threatening (Lewis, 1962, p. 102).

As one nears suicide, a self-absorption engulfs the individual and propels the drive toward premature death via helplessness, hopelessness, fear, and frustration. The bell jar lowers and suffocates (Plath, 1971). I suspect that, to some degree and at some level within herself, Katie realized her efforts to become authentic were unsuccessful and that she was moving in a direction that contradicted her intention and offered no identifiable point of return. Her episodes of periodic rage may have been manifestations to her of this regression. Perhaps the greatest disappointment for Katie was those times when she viewed herself as not loving others, the exact sentiment she seemed to hate in others, especially since it was lack of love by her parents that was perceived as contributing to her suffering in the first place. In the final year of her life, Katie's "selfish love" expressed itself in her increasing need to satisfy her own needs at the expense of others' needs (Lewis, 1962, p. 49). She became increasingly less able to cope with the demands of her everyday life and increasingly more deluded in the illusory belief that she would be able to transcend this painful experience through the love of another and through Divine Intervention.

The Ultimate Decision

A very fine line exists between the experience of despair-to-suicide and despair that leads to a transforming intimacy with life (Fournier, 1987). Doubt and despair are normal aspects of significant life change, as may be seen in the adaptive process after the death of a loved one. We question who and where we are, what we value, where we are going, and even whether or not we should go ahead at all. A normal tension exists within us as we attempt to transform our life to a healthier, better place—a tension between faith and faithlessness, trust and mistrust, hope and hopelessness, and love and hate. The successful outcome of this struggle is a personal transformation of life wherein life experiences are perceived as valuable opportunities for self-growth and intimacy with others and society. During this transformation, we develop self-mastery and self-esteem as we learn to create a "new life" with a "gift" acquired from the undesirable, despairing experience. In the aftermath of a traumatic life event, the opportunity exists to discover something better for our life, something that would not have existed had this not happened. And what is unable to be changed is accepted as meaningful and purposeful (Frankl, 1963). This insight about despair is a manifestation of our "intellectual sincerity and honesty," to be praised rather than brooded over, condemned, or raged against (Frankl, 1997, p. 134). Courage and patience are the means by which a person may discover the meaning that will transform despair into intimacy with life. Biblical characterizations of despair leading to intimacy with life may be found in the Old Testament story of Job and the New Testament story of Jesus in the Garden of Gethsemane. In these stories, the help besought from another, "God," was sought and received through human patience, courage, and perseverance.

The life-giving opportunity to discover meaning in despair appears to have gone largely unnoticed by Katie. Surviving each moment's obstacles and seeking elimination of immediate pain took priority over a faith and hope that she could transcend her despair. And, ironically, "unless life points to something beyond itself, survival is pointless and meaningless" (Frankl, 1997, p. 134). Katie was unable to "turn suffering into a human achievement and accomplishment" (Frankl, 1997, p. 142).

If left alone in despair, we are drawn toward deterioration and premature death. Suffering and pain appear as endless, and life becomes unbearable and meaningless. We see only more of the same pain for our future, shattering our illusion that all is well. Out of desperation for survival, we may perceive another person in an illusory fashion, perhaps as a miraculous savior, or as an omnipotent and omniscient god. Mounting life frustrations lead toward helplessness and hopelessness, with no perceived way out. When alternative measures fail and all does not seem well, self-surrender may occur (Lewis, 1962, p. 92) and suicide may become viewed as a desirable, alternative "strategy" for coping with life (Kushner, 1989, p. 144).

In the last five weeks of her journal-writing (book 5), Katie's writing appears to reflect greater sincerity and honesty, disclosing a truth that perhaps she hoped would set her free, perhaps an inner realization of her actual need for transformation and authenticity in life. In a somewhat similar fashion to the last weeks of explosively expressive poetry by another young woman who killed herself, Sylvia Plath,[2] it is this unleashed rawness of reality confronted in aloneness that may have directed Katie toward her premature death. The real and undisguised awareness of what now appears as an "absolutely endless" (June 2, year 2) burden of her struggle with the beast becomes consciously present in Katie's everyday life. Pain and suffering mounted in intensity and frequency.

I can't stand myself and my life anymore . . . don't have any control whatsoever in my life at all . . . (May 30) . . . pure rage . . . I feel like I've lost everything inside . . . feel like such a burden to everyone . . . (June 1, year 2) . . . going absolutely crazy . . . have to force myself to be open and nice (June 2, year 2) . . . hate all of this . . . tired and dry . . . given everything I can. I don't have any more to give . . . (June 7, year 2)

Katie expressed her innermost needs at this time, those needs that she believed might release her from her suffering and lead her to authentic healing and well-being.

I want to experience solitude, not alienation, nor isolation (June 20, year 2) . . . I want to feel whole inside, instead of being severed in hundreds of little pieces . . . (June 20, year 2)

Katie appeared to know that her change in college was counterproductive to her growth and unrepresentative of her real self. She craved now to return to previously used coping styles that she perceived were successful and healthy earlier in her life.

I always had the answer for everything. . . . I used to have boldness and a strong character and have an edge on everything in my faith (June 2, year 2) . . . so angelic, as a person of higher spiritual and living example to the world . . . seem to have had a good wholesome sense of myself

despite everything else around me. . . . I know it's still in me
(June 2, year 2)

Katie's realization that her past strategies for adapting in life were no longer accessible or usable led her into a self-absorbed, fantasized, if not psychotic-like belief that she could become healthy through spontaneous or Divine Intervention, human love, and self-will. Rather than help, this further separated her from the world of reality and life.

I can start all over (May 30) . . . it will all work out (June 1, year 2) . . . I'm not going to kill myself . . . perhaps only the old Katie, so a new isolated individual could rise up and emerge (May 30) . . . starting to feel strong finally—independent (June 9, year 2)

Katie's desperation became more apparent as she now rallied whatever means she could to change for the better. She tried to exercise, diet, and fast to beautify and strengthen her body, hoping this would "melt away" her problems (May 30). "Muscles make the human body . . . absolutely beautiful" (June 2, year 2). She tried to solve her identity and intimacy crisis by honestly confronting her "friends" and giving herself time and space apart from her boyfriend, Mark, to reduce her dependency on him and face her beast. Hard as she tried, she found herself resorting to mal-adaptive behaviors that confounded these efforts to survive, such as making love with Mark for security and acceptance, and eating excessively. Despite her efforts, she continued to experience the severe anxiety and fear that had been with her throughout her life and that had informed her persistently that all was not well: "fearful of being taken advantage of and hurt" (June 2, year 2), "afraid that I'm suffocating him" (June 1, year 2). Katie became more and more narcissistically invested, with each new moment of time presenting another crisis of despair, with fewer and fewer resources for coping (Maltsberger, 1986). Katie was, in lay terms, "losing it" and approaching her "suicidal moment" (Fournier, 1987).

The very things I believe in are starting to disappear (May 30)
. . . feel like I'm losing touch with everything, that I'm slipping
away without choice (June 18, year 2)

Katie's world narrowed. Failing in her attempt to resolve problems with her boyfriend and others, she had only her faith in God to turn to. God became the exclusive Provider for meeting her material provisions, establishing her identity, and achieving intimacy with life. Katie petitioned God in a last-ditch attempt to free herself from her suffering, asking for everything from "an A on that test" and the arrival of a desired "package" to health and happiness (June 20, year 2). Her needs appeared as ever growing and insatiable. Finally, with both Mark and God perceived as unable to solve her problems, she resorted to her own problem-solving—suicidal behavior. Katie, it seems, died succumbing to the illusory belief that she was alone, abandoned, and incapable of change in life.

☐ Concluding Remarks

Learning to experience life with well-being is not easy, especially when those who are entrusted to welcome us into the world and guide us have themselves been impaired in this learning experience. After traumatic life events, we experience life as uncomfortably different, like a new jigsaw puzzle with all the pieces for the picture scattered before us in apparent chaos. We do not know how, when, or whether the pieces to our puzzle will come together or exactly what the picture will look like when it is put together. In her life, Katie did not know how to order the chaos within and about her to create her own well-being. Katie tried to empower herself to develop her own self-esteem and self-mastery, so as to discover and express her own unique significance in life (May, 1972, p. 27). Her journal entries demonstrate vividly this struggle in the last year of her life, fighting the "beast" to discover the way to emerge victoriously into the joy and peace of intimacy with life. Her struggle is a message to us all of the painful yet desirable "becoming" which we are challenged to experience in our own unique way for intimacy with life.

Understanding suicide is a complex and difficult endeavor, possible only when considering the influence and interrelatedness of physical, psychological, social, and spiritual factors. And because of the unique mystery and creative power of a human being, understanding will always fall short of absolute truth. Even so, our human calling beckons us to seek truth and perfection, and believing in our self and disarming the illusory and imperfect obstacles in our life help us to do so. So what may we conclude from the words that Katie has left us? After all, despite what we may know or what we may infer, much of Katie will remain unknown, as mystery, even to those loved ones who were close to her. What, we may ask, are the messages or "gifts" that our understanding of Katie's life journey has left for us?

Several important messages for life emerge from Katie's writing, associated with the well-being that she sought, that is sought by us, and that will be sought by all those who come after us. Among these messages for life are the following:

1. We must appreciate the intrinsic and unique dignity, worth, and potential of human life. Katie's budding potential in life displayed the unique value of a human being that yearned to become whole and wholesome, contributing personally and socially with meaning and purpose. Katie was impeded in appreciating herself and life by the hurt bestowed upon her by significant other human beings, as well as by the shame and dis-empowerment that she experienced from this hurt.

2. We must become consciously aware of the power of the human presence to influence others constructively or destructively. Listening, understanding, affirming, guiding, and exemplifying healthy living provide essential support to another for achieving well-being. Having someone to witness and walk alongside us in our life journey, especially when traveling through our personal "hells" of suffering and pain, reinforces faith, offers hope, and extends love. Katie longed for someone who would guide her toward healthy living, teaching her about herself and life, providing emotional and material support, and helping her "process" or transform her hurt and suffering into a meaningful and purposeful life expression. As it was, she appears to have "assumed" that her friends and those around her modeled this healthiness in their attitude and behavior, propelling her often into a state of confusion and frustration.

3. We must realize the distinct vocational role and commitment needed for responsible parenting. The parental role involves the serious vocational responsibility of helping a child to become uniquely present in the world with distinct identity and intimacy. Parental love is a "human achievement" that provides the soul with substance for living and for meeting the stressful demands in life (Gough, 1997). This achievement requires continual self-awareness and self-reflection, including modification of who and what we are, and a life directed toward virtuous living. Katie's birth, her presence in life, was an invitation to her parents to respond with love, enabling her to discover, develop, and express her original gift in and for life, apart from their needs and desires. The unhealthy parenting that Katie reported having experienced reminds us of the power of a human being to influence others in a de-formative manner, including doing harm that may have lifelong, detrimental consequences.

4. We must understand that human suffering is more than a labor of pain and anguish. Suffering provides a human being with a potentially valuable opportunity for personal and social transformation. As undesirable as it is (some describe it as a "necessary evil"), suffering is a part of our natural life. Viewing suffering as including an opportunity for healthy change empowers a human being, enabling her or him to see what is hidden amidst the suffering—that is, the wonder and awe of life and what it has to offer us. Being stuck in life with a sense of suffering-as-only-bad,

as happened to Katie, leads to an escalating, narrow-minded, and nega-
tivistic view of life and, ultimately, to despair and premature death (Lewis,
1962). Education about trauma and successful adaptation after traumatic
events may help others gain a greater ability to see the role that "hurt"
plays in life, thereby avoiding being perpetrators and victims.

5. We must attend to the essential human need for a responsible attitude and behavior for suicide prevention. Time and time again, we hear
about or see others who are ignorant of what to do about suicidality, or
who passively stand aside, ignoring or oblivious to the "cries" of others
for help. The price to be paid for our ignorance and inaction is heavy—life
itself. Those who have lost loved ones by suicide become ever conscious
of the detrimental impact of suicide for all. Even before helping others,
we must understand and accept our own responsibility for life, by identifying our own relationship with life, death, and suicide and learning to
make responsible choices that facilitate well-being. Thereafter, we may
advocate and work for social change, including increasing knowledge about
suicide, reducing lethal methods, and improving effectiveness for intervention and postvention services.

6. We must respond willingly and passionately to today's essential challenge to satisfy the intrinsic and life-giving human need for spiritual formation. Becoming a healthy presence in the world is a responsible human
action that provides an invitation to others to do the same, as they witness and desire the well-being that is placed before them and seek to live
it out creatively, in their own way. Katie and others who have died by
suicide have spoken about this need, manifested through their "spiritual
hunger" for meaning, community, and transcendence. Katie knew of her
inherent need for virtuous or "good" living, yet moved off course. She
was tempted by the urgings of a social environment that she believed
possessed spiritual well-being, and by the learned helplessness that en-
gulfed her, including her view of herself as incapable and unworthy of
goodness and well-being.

It is our responsibility and choice to decide whether or not Katie's life
and death will become beneficial to our life and to that of others. Each of
us seeks to be ourselves, that is, to develop in life the initial originality
that we receive at birth, that power of "I am able to" (Van Kaam, 1972, p.
2). The world is an "ever-expanding horizon of possibilities" in which to
accomplish this life task (ibid., p. 115). The world also may be a source of
intrusiveness and distraction to this process, leading us to become afraid
to become our self, and teaching us to accept the fundamental lie that life
has no meaning and we have no value. Learning to appreciate life with
patience, courage, gratitude, and shared authenticity in relationship with
others enables us to transcend obstacles to originality and joyously become who we are meant to be.

☐ Notes

1. In the literature, the word *trauma* is used interchangeably to represent either the "source" of traumatic stress or its "effect." The latter definition is used throughout this chapter, emphasizing the definition of trauma as "wound," meaning the physical, psychological, social, and spiritual manifestations of stress in Katie's life in response to her past life experiences.

2. Several interesting and potentially significant factors may be observed in both the lives of Sylvia Plath and Katie, including the following: (1) the use of writing as an intimate medium for self-disclosure; (2) the belief that the suicidal act may serve as a wake-up call for others to listen and respond to suffering (Katie—"maybe I'll be listened to more now", May 30); (3) the dislike of the body and its perceived dislike by others; (4) the obsessive-compulsive need for perfection; (5) a fatal (Katie) or intended fatal (Plath) suicide attempt at age 20 (Plath committed suicide later, at the age of 30); (6) a strong negative sentiment toward "mother"; (7) Germanic ancestry; (8) a narcissistic investment in transcending severe mental distress alone; and (9) a yearning and quest for spirituality in life.

☐ References

Bloomfield, H. (2000). *Making peace with your past*. New York: Harper Collins.

Bryant, D., Kessler, J., & Shirar, L. (1992). *The family inside: Working with multiples*. New York: Norton.

Dunne, T. (1985). *Lonergan and spirituality: Towards a spiritual integration*. Chicago: Loyola University Press.

Erikson, E. H. (1963). *Childhood and society*. New York: Norton.

Fournier, R. R. (1987). Suicidal movement: An addiction to death or an invitation to spiritual formation. *Studies in Formative Spirituality*, 8(2), 175–185.

Fournier, R. R. (2002). A "trauma education workshop" on Post-traumatic stress. *Social Work and Health*, 27(2), 113–124.

Frankl, V. E. (1963). *Man's search for meaning: An introduction to logotherapy*. New York: Washington Square Press.

Frankl, V. E. (1997). *Man's search for ultimate meaning*. Reading, MA: Perseus Books.

Gough, R. (1997). *Character is destiny*. Rocklin, CA: Prima Publishing.

Helminiak, D. A. (1987). *Spiritual development*. Chicago: Loyola University Press.

Herman, J. (1997). *Trauma and recovery*. New York: Basic Books.

Kushner, H. I. (1989). *Self-destruction in the promised land: A psychocultural biology of American suicide*. New Brunswick, NJ: Rutgers University Press.

Leenaars, A. A. (1988). *Suicide notes: Predictive clues and patterns*. New York: Human Sciences Press.

Levine, P. (1997). *Waking the tiger*. Berkeley, CA: North Atlantic Books.

Lewis, C. S. (1962). *The problem of pain*. New York: MacMillan.

Maltsberger, J. T. (1986). *Suicide risk*. New York: New York University Press.

May, R. (1972). *Power and innocence: A search for the sources of violence*. New York: Norton.

Menninger, K. (1966). *Man against himself*. New York: Harcourt, Brace & World.

Merriam-Webster's collegiate dictionary (10th ed.). (1998). Springfield, MA: Merriam-Webster.

Merton, T. (1983). *No man is an island*. New York: Harcourt Brace Jovanovitch.

Myers, D. G. (2000). *The American paradox: Spiritual hunger in an age of plenty*. New Haven, CT: Yale University Press.

Pelzer, D. (1995). *A child called "It."* Deerfield Beach, FL: Health Communications.

Pelzer, D. (1997). *The lost boy*. Deerfield Beach, FL: Health Communications.

Pelzer, D. (1999). *A man named Dave*. Deerfield Beach, FL: Health Communications.

Plath, S. (1971). *The bell jar*. New York: Harper & Row.

Schwartz, M. (1996). *Morrie in his own words*. New York: Walker.

Shneidman, E. (1993). *Suicide as psychache*. Northvale, NJ: Jason Aronson.

Van der Kolk, B. (1987). *Psychological trauma*. Washington, DC: American Psychiatric Press.

Van Kaam, A. (1972). *Envy and originality*. Garden City, NY: Doubleday.

Wilbanks, D. W. (1990). Ethical perspectives in review. In J. T. Clemons (Ed.) *Perspectives on suicide* (pp. 59–78). Louisville, KY: Westminister/John Knox Press.

CHAPTER James Hollis

Not Waving but Drowning:
A Jungian Perspective on Katie

"I was much too far out all my life
And not waving but drowning."
("Not Waving but Drowning," Stevie Smith, 1983, p. 303)

"I commit utter honesty upon these pages."
(Katie, August 10)

So why do we read the diary of Katie? We have seen her story, in all its heartbreaking permutations, over and over. Her generation of young women seems especially at risk, caught as they are between imperatives that they grow up, be free and self-determining, and yet satisfy the competing expectations of so many others. What is our motive, then, in invading her privacy, her aspirations, her terror? Did she not ask her most intimate partner, Mark, to feel shame in reading her private thoughts and desist? So we offer our justifications: A greater knowledge of etiology leads to prevention, we say. Do we not have abundant literature of such etiology? A search for therapeutic strategies. Do we not have therapeutic protocols well rehearsed by now? Morbid fascination? Fear? Prurient interest? Self-indulgence? Condescension and judgment? Or could it be our secret hope that we may find a clue from Katie to assist in our own troubled transit, an apotropaic gesture to hold off our great personal darkness a bit longer? Who does not know the answer(s) to this simple question may unintentionally dishonor Katie in an invasion of her privacy, an incursion into her grief and glory.

More particularly, can we find the Katie within us? Do we discern her wild, frightened, poignant, longing, doom-bound vacillation in ourselves? Until we can, we can lay no claim to being psychological. Being psychological demands two things: that we have the capacity to take personal responsibility for all that we are, and that we can internalize, that is, see the dynamics of history at work within ourselves. Can we "commit utter honesty within these pages" as Katie sought to do?

Having once taught for many years in various colleges, I probably met a hundred Katies, some of whom no doubt went on to take their lives, and I never knew what they were enduring. Certainly there were troubled students who reached out, who saw me, and my colleagues, as potential parents and potential rescuers. And how many of them did I turn away, being too busy, too tired, or too preoccupied, saying that it was someone else's responsibility?

Certainly the Sturm und Drang of the adolescent passage is well known to every parent and every professor. And we also know that one of the chief precipitants of their suicide is the breakup of a romance—not drugs, not bad grades, not parent problems, but romance! Why is it the case, from Goethe's late eighteenth century *Sorrows of Young Werther*, with its suicide—inspiring two generations of love-struck teens to fling themselves off cliffs or drink a soporific—to the present, that romance plays such a prevalent role as an etiological factor in youthful suicide? I suspect the reason is that youths, having no meaningful rites of passage and few wise elders or mentors to shepherd them, tend to transfer the immensity of their individuation imperative onto what we might call "the magical other."

Their bodies, their society, and their own psyches implore that it is time to leave Mom and Dad, but their inherent dependencies cry out for rescue, succor, safety, and satiety. The immense agenda of the fragile, needy child, no longer the province of the parent, is transferred to the romantic surrogate. Unconsciously, each says to the other: "I expect you to meet my needs, understand me, protect me from growing up, and so on." No one says this consciously, of course, but it is the secret, compelling agenda of romantic love. We see in Katie her loathing of her partner, Mark, and, simultaneously, her desperate need for his affirmations and protections. She is so wholly at the mercy of the other that his all-too-human inconstancy occasions seismic tremors throughout her psychic system. And who among us has not known such dependencies? Her need and her frustration are not pretty, but they are universal and represent the chief impairment of relationships, namely, that one or both partners burden the other with the impossible agenda of unconditional love.

Not finding such impossible love in their parents, even less in the surrogate alma mater, they turn to their various Marks, who, not up to the impossible task, fumble them into the primal terror of abandonment. In the face of this terror, they sometimes take their lives, lest something worse happen to them! As James Hillman (1976) suggests in *Suicide and the Soul*, the implicit thought is not about an end, but rather the desire for instantaneous transformation. The faulty logic of the suicidal stratagem suggests that one will still be around to reap whatever benefit may accrue as a result of this desired transformation.

Those of us who stand outside this circular argument know that what is called for in such moments is not suicide, the death of the self, but egocide, the death of the attitudes that govern the conscious personality. These values need to die. If they can be slain, a more adequate adaptation to the world may replace them—if the person survives to carry the work forward.

In his 1912 book that denoted his split from Freud, *Symbols of Transformation*, Jung (1956) identifies the powerful autonomy of libido (by which he means psychic energy in general), which vacillates between progression and regression.

> The natural course of life demands that the young person should sacrifice his childhood and his childish dependence on the physical parents, lest he remain caught body and soul in the bonds of unconscious incest. This regressive tendency has been consistently opposed from the most primitive times by the great psychotherapeutic systems which we know as the religions. They seek to create an autonomous consciousness by weaning mankind away from the sleep of childhood. (Jung, 1956, p. 356)

In short, given a vital tribal mythos, a Katie might have other images to mobilize her libido in developmental forms, serving maturation and communal participation at the same time. For Katie, and our current children, the tribe has vanished, and the imagoes that linked the individual to the cosmos and to the community are replaced by information sciences, drugs, depersonalized sex, and general hanging-out with other lost souls. Their clustering together is in direct proportion to their understandable fear of life and all that it is beginning to demand of them. No wonder that, beneath their cool, we sense the gathering desperation.

Yet Katie's dilemma is more difficult than that of many of her peers. Not only is she abandoned by her tribe, which has no mythos to offer her, but she is betrayed by her parents as well. That separation from primal connectedness which we call birth is a trauma from which we never fully recover. No wonder that we seek to crawl back into the womb by remaining infantile, by addictions, or by joining groups and movements. The burden of separation is too great, and we slip back into the "Mother," whereby we seek the annihilation of painful consciousness. Among the tasks of the parents is, of course, the demand that they be some sort of model of how an adult navigates this world. In fact, Jung has suggested that the greatest burden the child must bear is the unlived life of the parent. By this he means not only the external, visible life model provided by the parent, but also the internal deficiences which have impeded the parent's development. Moreover, the task of the parent is to modulate the existential shock of birth and the many separations that constitute our growth process. Katie's parents added to her existential trauma. Her father betrayed her by his sexual depredations, alcoholism, and emotional abuse of the mother and children. Her mother betrayed her through her inability to protect her and failure to model how an adult refuses to accommodate abuse. Her father's substance abuse, and her mother's schizophrenia, further destabilized her world. Upon what floor can a child thus stand and build a nascent personhood, if not the parent? Her loss of her home and her foster surrogates further destabilized her world. All things considered, we may pause to admire how heroic Katie's effort was, in the face of these formidable obstacles, to create a consistent, coherent, productive personhood. She was mostly self-supporting; she met her classes and friends halfway; she sought to hide her terror from others—hers is an heroic assertion not many of us can match.

At the heart of Katie's psychic mythos lies the pathologically charged primal imagoes of Mother and Father. Possibly only her genetic inheritance could rival the power of their influence. Yet, over neither nature nor nurture did she have any choice whatsoever. As William Faulkner once observed, the past is not only not dead, it is not even past. Or, as T. S. Eliot put it, what concerns us is not the pastness of the past, but its presence. Though dead or distant, Mother and Father are always present as psychic specters: models, influences, choices, and value systems. Dark Mother, always near, slipping by on timorous feet; Saturnian Father, always near, breaking and entering. We see in her desperate attachment to Mark, her boyfriend and parental surrogate, the need to please, just as the child had to contort her inner reality in service to that inconstant environment, seeking to attract love and support from her narcissistically wounded parents. The futility of healing them is repeated in her desperation to manipulate the constant object her boyfriend represents, using him as a remote possibility for the revisioning of history.

The internalization of these parental influences is central to a child's concept of self and other, and the transactions between them. We are all victims of the fallacy of such overgeneralization. We form core ideas of who we are, who the other is, and how we relate to each other in those earliest of times when we are without comparative possibilities or alternatives. These core ideas are what Jung called *complexes*. The idea of the complex has been so mainstreamed that we forget its origin in analytic psychology and its radical utility for understanding history and the usurpation of the present moment.

A complex is an affectively charged "idea" which comes to us through the fortuities of our lives. Some of them have the power to affirm us and support growth, without which we could not love or value beauty or justice, for example. And some of them have the power to undercut the ever-new present with the agenda, message, and behaviors of the disempowered past.

Every moment of history is new, of course, but our psyche functions as an analog system. In its effort to convert the unfamiliar, anxiety-provoking, present moment into something known, it asks, in effect: "Where have I been here before?" "What does my experience tell me?" "What is the familiar coping pattern?" This analog process, which imposes (1) the sense of self and other, (2) the value system and worldview of that time and that place, and (3) the replicative actions attendant upon survival or adaptation, is the source of our repetition compulsion. Not only does a Katie impose her sense of self and others upon Mark, she falls prey to the demoralizing, dependent, and destructive valences which her primal relationships with Mother and Father inculcated. The more these values are unconscious, the more powerful they are. The one question that Katie could not answer, nor can the reader, is: "Tell me, now, of what are you unconscious?" Yet what is unconscious owns, guides, and chooses for each of us in any given moment.

The therapeutic question for each of us then becomes: What are the unconscious imagoes that direct my libido, make my choices for me, and tend to produce the patterns of the same old, same old? (Since we cannot consciously know these core ideas, affect-laden and autonomous, we can only surmise their silent hand in our lives through a conscientious examination of their possible presence in the patterns we created.)

As an analyst, my experience has been that it usually takes a considerable period of ego development for a person to be able to become psychological, that is, take responsibility for the patterns that have accumulated. To the forty-year-old it may seem common sense to acknowledge that "I am the only one present in every scene of that drama I call my life; therefore, it may be that I have some responsibility for how it is playing out."

For the youth, the culprit will have to be, and not without cause, Mother or Father, or some such occult agency. Katie alternatively rages against her parents for their abuses of her and cries still for their support. While a supportive therapy would have helped her see alternatives, strengthened her ego for a wider range of choices, and quite possibly given her a positive parental transference, her psychic existence would be up for grabs for a very long time. Certainly, she would have been a candidate for an SSRI antidepressant that would have helped modulate her obsessive thinking and the agitated depression of her bulimia. But also, either through some sort of absurd lottery or grace that would have permitted her to survive this passage into the first adulthood, she might have had a shot at what we might call "the second adulthood," that place where we have achieved a history, an ego strong enough to stand up to it and take a long hard look, and the potentially liberating capacity to discern the role of those complexes at work within (cf. my larger studies of the possibility of midlife transition in Hollis [1991, 1998]).

Leaving home during the adolescent passage is relatively easy. One goes away to college, gives over to the system in hope that its ministrations will be supportive, and seeks a lover who will carry all the rest of the impossible agenda. Leaving home from midlife onward is much tougher. It means that one is obliged to separate who one is from the powerfully ingrained parental imagoes. In the face of the autonomy and ubiquity of these primal mediators of the life force, self, and world, one has only three choices: to repeat the implicit mythos that each complex embodies, to run in the opposite direction, or to try to find a treatment plan for them.

In most cases the first strategy is followed. We repeat even the abusive, wounding experiences because therein we already know, by analog, who we are, who the other is, and how we are to comport ourselves. Mark betrays Katie, but, unlike her Father, he does not seem evil; he presents as another confused adolescent, somewhat narcissistic, and at the mercy of his own dark winds. How could he not betray her, given the immensity of her need for constancy, stability, and unconditional affirmation? Who among us could, or should, meet such an agenda without developing a dependent personality disorder in return?

The inconstancy of her parental relations creates the classic borderline psychology whose primal terror is abandonment, and yet whose frenetic search for reassurance drives others away. Her vacillation between idealization of and rage toward Mark mirrors the constant shifting of her own inner sense of self. (Rather than label her a borderline personality disorder, which comforts us with its clarity and its dismissive finality, we might utilize the more ambiguous "disorder of self," a category that, in greater or lesser degree, includes all of us.) If her relationship to the self has itself been subject to inconstancy during her formation, how can Katie ever present a coherent sense of self to others, be drawn to someone relatively stable, or be able to hold or bear the terror of abandonment without desperate measures for its avoidance?

Secondly, a Katie, or any of us, can run from those primal imagoes, believing "I am anything but like my mother," or "I am not at all like my worthless Father." And the more we flee these historically generated definitions, the more we are owned by them. We are prisoners of what we flee and thus can only find what we flee everywhere.

Or thirdly, we evolve some sort of treatment plan for the wound that will not go away. We find that which temporarily assuages the pain—

substances, sex, work, mindlessness of various stripes and cultural access—whatever offers temporary respite. Katie runs the gamut of treatment plans in her honest account. If she were especially clever, facile, or gifted by fate to survive, she might become a psychology major, learn a great deal from her abnormal psychology class, and perhaps even become a therapist. Few professional caregivers, if any, are free of their own wounded origins. They seek knowledge and comforting ritual, sometimes distance themselves through condescension and superiority from their patients, and unconsciously seek healing of their own wounds by working with the wounds of others. (The ideal of "the wounded healer" goes back at least as far as the myths of Chiron and of the Temple of Aesclepius at Epidaurus. Paradoxically, the snake that bites us may in fact bring a painful wisdom that may be helpful to others.) The primal wound, and its psychodynamic script, which seems so long past, renews itself through the enactment of the countertransference dynamics present in all intimate encounters. Therapy is a special arena for such reenactment. Precious little attention is paid to the psychological origins and dynamics of the therapist in training; accordingly he or she is personally at risk in the work. Moreover, the autonomy of such dynamics often places the patient at risk of boundary violations. Whatever "the treatment plan" and its naïveté, each party stays tied to the power of the original imago, the primal complex. More than one professional caregiver has burned out or compounded harm to self or patient. Some fewer tumble to this secret connection between their work and their wound and find greater healing by walking away.

Katie and her putative therapist are up against primal forces. Such highly charged imagoes, again, represent an archaic "idea" of self and other and of the repetitive transactions between. (The greater the traumatic origins of the complex, the greater its intractable power; the earlier, the less conscious; the less conscious, the more autonomous its influence.) For all of us, such core complexes have suzerainty in our lives until they become conscious. Even with insight, a titanic struggle ensues for a conscious purchase on the moment. For Katie, bereft of wise mentors, supportive tribal rituals, and feeling overwhelmed by the twin wounds of invasion and abandonment, the odds of survival are slim to difficult at best. As Viktor Frankl amazingly observed of Auschwitz—that the concentration camp was a metaphor, hyperbole perhaps, for everyday life—so we can say that Katie is a hyperbolic portrait of each of us in the struggle for survival, for a broadened spectrum of possible choices in the face of powerfully charged history.

Simply making such history conscious is only the first step. After that comes repetition, support, more repetition, insight, other choices attempted, and finally, from time to time, occasional healing through enlargement. It is clear to anyone who has undertaken this process or who is a therapist: the process of healing does not mean leaving such core complexes behind—would that one could do so. It means that a more capacious, a more compendious personality has emerged which can hold, even contain, the original traumata and operate out of other, broader, more enabling complexes.

From time to time we see Katie has an intimation of her possibilities.

I will allow, I will let myself be free today, to feel, breathe, move and create, discover and feel the strong sense of the universe within myself. (June 17, year 1)

And later,

I may actually have to trust myself and my life. . . . I can't deny where I come from and where I have been, but I can change where I am and where I am going. (July 4)

And in her last recorded passage:

. . . let me feel an ever encouraging life force in my everyday existence from the time I wake to the time I sleep. Let my voice become strong and defined along with my character . . . (June 20, year 2)

One senses that some energy within, perhaps the natural instinct for survival and growth, or the teleological imperative of the Self, is rising to support her. Yet she quickly adds, "And please let Mark call soon, because I want to go to sleep soon and be uninterrupted" (June 20, year 2).

In these passages one senses an ancient drama that courses within each of us. The force that sets us out on the high seas, toward necessary, distant shores, is equally opposed by the siren-longing to drown in those same billows that offer surcease of pain even as they annihilate. Our ancestors dramatized this conflict in the archetypal "night-sea journeys" of Jonah and the whale, Odysseus, and many other archetypal carriers of libido. Each of us is a reluctant Jonah, summoned to bear witness to our lives on these alien shores, yet desirous of annihilation in the leviathan of fear and longing.

Each day is high drama on high seas; each day offers defeat or victory; each day the stakes renew. Each new morning the grinning gremlins of fear and lethargy sit at the foot of the bed. No matter what was achieved yesterday, they reappear today, and will be there tomorrow. First they nibble at a toe, then they ask for a leg, soon they demand the soul. Where fear of the world forces us back into dependency, where longing for protection gives over to lethargy, life is defeated. The gremlins win. As Keats reminded us, we are "half in love with easeful death." There are many ways of dying, and physical death is only one of them.

Katie's struggle is ours as well. Why do we voyeuristically visit her sufferings? We cannot save her. Can we learn something from her travail to help others like her? Possibly. Can we bear to see Katie in the person in the room next door to us, this very minute? Can we remember Philo of Alexandria's advice, centuries ago, "Be kind, for everyone you meet is fighting a great battle."

Can we learn something in her suffering that touches our own, something that offers insight, encouragement, or resolution? And why, anyway, should we prolong this journey with its certain mortal end? Albert Camus observed that suicide is the only truly philosophical conundrum. To be, or not to be, that is the question. In the suffering of this girl who is our daughter, our sister, ourselves, we are obliged to find our own reasons for living and our own resources for combating the gremlins of fear and lethargy.

Can we "commit utter honesty" on these pages that we call our life, the story that we write every day, or in which something is writing us?

☐ References

Hillman, J. (1976). *Suicide and the soul*. Zurich: Spring Publications.
Hollis, J. (1991). *The middle passage: From misery to meaning at mid-life*. Toronto: Inner City Books.
Hollis, J. (1998). *The Eden Project: In search of the magical other*. Toronto: Inner City Books.
Jung, C. G. (1956). *Symbols of transformation: An analysis of the prelude to a case of schizophrenia*. Princeton: Princeton University Press.
Smith, S. (1983). *Collected poems*. New York: New Directions.

Lisa Firestone

Separation Theory and Voice Therapy Methodology Applied to the Treatment of Katie: A Diary-Based Retrospective Case Conceptualization and Treatment Approach

FIRST ENTRY: June 8, year 1

I am so depressed and suicidal. My body feels restless and tired. I don't know who to turn to for help. I don't want to bother anyone with my battles. I just feel like crying. . . .

I really hate my body. I really hate my life where it is, with everything I am.
God give me strength. Help me today. I feel so unbelievably lonely and battered.

LAST ENTRY: June 20, year 2

Please help me through this and next week especially; things are so bad right now.

These passages from Katie's diary hold clues to the roots of her self-destruction as well as a possible key to her survival. The first two quotes from her initial diary entry, and the next quote, taken from her final entry nine days prior to her suicide, clearly reveal her desperation, pain, and cry for help. Unfortunately, this young woman, who was 20 years old when she hanged herself, apparently never turned to anyone for help or, at least, she failed to receive the help she needed.

In many of her journal entries, Katie wrote of her struggles and her prayers to be delivered from her pain so that she might attain her perfectionist goals, such as losing forty pounds or getting straight A's the next semester. She described her longing to be "strong, warm, distinct, good, and downright real" in her relationship with her boyfriend, Mark, her desire "to become awesome and wholesome," and her wishes "for their minds and hearts to soar." The unrealistic goals that Katie established for herself invariably resulted in failure. Her plans to "fix everything" about herself were followed by feelings of hopelessness and thoughts of suicide. Yet it appears that she failed to seek aid or guidance in her battle with her internal demon, the part of herself that ridiculed and tortured her and that ultimately wanted her dead. What treatment would have helped her understand this demon so that she could have effectively combated it? What could have been done to avert the tragedy of her suicide?

☐ Suicide and the Inner Voice

Separation theory (Firestone, 1997a, 1997b) can help provide a framework for understanding the development of the suicidal process, as it occurred in Katie and as it evolves in most suicidal people. Voice therapy methodology (Firestone, 1988, 1990, 1997a) and the *Firestone Assessment of Self-Destructive Thoughts* (FAST) (Firestone & Firestone, 1996) provide techniques for accessing what is going on in the mind of an individual who is suicidal and allow another window into the self-destructive process. In terms of intervention, voice therapy is an innovative cognitive-affective-behavioral methodology for treating individuals who are in a depressed, suicidal state, such as Katie was apparently experiencing in the months preceding her death.

A division existed in Katie between a self that had goals and aspirations, loved other people, and valued feelings, and an anti-self that was self-attacking, self-defeating, and, at its ultimate extreme, self-destructive. An example of Katie's anti-self can be gleaned from this diary entry:

I sit here with my untamed piano, untamed mind, untamed heart, with the music I only know, within myself. My mother is alive! Screaming viciously, laughing viciously, Jekyll and Hyde. Mommy Dearest. (June 25, year 1)

Katie described in one journal entry how she had lost touch with a sense of her real self:

I see how my interests & drives as a child have honestly disappeared. It all makes me very angry. There are a lot of things & people to blame for this. I never picked my circumstances. Besides, who in their right mind would actually choose to live where I did—honestly now—come on. It's not very healthy—but I can't ignore everything either. I think what would make me very happy would be—hm—do all my homework to the best of my ability today. Take little circumstances as they come, act as productive as possible—also—hm—be real, funny, mature, serious (intellectual), spiritual. (November 5)

She speculated that what could make her happy would be to become a perfect self and then, in her next diary entry, reported her feelings of failure when she didn't live up to this ideal.

I have done absolutely no homework. Can't get down & focus. I have so much going around my head & heart. Feel so disoriented. (November 6)

☐ Diagnostic Picture and Psychodynamics

Major Depressive Disorder

Beginning with her first journal entry, Katie reported feeling depressed and suicidal. Over the course of the year covered in her journal, it seemed that her depression waxed and waned, although she was never completely free of her depressed state for any substantial period of time. The diary also provides valuable information regarding Katie's emotional state, thought processes, and self-image. For example, she described symptoms indicative of a major depressive episode:

This life is so empty—didn't even get a quick fix this time—just uneasiness and emotional eruption. I felt like I died—all my dreams died—felt like a different person—completely isolated from other selves in other parts of my life—still feel that way now—feel dirty now—not only because I was abused when I was young, but because I abuse myself now—mutilate, destroy, manipulate, lie, control (sickens). (July 4)

Eating Disorder

Katie described herself as having an addiction to food, which coincided with her sister's report of her anorectic and bulimic tendencies. She even joined a self-help group in an attempt to overcome this behavioral pattern and in a few entries referred to making contact with her sponsor. Katie's feelings about her weight and her negative comparisons of herself with other girls played a large role in her life, as did her efforts to diet and severely restrict her food intake. Numerous diary entries revealed her repetitive pattern of setting a goal to lose a large amount of weight, carefully recording her dieting plan, failing to follow through, and then attacking herself with bitter self-recriminations when she binged.

Borderline Personality Disorder

Katie also manifested symptoms consistent with borderline personality disorder:

But then, what is always going on inside me? I can feel so damn restless and irritable talking about it. Obsessing aimlessly. It's ridiculous. But mainly I have inner fears and abuses. Things I do to myself. I act out horrible ways with myself. I act very unconstructive. Whether it's lying to people, or stealing, or being cruel by hurting my body. Whether it's all the helplessness I had to accept—lack of control which both of these were imperative factors. (June 24, year 1)

Katie's sense of self appeared to fluctuate considerably. She often thought of herself as superior to other people, but could quickly revert to depreciating and hating herself. She tended to think in terms of extreme absolutes, good and bad, alternately idealizing and tearing down both herself and others.

In her personal relationships, Katie's cynicism toward others, following a period of idealizing them, could be quite venomous. Many journal entries showed her chastising people and giving full vent to her rage. Subsequently she felt guilty and turned her anger against herself. Katie habitually criticized herself for having needs and desires. At the other extreme, she described a voice of vanity insisting that she must be the best, the sweetest, the thinnest, and so on. These thoughts of self-aggrandizement, which on the surface seemed friendly toward her, merely served to set her up for the inevitable crash whenever she failed or acted out. At those times, she inevitably viciously attacked herself. "I'm 20 years old and I still don't know who the hell I am and actually where I am and where I fit in" (September 18).

The diagnosis of borderline personality disorder is often perceived as a pejorative label. However, what this disorder appears to represent is a cluster of symptoms resulting from trauma history. Katie had such a traumatic history. Her father was abusive, and her mother's mental illness rendered her incapable of providing any semblance of stability or safety for Katie. As a result, she felt that she had to care for her mother, but she was also convinced that she had failed miserably in living up to her filial responsibilities. In her diary she acknowledged her hurt at never having a mother who could take care of her and expressed that she felt violated physically as well as mentally by her mother and her alcoholic father. It is likely that the early traumas contributed to Katie's symptoms that are consistent with the diagnosis of borderline personality disorder.

I don't need my mother in my life anymore. I never needed someone who was so sick and raped me—my mind, heart, soul. But why do I love and miss her so much? Boohoo. Boohoo. (June 14, year 1)

Never write about my Mom. She's killing the gentle structure of healing I've built in my mind—along with my Father. God I can feel them here. I can feel them everywhere. I'm flashbacking— won't let anyone know. OH GOD. Want to be the best for and to Mark. Having a hard time becoming perfect—or as close as humanly possible. It all kills me so much. I'm such a terrible friend and girlfriend. OH GOD! I HATE & CAN'T forgive myself for messing up. (September 28)

Post-traumatic Stress Disorder

Katie also described how she dissociated during times of stress. These symptoms warrant a consideration of a diagnosis of post-traumatic stress disorder.

I know where I've been, and I can tell where everybody else has been and who they are. . . . But me—fully me—only partially rises to the surface—voices cluttered by bombing milestones— skies crashing to the seas & me lost somewhere in between all of it. I don't feel fully alive—that's the truth. I think I did when I was younger, but now and then I really didn't live with me. (September 18)

I can feel escape in my mind—in my heart to go within—or go way outside—but I want to experience with my body—feel the earth—be the child of the earth. (September 18)

Furthermore, during sexual encounters with her boyfriend, Mark, and at various times when she felt personally hurt, Katie reported having flashbacks to early sexual abuse.

I also had flashbacks, and Mark held me. I was shaking so badly, but I didn't want help because we broke up that night. . . . I feel so vulnerable emotionally to him. Well, it just has to stop. (June 22, year 1)

I awoke to police sirens. It's so confusing. I'm petrified. Reminds me of my Dad. When neighbors would call police on him, when he was beating my Mom. I was so scared all the time. Every time I thought would be the last I'd see my mother. I figured one of these times he would actually kill her, or vice versa. The first always seemed more likely. Oh, I hate this terror. I hate this fear. I'm so afraid someone is going to come down here and hurt me. Not the police but my biological father. Oh, all the nights being afraid. (June 26, year 1)

Disordered Thought Processes

At times in the diary, Katie's writing took on a psychotic quality. This writing style, combined with her sister's speculation that she hallucinated at times, indicates the possibility that Katie manifested psychotic symptoms. It is difficult to determine, from her use of language, the degree of rationality and logic in her thinking. Are certain of her entries merely representative of an artistic, free-associative style of writing in one's personal diary? Are they indicative of a psychotic, severely disordered thought process? We will never be able to make this distinction conclusively.

When I look at my reflection—I say—death becomes her—death embraces her eternally—bloody sheet float around my body trembling—death is my angel. She wears my blood stained sheets—Ha! Ha!

ARGH! (September 2)

☐ Suicide

Katie's life was characterized by a series of ambivalent relationships with significant people in her life. Initially, she would idealize a particular person and then begin to feel let down or betrayed by him or her. She would strive for and demand perfection from herself and others. When they, or she, ultimately failed to live up to those standards, she would turn on them and on herself. Her basic lack of trust prevented her from sharing her deepest feelings and thoughts with anyone other than her diary. She isolated herself from other people in terms of her most personal thoughts and feelings: "I have such a problem with loss. Fear of losing someone. Fear of loving someone. Fear of trusting someone" (October 17).

Katie's suicide occurred nine days after her last diary entry. At this point in her journal, she became grandiose in writing about her desires, longing, and goals. She envisioned a transformation in her character to that of a "perfect being" and imagined her relationship reaching unrealistic highs. At the same time, she feared losing everything and felt as though she were "being severed in hundreds of little pieces for her own and others' actions." She longed for "a good number of encouraging friends who would help show the way. A group of wonderful people, open, that have good social status, nice people, and giving."

In the same last entry, she recorded what she perceived as a personal insult from an acquaintance regarding her weight and went on to describe her emotional reaction:

They hurt so much. I want to be proud of my body, not shameful about it. All the things my sister, Jena, Beth, etc., have said come back up from where I locked them down. I hate when I feel shut out from life. It's such a dreadful feeling . . . isolation, alienation. It's sickness, mind-altering and life-altering at times also. (June 20, year 2)

What triggered Katie to take action on her suicidal thoughts and feelings? Was there yet another instance (during her final nine days of life) where she felt disappointed, hurt, or betrayed by Mark? Did Mark show some human weakness or express his own ambivalence about their relationship at a certain point? Did Katie fear the loss of a "fantasy bond" or the illusion of connection with another person (Firestone, 1984, 1985; Firestone & Catlett, 1999)? Feelings of overwhelming dread, despair, and pain can accompany the threat of such a loss, and those feelings can feel life-threatening. Most importantly, what self-destructive thoughts or feelings were unleashed by events that occurred? Throughout her diary there is evidence that when negative events occurred between her and Mark, she turned on herself viciously and experienced extremely destructive critical inner voices telling her that she "did not deserve to live," that she "should just die, kill herself."

I feel so on edge lately. I want to go and dance all night. Somewhere alone where no one can touch me anymore. I owe so much money now. What am I going to do? I really want all this madness to disappear. I'm sick of people using me. I hate people for that. There is no one to trust . . . not even myself. I can't take this anymore. (September 6)

I feel so abandoned and unconnected with everyone, everyone. I feel like I'm going to die. . . . I did try reaching out again for the last time. People are so mean and selfish. I want to kill myself on my birthday. I have to. (June 14, year 1)

Did Katie feel that she had failed again by engaging in behavior that she did not approve of? We can only assume that some interaction or event (while not the actual cause of her suicide) escalated a powerful self-destructive process that had been active inside Katie, at least throughout the last year of her life. This process is evident in the self-revelations in her diary. It was a process in which suicide became the only choice, a definitive action she could take that would solve all her problems, allow her to escape the pain of being herself and living her life, and the choice that Katie felt she deserved. At this juncture, her perceptions were seriously distorted through the lens of her self-critical thoughts and her inner demon that demanded perfection and chastised her when she failed to achieve it.

I've got to make it end tonight!! I HATE MYSELF SO MUCH. I'VE TRIED to learn how to love myself . . . but I can't because people

*always want more than me. God, I wish I could torture myself—
not subtly but viciously. I feel so sick. I CAN'T TAKE ANY
MORE!! Please God Help Me! (September 6)*

The voice process, as evidenced in her writing, gained more and more
control over Katie's behavior until she ultimately killed herself.

*I feel like such a savage lately with all the rage I feel—feel
almost like an animal—when it comes to human closeness and
freedom. I am savaging everything around. (September 18)*

*I so very much want to become what people—what I—worship. I
feel so damn depressed—tears fall from my eyes. They feel so
damn endless. My void seems endless. I want so much for true
love to be my hero. If screams could carry me to the heavens
and heal me right now—. Our hearts feel so separate. I will diet
until I die. I'm sick of people not loving me. (October 2)*

☐ Theoretical Approach

Separation theory (Firestone, 1997a) posits that the basic defense is a
"fantasy bond," an illusion of being connected to another person (Firestone,
1987).

*Where does freedom go? I feel so bound up inside and trapped
in the feelings of my childhood, trapped, not able to move. Lying
motionless on the floor because it's told it's safe. Is it really
safe? Every morning I want to feel my freedom. Argh! Oh, still
frustrated, oh so frustrated. Nothing is resolved! (June 14,
year 1)*

Katie's upbringing in the hands of a mother with a psychotic disorder
and a brutal alcoholic father probably resulted in her becoming dependent on fantasy as a survival mechanism.

> For the infant, this fantasized connection alleviates pain and anxiety by
> providing partial gratification of its emotional or physical hunger. In other
> words, the fantasy bond is a substitute for the love and care that may be
> missing in the infant's environment. (Firestone, 1985, p. 37)

Katie's addiction to food was how she supported this fantasy process.
Food was how she comforted and numbed herself.

Children support this illusion of being self-sufficient with behaviors that relieve tension, a thumb-sucking, rubbing a blanket, and, later on, behaviors that help them numb painful feelings. (Firestone et al., 2002, p. 13)

Katie's Original Fantasy Bond

Katie's journaling indicated that she had a strong fantasy bond with her mother that she may have originally developed in response to her mother's limitations. The mother's mental illness prevented her from providing an adequate environment for her children. She failed to provide sustaining nurturance and direction, that is, the "love-food"[1] necessary for Katie's optimal development. Many entries alluded to physical and sexual abuse which her mother was unable to protect her from. In fact, Katie's mother may have been one of her abusers.

Other journal entries depicted an idealized mother for whom Katie desperately longed. As a young adult, she still wanted to be taken care of by her real mother as well as by a series of mother substitutes. In her mind, Katie maintained a strong connection with her mother. It appears that she found it extremely difficult to face her mother's limitations or to adjust to the reality that she (Katie) would never get the love and care she wanted in her adult relationships.

Is it so wrong to want to have a family? It's always been such a big dream for me. But my old family life seems to come up now, being alone, abandoned, rejected, and neglected. . . . I guess as long as I feel this and have felt this, everyone I know has rejected this and me along with it. So I guess I will still continue to punish myself sometimes for such cravings, and everything will come full circle. I'm scared, but I have to tell myself I'll be all right because I've always been by myself and I need to hold myself and carry myself a little while. (June 18, year 2)

The Fantasy Bond as Manifested in Katie's Romantic Relationship

I miss my Mom. I really wish she was better. Oh, how I wish she was my Mom. I need her to love me—so deeply. I don't feel anyone will ever love me so deeply. The only person who has given me this kind of depth is Mark, and I love him so much for this. I feel like I was dying inside—my heart drowned out of my breath—and he has been restoring it bit by bit, breath by breath. (June 17, year 1)

The extension of the fantasy bond into Katie's romantic relationship is quite clear in her writing. In her relationship with Mark, she alternately built him up as her savior—a perfect man—and then when he let her down, as he ultimately did, she tore him down. At these times, she was determined to reject him and to rely only on herself. However, as soon as he showed a renewed interest in her, she threw herself full force back into her fantasy of Mark as the ultimate rescuer. Indeed, a great deal of Katie's writing focused on Mark and described both her desire to be close to him and to please him, as well as her resentment and anger at him for hurting her and betraying her trust.

When it comes to relationships I'm a lot more walled up— removed—restrained. I really have hated men & women relationships since I was a child. I know mostly all of it came from my Mom & dad. It makes me want to scream. I can't pretend that these brain washings don't affect me. But my view is cluttered all the same—especially if one tried to touch my heart, mind, & body. My hatred deepens with all of me. I plot against them for when we argue. (September 27)

Katie's desire for a perfect relationship was demonstrated in her last journal entry, as she described how she prayed to either meet someone who would love her deeply or achieve a perfect love with Mark, and to become a perfect being herself.

However, Katie alternated between a strong desire to achieve a perfect union with Mark by being open and vulnerable to him and a desire to be independent and totally self-reliant. In the latter state, she fought against her desire to become dependent, hated herself for "needing him," and attacked herself for becoming vulnerable to Mark or anyone else.

I don't know what's wrong with me. I've been so damn callous since I've started to date Mark. I know I felt that he was only toying with me very strongly from the very beginning. I resented him for these feelings. I see him now as more true and loyal. . . . I know what to do with such blocks to closeness— stable closeness—peaceful relationships. I was looking at these girls in the gym, these cute healthy girls. I wished so much to have their pure heart inside of me—their free minds & hearts—to love a man without restraints.

Where the hell is my freedom? I feel anorexia at my door, more strongly today than ever. I feel this cold isolation feeling, abandoned, alone, with nowhere to go, no one to go to. It's all a facade with Mark. That's all it is. I thought it was more than that maybe I just made it up in my mind. (September 27)

During Katie's frequent arguments with Mark, she sometimes hit or bit him:

I can't believe I hit another human being. Want to die because of this—it kills me inside—what the hell is wrong with me? All so painful. I'm going to punish myself severely for my lack of morals and inability to control my feelings and life. I'm going to purge myself of all of this. I will shed the excess baggage of mortality and lean upon a higher existence—not the one with and out of hell. (September 28)

   Sex was a complicated issue for Katie. She wanted to be sexual to please Mark, to make him feel more tied or connected to her. Yet she often had negative reactions after a sexual experience. She wrote of never wanting to "do it again," insisted that she was not ready for sex, and revealed that being sexual stirred up too many feelings from the past.

Mark and I made love just this morning. It was nice. I just started to get panicky for a while. I didn't want to have sex with him this weekend because I was feeling a lot from my past with my body. But I love him very much, and I wanted to be physically close to him. I wish I didn't get this panicky. I still get half grossed out about sex. I get scared. I wish my Mom never said and did certain things to me. (June 17, year 1)

I couldn't bear to be with someone I loved so much. It brought up all the old pain of ever loving anyone. I got so horribly messed up with sex. (November 28)

Toward the end of her life, Katie reported feeling that she had taken on Mark's pain and depression and was bearing his negative feelings as well as her own.

I feel so alone &., when the bridge of intimacy is being crossed, I feel baffled, tormented, abused, unsure of the safety, and I once again throw myself to the wolves for love. (October 2)

Katie's relationship with Mark, as she described it in her diary, fits with the conceptualization of a fantasy bond described above. She often perceived herself and Mark more in terms of the past than the present. She used Mark to reinforce negative images of herself that she probably originally formed in her family.

The Voice

The voice refers to a generalized hostile attitude toward self and as such is the language of an overall self-destructive process. It is an overlay on the personality that is not natural, but learned or imposed from without. In general, under traumatic conditions, children tend to depersonalize in an attempt to escape from painful emotions. At the same time, they internalize or incorporate the hostile attitudes and feelings that are directed toward them. These negative parental introjects or voices determine a basic split between the enemy within and the real self. All people, not only depressed, addicted or suicidal clients, have internalized negative parental attitudes during childhood that are part of a self-destructive process. The voices in suicidal clients differ only in degree, not in kind, from those experienced by "normal" individuals. (Firestone, 1986)

In Katie's case, the terror aroused by her abusive, often intoxicated father's violent outbursts, both toward her mother and toward Katie and her sister, would have created the conditions for incorporating the self-destructive voices Katie evidenced in her writing. Her mother's mental illness, with its psychotic episodes that resulted in abuse and neglect of Katie, also provided incidents where Katie felt terrified, and she evidently took on her mother's aggression toward her at those times of stress.

In Katie's case, her diary provided many examples of the form these critical inner voices took. At the most extreme, her critical inner voice was extremely self-punitive and, at the end, suicidal.

☐ Assessment and Treatment[2]

This tragedy might have been averted if Katie had sought treatment, if she had been convinced by friends, acquaintances, or family members to obtain professional help.[3] What steps could have been taken by Katie's treating clinician within the context of crisis intervention and long-term treatment that might have led to a different outcome? Necessary steps (Firestone, 1997b) consist of (a) establishing rapport in the clinical interview; (b) assessing risk factors and performing a mental status examination; (c) inquiring directly about suicidal thoughts and behaviors; (d) documenting medication, hospitalization, and treatment plans; (e) arranging medical consultation and consultation with colleagues; (f) gathering collateral information from family and significant others; (g) determining the necessity for hospitalization; (h) writing a no-suicide contract; (i) providing knowledge of community resources; and (j) considering the effect of attempted or completed suicide on self and others.

Establishing Rapport

Any treating professional would have faced a major challenge in building trust with Katie. Her difficulty in trusting people undoubtedly contributed to her failure to seek the treatment she needed. To build trust and establish an effective therapeutic alliance with Katie, her therapist would have needed to become a stable, caring force in her life and been willing to understand her rages and feelings of hopelessness as well as her lies and the special meaning they held for her. To be effective, her therapist would have needed to possess a tolerance for Katie's expression of strong emotions and would have needed an ability to convey concern, warmth, and compassion through his or her responses.

Assessing Strengths and Weaknesses

Katie's diary demonstrated that she possessed a number of strengths. It would have been important for her therapist to understand her resilience, strong points, and resources. In her writing, Katie displayed a keen intellect and psychological mindedness or sophistication, and an ability to make connections between her past and her current behavior. These are all traits that would have made Katie an excellent psychotherapy client. It would have been vital for the therapist to have worked with her creativity and intelligence in order to strengthen Katie's sense of self.[4]

Assessing Risk Factors

Although Katie had no known history of suicide attempts, either reported in her journal or by her sister, she nonetheless wrote about a great deal of suicidal ideation. She also displayed signs of despair and feelings of being fragmented. Sometimes suicide appeared as a relief to her, a last resort, a way out of her pain and torment. At other times she felt that the world was not a place in which she could live. These thoughts were often accompanied by intense rage toward herself or other people. Her suicidal ideation also focused on the self-punishment that she felt she deserved.

Her perfectionism fit a profile that research studies have linked to suicidality. As she approached the end of her life, Katie was increasingly immersed in fantasy about her goals in life—a perfect relationship, ideal thinness, good grades, and positive changes in her own character. Yet in her last entry she also felt as though she were being severed into a million pieces.

Katie's family history of major mental illness is a risk factor, although we have no knowledge of family history of suicide attempts. Early in the course of major depressive episodes (which Katie was experiencing), the risk of suicide is especially high. From her diary entries, Katie appeared to have begun using alcohol to excess more often. Increased use of alcohol is a risk factor for suicide, and a history of sexual abuse in and of itself has been linked to suicide in women.

Katie also lacked a consistent support system. Her relationships were fragile—at least she perceived them as being fragile, as reported in her diary. She had alienated many of her friends and acquaintances and ended numerous friendships by lashing out at people. She was distant from her sister, her relationship with Mark was strained by her consistent acting-out, and she had no sustaining resources or support network. As mentioned before, she would rage at Mark and on several occasions physically attacked him. Following each incident, she berated herself with self-recriminations, feeling like a savage with no morals.

Toward the end of her life she described episodes of self-mutilation in several diary entries, another behavior that has been linked to suicide. In one such episode, she apparently cut her breast and her wrist, and she alluded to having done much worse harm to herself in the past. Two of these episodes occurred in Mark's presence, and evidently the effect was to make him pull away from her.

Katie also described feelings of being a burden to other people. This is a common theme with suicidal individuals, many of whom believe that their family and friends would be better off without them. Katie's personality style and trauma history also added to her risk, especially since these appear to have resulted in a borderline personality disorder and dissociative states. Recently, some suicidologists have come to believe that, although suicidal individuals are in great distress and desperation leading up to the attempt, they are in a dissociated state at the actual moment when carrying out the act (Maltsberger, 1999, 2002; Orbach, 2002). In this state, as conceptualized by separation theory, Katie would have been at one with her critical inner voice and dissociated from her real self. She would have been acting as the punishing parent toward the helpless child, essentially acting out the extreme end of her critical inner voice's murderous rage toward herself. Katie repeatedly reported experiencing dissociative states.

Lastly, Katie's unregulated aggression often emerged impulsively toward herself and toward the people closest to her. Many journal pages contained long passages in which she vented her rage toward acquaintances, friends, and especially toward Mark and her parents. The frequency of her outbursts of rage seemed to be on the increase toward the end of the diary. She also reported hating herself and castigated herself severely following these outbursts. Katie often expressed the need "to fix herself" (common in suicidal people), as though there was something inherently bad about her. She had strong feelings that she was "damaged goods" as a result of her childhood experiences.

Gathering Collateral Information

In Katie's case, it would have been difficult to access resources for collateral information.

Determining Objective Measures

Given the seriousness of Katie's risk factors, objective measures of suicide potential would have added valuable information, such as the Beck Depression Inventory (Beck, 1978a), the Beck Hopelessness Scale (Beck, 1978b), the Beck Suicide Inventory (Beck, 1991), and the Firestone Assessment of Self-Destructive Thoughts (FAST). The FAST in particular would have provided direct access to the voices driving the suicidal process. Research has demonstrated that people tend to be more open and honest on a paper-and-pencil test than in a personal interview. Because of her trust issues, Katie may have avoided sharing her suicidal thoughts and feelings directly with her therapist. In asking her to complete the FAST, her therapist would have been able to observe her reactions to the items, looking for comments or body language during the testing that would have reflected her state of mind.

Developing a Treatment Plan

Any initial treatment would have required serious consideration of hospitalization for Katie in order to protect her from harming herself. A mental status exam would have helped clarify the quality of her thought process in order to rule out psychotic features. Psychiatric evaluation to ascertain the best possible medication or combination of medications for Katie would have been indicated. Her depression, anxiety, and disturbed thought processes might have improved considerably if she had been stabilized on appropriate medication.

The primary treating clinician could have helped monitor Katie's medical compliance with her psychiatric medications. It would have also been important for the clinician to take note of Katie's reactions to medications and facilitate her communication with her psychiatrist, perhaps providing helpful feedback to her psychiatrist in order to achieve the optimal benefits of medication.

When treating Katie, the intensity of treatment would have been an important issue. At the beginning, several sessions a week might have been necessary. In addition, a valuable adjunct to treatment would have been some type of skills-building class to help her acquire the affect regulation and affect tolerance skills she lacked. Marsha Linehan's Dialectic Behavioral Therapy (DBT) approach would have been helpful (Linehan, Armstrong, Suarez, Allmon, & Heard, 1991; Rudd, Joiner, & Rajab, 2001). Katie might have benefited from attending a class with others who were experiencing problems similar to hers. There she might have learned skills to help regulate and tolerate disturbing affective states.

Initially, it would have been important for her treating clinician to have been available for telephone contact on a 24-hour basis. Community resources such as local or national hotline numbers could have been used as backup if she was unable to reach her therapist immediately. These resources would have provided her with a person she could talk to who would be trained, understanding, and caring. Phone calls from the therapist between sessions might have been a necessary adjunct to treatment. The initial treatment focus would have been to reduce her lethality. A variety of methods could have been employed to accomplish this objective. Voice therapy is one such approach.

Voice Therapy Methods as Applied to Katie's Treatment

In order to determine whether to utilize voice therapy, Katie's therapist would have needed to assess her ego strength. In various sections of the diary, it appeared that she possessed a great deal of ego strength. However, an underlying fragility also manifested itself.

Voice therapy methods could have helped Katie gain insight into how her negative thoughts were impacting her life and affecting her behavior, including the injunctions she was experiencing about committing suicide. The deep emotional release would have permitted Katie to give vent to the many pent-up feelings she was experiencing and would have offered her an environment where expressing those deep emotions was acceptable. Had she become aware that she was experiencing life through the filter of her critical inner voice, she might have developed a different perspective and gained a measure of compassion for herself. Normalizing Katie's feelings would have been important. She could have realized that her strong emotions were neither abnormal nor evidence that she was "damaged goods."

One of the most important issues for Katie would have been to establish hope that her life could be different, that she could feel differently toward herself and others, that she did not need to continue tormenting herself, and that she could come to understand her emotions and behaviors and make better choices. In an effective therapy, Katie could have collaborated with the therapist to change behaviors that were directed by her voice and develop the capacity to act more in her own self-interest. Initially, her progress would have caused her anxiety, and her voices would have temporarily become more intense, more insistent, or louder in her mind. If she had stuck it out, that is, endured the increased anxiety and tolerated the intensified voice attacks, she gradually would have become comfortable with the new behavior and could have expanded her boundaries.

Katie's journal provided evidence that she was progressively more tormented and governed by self-destructive thoughts. These thoughts were driving her toward punishing herself, hurting herself, and eventually killing herself. A therapist who showed an understanding of the "voice" (negative thought patterns) she described in her journal would have had tremendous leverage in establishing the rapport necessary to sustain the treatment, and could possibly have saved her life.

Following a thorough assessment of Katie, the therapist could have introduced the concept of the voice and explained how negative thoughts might be contributing to the psychological pain she was experiencing and to her self-destructive behaviors. Katie's ability to express her thoughts and feelings in her diary is an indication that journaling would have been an important and effective tool for her. In addition, the process of administering and scoring the FAST would have facilitated treatment by providing the therapist with information regarding the content of the voices Katie had endorsed on the scale. Subsequently, these specific self-attacks could have been addressed in therapy sessions.

As Katie began to talk about herself in the session, the therapist could have been sensitive to indications of voice attacks. In other words, as Katie talked about what was on her mind, the therapist could have listened for self-critical statements or attitudes and asked Katie to elaborate on them.

The therapist also might have introduced the first step of voice therapy by asking about a situation or interaction that had occurred during the past week that Katie had experienced as painful or that she felt had intensified her suicidal thoughts. Next, the therapist could have asked her what she was telling herself during or after the specific interaction. The therapist would then have asked Katie if she could say these thoughts as a "voice," as though someone else were saying them to her, in the second person. For example, if Katie revealed, as she did in the diary, that she had had a fight with Mark and afterward was thinking "I'm no good, of course he doesn't love me. Look at how I behaved, I deserved to be punished," the therapist might have suggested expressing the voice in the second person: "You're no good, of course he doesn't love you. Look at how you behaved, you deserve to be punished, you deserve to suffer!"

Next, the therapist would have encouraged Katie to say these statements with whatever feelings were behind the thoughts. Often clients express considerable rage when they verbalize their self-critical thoughts in this form. The therapist might have encouraged her to say her self-attacks louder if Katie appeared to be holding back the full expression of her thoughts or feelings. When people express their voices in this abreactive format, material often emerges that they were not fully aware of prior to the session. For example, Katie might have started with thoughts she was aware of on the surface, but would have probably continued by expressing voices she was not fully conscious of prior to the session.

In Katie's case, one of her core beliefs appeared to be that she was "bad" or damaged in some way that she could not fix. Katie held a deep-seated conviction that she could not escape her past.

The next step of voice therapy consists of the client developing insight regarding the sources of these destructive thoughts. Often, when people have expressed their voices in the abreactive method, they spontaneously have insights. Many make statements such as "That's exactly what my mother said to me," "That's the way my father treated me," or "That was the atmosphere in our house." Again, the therapist waits. If the client does not spontaneously come up with his or her own insights, the therapist may inquire: "Where do you think these thoughts came from? How did you get to feel this way about yourself?"

The value of developing insight is not to establish blame, but rather to help the person develop compassion for himself or herself, to understand on a deep level that he or she did not develop problems, limitations, or disturbing behavior patterns for no reason; in other words, he or she was not born bad. In Katie's case, excerpts from her diary demonstrate that she was aware of her parents in her head and had some insight regarding the source of her bad feelings toward herself. Developing compassion for herself, and others, as hurt human beings would have interrupted her negative way of seeing herself and others and counteracted her feeling that she deserved punishment and torture.

☐ Voice Therapy Session

The following hypothetical voice therapy session was compiled from actual voice statements gathered from subjects and patients who had a diagnostic picture similar to Katie's. It is also composed of actual material from her diary illustrating the types of voices (attitudes and beliefs) that might have been elicited and identified if Katie had participated in voice therapy sessions.

Therapist: How are you doing today?

Katie: Okay. I've really struggled with the eating this week. I binged a couple of times and I feel out of control again. On Thursday I overheard these girls at school talking about me and it made me feel really, really bad. They looked at me and, as they walked by one of them said: "She sure could use a walk." They think I'm a cow. The way they looked at me I can tell they think I'm disgusting. It made me feel so low. I am determined to lose at least 30 pounds before my birthday in two months. I was starting a new diet that day but, when I heard that, I felt so bad that I went and ate. That's what always happens—I feel bad, then I eat, then I diet and eat. It makes me crazy.

Therapist: What were you were thinking about when you overheard those girls make the comment about you?

Katie: That they were right. I am a fat cow, and I should be walking and working out all the time. I shouldn't be this fat. I am disgusting and shouldn't even be out in public till I can get rid of this huge stomach. Also, that I'm a loser who can't even stick to a stupid diet. It's supposed to be so easy—stop eating, lose weight. So why can't I stop eating? Because I'm a pig and a weak person and I don't deserve anything good.

Therapist: It sounds like you have a lot of negative thoughts about yourself. Try saying that again. "I'm a pig and a weak person and I don't deserve anything good"—only this time, say it as if another person was saying it to you about you.

Katie: Okay. "They were right. You are a cow. A fat disgusting cow. You shouldn't even be out and about the way you look. Go work it off before you show your face and your fat stomach in public again. All your rolls and rolls of fat. You should be ashamed of yourself. How can you even get out of bed?"

Therapist: Really let go. You might as well say it all, get all the feelings out.

Katie: (*Louder voice*) "What is wrong with you? You can't even stick to a diet for one week. You should starve yourself! Eat nothing, you don't deserve anything. You're a loser! Not worth ANYTHING! (*screaming*) No one is ever going to care about you." (*cries deeply, for a long time*)

Therapist: (*after waiting for the full experience of her emotions*) Where do you think that way of thinking about yourself came from?

Katie: It was strange to hear myself say some of those things. (*Sad*) I can remember my mom saying things like that to me sometimes—that I wasn't worth anything, that no one would ever love me. Sometimes, like when I'm writing about her, I can almost feel her hating me. I feel like she used me, like she needed me there to yell at, so she could make sense of her own horrible life by blaming me for it. Like dad hit her and us, and everything, and she needed some way to explain it, so she blamed me. If I was horrible and deserved to be hit and hated, then it wasn't so bad. Sometimes it feels like the way she was toward me was like a rape of me—of my mind and heart and soul. And now it's like she used me up. So did he. That was what I was there for. Either they hated me or they ignored me. I don't know which was worse.

Therapist: How are these thoughts affecting your life now?

Katie: I think they make me hate myself all the time. They make me feel like I'm never good enough. I think it makes it very hard for me to trust anyone. It makes it hard for me to be close to Mark.

Therapist: How so?

Katie: It's like I have to be perfect, like I have to be thin and perfect and sweet and wonderful. And I plan to be just that, that I will make it all perfect if I get thin. If I'm sweet and have sex with him. But then it doesn't work. I fuck it up and say the wrong thing, or get mad and yell at him, or ask him to just leave me alone, to stop touching me. And I ruin everything. It's like I become this savage beast, and I end up hating him. Sometimes even hitting or biting him. It's like I treated myself and have treated myself for so long. Then I torment myself for what I have just done. With all these outbursts and the confusion, I am just pushing him away all the time. And all I want is for us to be close. The other day we had a terrible fight, and I started screaming and ranting and raving. I was torn up with feelings, and I ended up hating him.

Therapist: If you were to put into words the anger behind your outburst, what would you say? Try to say it as if someone else is talking to you, like you did before about your weight and the eating.

Katie: It would say, "Look at what he's doing to you. He is making a fool of you. He's never really loved you. No one will ever love you. Never. Never. You don't deserve to be loved. You're only good for one thing. You are here for me. Don't think you're worth anything! Don't think you have anything good. He will never love you. All he wants from you is sex. That's all you can give him. And you'd better give it to him or he'll leave you and then you'll have nothing. And you deserve it. You hurt him so badly. You hurt everybody you get close to. You're poison! You deserve torture and punishment. You don't—deserve to live. Just kill yourself. Smash yourself! Get yourself off of the earth!" (*Sad, crying*)

Therapist: (*after a pause for the emotions to be spent*) Saying this made you feel really sad.

Katie: It's like there's this other person living inside my head. Sometimes it feels like Mom, Sometimes though it's like my Dad. Maybe it's both of them, ganged up, trying to kill me. It's like Dad hit me, and I swallowed his rage. I ate it up, and now I hit myself, but even worse, then I hit someone else. I feel like I can't control the anger sometimes, and I attack him. It scares me so much. I scare myself. (*Crying*)

Therapist: It seems like you are treating yourself as you were treated.

Katie: Yes, I am. You know, this makes me realize that it's not really me who wants to kill me, it's them. I don't have to act on these thoughts and feelings. I'm beginning to get the sense that I don't have to torture myself like this.

☐ Discussion

We have found that clients often report an immediate reduction in depressed feelings after identifying the contents of the voice and releasing the affect associated with the thoughts. In voice therapy, they come to their own conclusions, identify their destructive voices, and develop insight about their sources. The therapist merely supports the client's interpretations of his or her own material.

Depressed individuals in particular have commented that they felt uniquely understood by therapists working with voice therapy methods.

They begin to make a separation between their real motives and desires and thoughts that are opposed to their ongoing wants, or even their survival. In Katie's case, it would have been crucial for her to make this kind of separation, that is, to be able to distinguish between her destructive voices and a more compassionate and realistic point of view about herself, to see herself as not perfect but having both the strengths and the limitations she actually possessed. Understanding that she was divided within would have helped her take back many of the projections she had made on to Mark, which could have led to considerably less conflict in their relationship.

At the end of each session, the therapist would have helped Katie plan actions to counter the dictates of her voice (for example, taking steps to begin a realistic diet plan, perhaps consulting a nutritionist). Katie's tendency to think of behavior changes in grandiose terms, losing thirty pounds, etcetera, could have been countered with suggestions to keep the behavioral change to more achievable, realistic goals—small steps—because anxiety would be stirred up with each action taken to break with her voice's prescriptions. Katie could have been educated about the fact that anxiety would be a natural result of breaking with this familiar habit pattern. The initial steps taken toward constructive behavioral change invariably increase the intensity of the "loudness" of critical inner voices. Actions that are instituted against the voices temporarily bring out their full fury, almost as though a parent were yelling at the person, trying to get them back in line. However, if Katie had learned to recognize this anxiety as a sign of positive change, and if she had been able to stay with the behavior change, she would have understood that eventually the voices would fade in intensity, almost like a parent who gets tired of nagging. At this point the voices would no longer be controlling her behavior.

Most important, as described earlier, Katie's therapist would have helped her resist urges to hurt herself by encouraging her to go against the voices that are telling her that she deserved punishment and that she should be dead. Instead of trying to be perfect for Mark, she would have gradually attempted to be more herself, more authentic, in interactions with him. Hopefully, she would have learned to tell him (and others) directly when she was angry rather than allowing her feelings to build up and then explode. This behavioral change probably would have eventually led to significant improvement in her relationships, which, in turn, would have allowed Katie to fulfill more of her real needs and desires.

This hypothetical session illustrates how voice therapy methods quickly uncover the core issues in an individual's life. This partially unconscious material would have been more difficult to elicit with traditional methods, and treatment might have taken considerably more time. A clinician's interpretation would not have had the impact on Katie that voice therapy techniques might have had, that of enabling her to identify and understand for herself the sources of her suicidal impulses, psychological pain, and depressed mood. Traditional techniques would not have provided her therapist with any indication of the power of the destructive voices that were holding sway over her life. In the case of suicide, these voices often lead to a trance-like state of mind, a kind of dissociated state, in which they become the only stimuli that the individual is attending to in his or her downward spiral toward self-destruction (Firestone, 1986; Heckler, 1994). If suicidal clients are allowed to express such negative thoughts in a session, they are better able to perceive these cognitive distortions as coming originally from an external source and may begin to question and challenge their validity.

It is clear from her journals that Katie believed this internal voice was her own point of view and that she had achieved no separation from it. During the session, by giving vent to voices that revealed the key issues, she would have been able to become aware of the death wishes, whether conscious or unconscious, that her mother or father must have felt toward her during her childhood, death wishes she could now separate from her real feelings for herself. If Katie had gained an understanding of the division within herself and its sources, it might have facilitated her struggle to separate from this destructive overlay on her personality. She might then have been better able to focus on identifying her real interests, priorities, and wants and develop a stronger sense of her own identity.

☐ Further Considerations

Voice therapy techniques allow for behavioral changes that often go beyond what is possible in many other therapeutic formats. As a part of her therapy, Katie would have been involved in breaking with powerful defenses that had drained her energy (e.g., her inward, isolated lifestyle, her reliance on Mark for a sense of worth, her addiction to bingeing and dieting). It would have been vital for the therapeutic approach to offer her maximum support and for the therapist to be a stable, caring force that provided her with a "transitional object" while she was relinquishing her self-nurturing, self-parenting, internal fantasy bond and expanding her personal boundaries.

An overall goal in psychotherapy (as it would have been in Katie's treatment) is to help clients come to terms with the painful feelings and frustrations that cause them to retreat to inward, self-nurturing patterns and self-destructive behaviors. The crux of the therapeutic task becomes one of supporting the growth of the client's self system, which involves helping them become aware of their ongoing desires and priorities and to use the therapeutic situation to ask directly for what they want. The limits to personal gratification in the therapeutic relationship lead to frustration of the client's wants, which in turn arouses anger. Clients gradually learn how to handle their angry responses and come to realize, on a deep emotional level, that they can survive without having the therapist gratify their needs. The issue of dealing with anger is obviously central in the treatment of addicted, depressed, or suicidal clients because of their strong tendencies to turn their aggression against themselves.

If Katie had been involved in such a therapeutic endeavor at the time she was writing her last journal entry, we may speculate that she might have been able to take advantage of the opportunity to break free of her inner demon and become a strong person who could experience and deal with her feelings appropriately. Hypothetically, with this type of intervention, Katie could have developed her capacity for pursuing satisfaction and fulfillment in the real world.

☐ Notes

1. Love-food refers to a psychonutritional product whereby the parent has both the intent and the capacity to gratify the needs of the growing child and help him or her adjust to the socialization process necessary to flourish in a particular culture (R. Firestone & Catlett, 1999, p. 101).

2. The reports of various hospitalizations indicate that Katie did in fact receive some form of treatment early in her life. However, it is difficult to ascertain whether this treatment had any impact on her because she failed to mention it in her dairy. In the second book of her diary she wrote about meeting with someone (it is unclear whether or not this woman was a mental health professional), possibly in an attempt to obtain some type of help with her problems. During the meeting she lied to the woman about her family history and said that her mother had committed suicide. In fact, her mother was still living. During this period, she evidently informed several other people of her mother's death. She described in diary entries how she wanted the false account of her mother's fate to be a curse that would eventually come true. The woman with whom Katie met assured her that she would try to help her obtain funding for therapy and Prozac. Katie may have been able to acquire the medication, because in a subsequent entry she reported being "wasted" one night on Prozac and alcohol. Besides these few entries she made no further reference to any treatment, nor did she again refer to taking medication.

3. Hypothetically, if Katie had read the book *Conquer Your Critical Inner Voice* (R. Firestone et al., 2002), she might have gained considerable insight into her voice process. Had she followed the book's suggestion to seek counseling (for readers experiencing her level of depression and self-hate), she might have received the help she needed. The self-report questionnaires and exercises in the book might have alerted her to her level of risk and might have prompted her to seek treatment.

4. Katie's ability to write about her thoughts and feelings as evidenced in her journal indicate that the exercises in *Conquer Your Critical Inner Voice* would have provided an excellent tool to enhance the therapy process.

☐ References

Beck, A. (1978a). *Beck Depression Inventory*. San Antonio, TX: Psychological Corporation.

Beck, A. T. (1978b). *Beck Hopelessness Scale*. San Antonio, TX: Psychological Corporation.

Beck, A. T. (1991). *Beck Suicide Inventory*. San Antonio, TX: Psychological Corporation.

Firestone, R. W. (1984). A concept of the primary fantasy bond: A developmental perspective. *Psychotherapy, 21*, 218–225.

Firestone, R. W. (1985). *The fantasy bond: Structure of psychological defenses*. Santa Barbara, CA: Glendon Association.

Firestone, R. W. (1986). The "inner voice" and suicide. *Psychotherapy, 23*, 439–447.

Firestone, R. W. (1987). Destructive effects of the fantasy bond in couple and family relationships. *Psychotherapy, 24*, 233–239.

Firestone, R. W. (1988). *Voice therapy: A psychotherapeutic approach to self-destructive behavior*. Santa Barbara, CA: Glendon Association.

Firestone, R. W. (1990). Voice therapy. In J. Zeig & W. Munion (Eds.), *What is psychotherapy? Contemporary perspectives* (pp. 68–74). San Francisco: Jossey-Bass.

Firestone, R. W. (1997a). *Combating destructive thought processes: Voice Therapy and separation theory*. Thousand Oaks, CA: Sage.

Firestone, R. W. (1997b). *Suicide and the inner voice: Risk assessment, treatment, and case management*. Thousand Oaks, CA: Sage.

Firestone, R. W., & Catlett, J. (1999). *Fear of intimacy*. Washington, DC: American Psychological Association.

Firestone, R. W., & Firestone, L. (1996). *Firestone Assessment of Self-Destructive Thoughts*. San Antonio: Psychological Corporation.

Firestone, R. W., Firestone, L., & Catlett, J. (2002). *Conquer your critical inner voice*. Oakland, CA: New Harbinger Publications.

Heckler, R. A. (1994). *Waking up, alive*. New York: Ballantine Books.

Linehan, M. M., Armstrong, H. E., Suarez, A., Allmon, D., & Heard, H. L. (1991). Cognitive-behavioral treatment of chronically parasuicidal borderline patients. *Archives of General Psychiatry, 48*, 1060–1064.

Maltsberger, J. T. (1999). The psychodynamic understanding of suicide. In D. G. Jacobs (Ed.), *The Harvard Medical School guide to suicide assessment and intervention* (pp. 72–82). San Francisco: Jossey-Bass.

Maltsberger, J. T. (2002, March). Affective states in suicide. Paper presented at the 2nd AESCHI Conference, "Understanding and Interviewing the Suicidal Patient," Aeschi, Switzerland.

Orbach, I. (2002, March). The role of dissociation and bodily experiences in self-destruction. Paper presented at the 2nd AESCHI Conference, "Understanding and Interviewing the Suicidal Patient," Aeschi, Switzerland.

Rudd, M. D., Joiner, T., & Rajab, M. H. (2001). *Treating suicidal behavior: An effective, time-limited approach*. New York: Guilford.

PART

Conclusions

CHAPTER David Lester

Final Thoughts: Did Writing a Diary Help or Harm Katie?

The brilliant commentaries above have given us a rich understanding of Katie and provided suggestions for how a good psychotherapist might have helped her out of the depths of her despair. Lisa Firestone (chapter 11) illustrates how a psychotherapist might work with a client like Katie using voice therapy. Thomas Ellis (chapter 6) identifies several cognitive styles and distortions in Katie's thinking that a cognitive therapist would focus on in therapy sessions. Antoon Leenaars (chapter 7), Robert Fournier (chapter 9), and James Hollis (chapter 10) also discuss issues that are important from their perspectives on suicidal behavior that a therapist could explore with a client like Katie.

But Katie was not in psychotherapy. She wrote extensively in her diary, and so one question remains: Did writing the diary help Katie or harm her? This is the question I shall address in this final chapter.

☐ Is Writing a Diary Good for the Writer?

In recent years writing a diary has come to be considered an interesting and even a useful activity. It can be rewarding because people get to tell their own stories and "celebrate each moment of being alive" (Simons, 1978, back cover). People may be able to "come to a clearer sense of [themselves] through a gentle and nonthreatening process. It can also be a source of freedom, relaxation, and fun" (Simons, 1978, inside front cover). Along with this orientation, several books have been published advising people on how to keep diaries (e.g., Simons, 1978).

Writing a diary for the purposes of psychological growth was stimulated by Ira Progoff (1975). Progoff wrote a book on the process (*At a Journal Workshop*) and gave seminars on the technique (organized by Dialogue House in New York City). Progoff's "journal" was guided by Jungian theory and was designed to allow our unconscious access to information that would facilitate our finding the right path for our life.

More recently, a new activity (or perhaps it should be called a hobby) has been defined, called *journaling*, with many books published and seminars offered, which has no theoretical bias, but which simply promotes the idea that we should keep a diary. Most recently, Neubauer (2001) has written a *Complete Idiot's Guide to Journaling* that suggests various types of diaries that people might keep. Neubauer suggested that diaries could take the form of: (1) a log, that is, a running record of your life, a task that is made more useful if you state a goal and orient the log around your efforts to reach that goal; (2) a healing journal for which the aim is to heal yourself emotionally, physically, and spiritually and which consists of writing things that you would tell your therapist if you had one; (3) a cathartic journal in which you can get your emotional baggage off our chest; (4) unsent letters, in which you write letters to significant others in your life that you do not send to them (and which can express love, forgiveness, anger, anxiety, or any other emotion); (5) a theme journal that is oriented around a task or situation, such as a wedding or the renovation of your house; (6) a reflective journal in which you write down reflections on yourself; (7) a spiritual journal in which you explore religious and existential issues, such as the purpose of your life; (8) a family journal in which each member of the family contributes entries; (9) a dream journal in which you record your dreams and your reflections on them; and (10) a historical journal for those who start their journal late in life in which you recall your memories and elaborate them in the diary.

Of interest to us are the journal types involving healing, catharsis, and reflection. Neubauer notes that these types of journals can be helpful to us, but what is of interest in the present context are such questions as these: To whom are such journals helpful and to whom might they be harmful? How can such journals be constructed (or guided) so that their effects are helpful rather than harmful?[1]

☐ Does Creative Writing Harm Suicidal People?

I have written on a related question to that guiding this chapter with regard to the poetry of Sylvia Plath and Anne Sexton, two American poets who killed themselves. Did their poetry-writing help them or harm them? Is writing therapeutic for creative writers or it is a stressor that contributes to their psychological disturbance?

Silverman and Will (1986) analyzed the life and suicide of Sylvia Plath and concluded that, although she tried to control her suicidal impulses by means of her poetry, she failed in this endeavor. Silverman and Will argued that poetry is successful when it bridges the inner worlds of the creative person and the audience. (Presumably they mean critically successful, for even poor poetry can serve a useful psychological function for the writer, even if it is merely cathartic.) To be successful, poetry must first achieve a balance between the writer's use of the audience to serve his or her own narcissistic needs (a type of exhibitionism) and the desire to give others a way of structuring the terrors and anxieties that afflict us all (a "homonomous desire" on the part of the writer, to use a term coined by Andras Angyal [1965]).

The writer must also achieve a balance between the potentially destructive conscious and unconscious forces motivating the writing and the constructive desires to harness these forces for the purpose of writing creatively. Related to this, the writer must balance primary and secondary process mechanisms. The writer must also compromise between the fantasy permissible in writing and the acceptance of reality necessary for successful living.

When they applied their ideas to Sylvia Plath, Silverman and Will asserted that the creative process is successful only when the unconscious forces in the writer operate silently and remain hidden from view. This assertion represents a rather traditional view of creative writing. It would seem to express a preference on the part of Silverman and Will for a particular type of literature rather than expressing a universal truth. For example, the unconscious forces motivating Ernest Hemingway may be under control in his writing, but they are certainly not hidden. More pertinently, the confessional style of poetry developed by W. D. Snodgrass and Robert Lowell and pursued by Anne Sexton is in direct opposition to Silverman and Will's view.

Silverman and Will saw the transitional period in Plath's poetry as being her final years in the United States. Plath may have had her confidence undermined by the frequent rejections that writers must endure, and so she changed her style. In her new style, she revealed her deepest feelings in her poems, using her experiences to create the poem rather than to simply transform it. Silverman and Will noted that she described her early poems as "proper in shape and number and every part" but not alive. Her poems moved from being a reordering and reshaping of experience with a poetic purpose toward becoming expressions of herself. She identified with her poems, which made their rejection even more painful, and Silverman and Will labeled this change as a "narcissistic regression."

The causal sequence that Silverman and Will propose for Plath has no evidence for or against it. It is simply one reading of Plath's life. Other, equally plausible, paths can be proposed. For example, it is quite likely that Plath's participation, along with Anne Sexton with whom she became very close, in a poetry workshop run by Robert Lowell had a major impact on her writing style. Several members of his workshop adopted a more self-revealing content for their poems, and two received Pulitzer prizes for their work (Lowell and Sexton).

Furthermore, Plath, as she herself clearly recognized, was prone to recurring depressions. In all probability, Plath had an affective disorder, possibly bipolar, and her depressions were likely to reoccur periodically. It is evident from the severity of her depression in 1953, which led to a very serious suicide attempt, that she would likely become suicidal again with each new depression (in a way similar to Virginia Woolf).

What is interesting is that, whereas in the early 1950s, her writing may not have helped her cope with the stressors, external and intrapsychic, with which she was confronted, in the late 1950s her switch to a more revealing and personalized style of writing may have helped her survive. Silverman and Will claimed that her writing failed to prevent her suicide. Perhaps it may have postponed her suicide?

In the months prior to her suicide, Plath wrote feverishly, sometimes producing several poems in one day. (This feverish activity in the months prior to suicide was apparent also in Anne Sexton's life.) What would Silverman and Will suggest as a more appropriate strategy for a person confronting intrapsychic turmoil who is not under professional care? It is very likely that the writing helped Plath control her inner turmoil, and some commentators think that the poems she produced were among her finest.

In seeking to formulate a *general* hypothesis about the role of writing for the depressed and distressed person, it is obviously important to discuss more than one case. In the present context, the life and suicide of the poet Anne Sexton is relevant.

Lester and Terry (1992) argued that writing poetry can be useful with suicidal clients. Writing poems per se may not be helpful to the client, but the revision of the initial drafts of poems may be therapeutically useful. Revising poems may serve a similar function for clients as the journal assignments devised by cognitive therapists by giving the clients intellectual control over their emotions and distance from the traumatic memories.

Sexton revised her poems extensively and, in the process of revision, had to concentrate on form rather than content. This allows for both the action that therapists deem to be therapeutic and the distancing of the self from one's problems. Because Sexton ultimately chose the moment of her death, one should not discount the therapeutic help her writing afforded her.

Anne Sexton illustrates the dialectic in poetry as therapy, between expression and catharsis on the one hand and cognitive control on the other. Sexton, as long as she was able to stay psychiatrically stable, was able to apply the craft of poetry to her creative productions. Both Sexton and Martin Orne, her first therapist, believed that her poetry had helped her recover. Only toward the end of her life, as her ability to craft her poems declined, did her mental stability dissipate.

Interestingly, both Plath and Sexton showed manic trends prior to their suicides, writing poems furiously, poems with more emotional expression and less poetic crafting. Rather than arguing that writing poetry contributed in part to their suicides, it makes much more sense to say that, in their final breakdowns, poetry was no longer able to help them deal with the intrapsychic forces driving them as it had in the past. As their inner turmoil increased, both wrote feverishly, almost as if the writing were a safety valve letting out the steam under pressure in a boiler, but to no avail, since the pressure was building up faster than they could release it.

But this final failure of the craft of poetry to keep Sylvia Plath and Anne Sexton alive does not, as Silverman and Will argue, signify total failure. Both were outstanding poets and functioned quite well given their probable affective disorders. I would argue that the craft of poetry kept both poets alive for many years after their self-destructive impulses first manifested themselves and so signifies success.[2]

Similar arguments can be made for Katie's writing. Her suicide does not necessarily mean that her diary writing was harmful. Had she not written in her diary, she might have killed herself at an earlier time than she did. If writing in her diary postponed her suicide, then it increased the chance that some event or experience might have occurred which would have diverted her life course from its destination of suicide into a more life-affirming destination. The fact that no such event or experience did occur need not invalidate the usefulness of the diary.

There are many ways in which writing, including diary writing can be helpful. Let us look at these.

☐ Can Writing Be Therapeutically Useful?

Schustov and Lester (1999) discussed the possibility of counseling people in crisis by means of letter writing. The client contacts a couselor by writing a letter that is delivered by the post office; the counselor responds; and so on. Similarly, Wilson and Lester (1998) discussed conducting crisis intervention by means of e-mail. Although e-mails (and instant messaging) can speed up the communications between client and counselor, Wilson and Lester described a system of counseling in which the counselor does not respond immediately, but rather responds within 24 hours to communications from the client.

Schustov and Lester discussed the ways in which letter writing can help clients. One way of looking at this uses transactional analysis (Berne, 1961). The acts of organizing one's thoughts and putting them down intelligibly on paper for someone else to read forces the Adult ego state to assume control, temporarily suppressing the Child and Parent ego states. In contrast, Schustov and Lester speculated, writing one's thoughts down in a diary that will be read only by oneself permits the Child or Parent ego states to stay in control.

On the other hand, making a permanent record of one's thoughts does allow reference back to what one has written which could increase the likelihood that the Adult ego state will be in control when the letters are reread, if they are ever reread.

Several years ago, I taught a course on deviant behavior that was broadcast on the local public television network. I began to receive letters, anonymously, from a viewer. Here are some extracts (Lester, 2002).

Friday, September 26

I write this for the edification of any who care to read it and so that everyone will know that there is no one to blame—unless one is to blame all of society for its failure to provide care and treatment for those it so foully abuses and allows to be abused. And for its attitude toward the mentally ill which made my mother too ashamed to admit I needed psychiatric care at the age of fourteen, and for society not bothering to see that it be provided nevertheless. . . . I grow so very tired of fighting. I am so alone. Surrounded by my family, who don't know how to help me, I still am so alone because there is no one willing and able to help me. I don't want to die!! But die I will. There is so much pain. And I can't even cry.

Saturday, September 28

7:30 A.M. A semblance of sanity returns. Perhaps as the result of writing last night I feel much better this morning. Perhaps it would even be possible to relax. When I can go into a trance for a while, life becomes much more bearable.

Friday, late

I have decided to send this to the Professor of the Deviance course (being very careful, of course, to make very sure he has no way of identifying me) because he expressed a strong interest in suicidal behavior patterns. No one should have to die in this country because of the lack of medical care and knowledge. At least, this way my death might contribute in some small way to psychology.

Why do so many suicides keep diaries? Is it perhaps part in the hope that someone will find it in time? Partly, undoubtedly, as mental catharsis to help prolong the end. And, undoubtedly, in part to try to spare others the suffering he is so acutely familiar with. And, with that last in mind, Professor, I am going to leave word with my husband to contact you when all is over so that if you want to know the trauma that led to my death, he can tell you where it is available. And in turn you can inform him that there was nothing he could possibly have done to prevent or help me, though God knows he has tried. For this time it is no idle threat meant to alleviate temporary pain and anxiety. This time there will be no food to slow things down. I shall accumulate the phenobarbital until I have a minimum of 200 tablets and then go to a motel.

Incidentally, I take care to include nothing that would give away my identity to you, not because I am fighting getting real help but because I fear incarceration in a mental institution. I spent five months in one 20 years ago and prefer death to torture.

Niggling away at the back of my mind, however, is the thought, "What if he did find me and could really help?" But, because I know conscience and training would undoubtedly indicate commitment, I take great care that there be no way to trace me. I shall probably even mail this from another town. . . .

Later

God, by the time I get through with this it's likely to be book length. Except that I mailed the others today. I wonder if the Professor will receive them. As I put them in the mailbox I thought "L. you're crazy." I've written before, but never mailed them to anybody. Make what you will of that, Professor. Incidentally, in case your conscience dictates that you make some effort to find me, forget it. I am not even enrolled in your course. And no way would anyone get me near a second M.D. Nor would my husband consent to commitment. I extracted that promise from him years ago, and he knows that to violate it would terminate our marriage.

Incidentally, Professor writing this out helps. I become no less sick, but less desperate. It provides not only mental catharsis but distraction as I wonder just what you will think if and as you read these. Would you stop me if you could? Or, would you just coldly observe knowing there is nothing that can do more than delay the eventual outcome? Or, just toss these into the wastebasket? . . .

Writing these letters to me helped the writer. As she says, she became less desperate, and the writing was cathartic. She was also able to play with the idea that I might track her down and rescue her, a pleasant fantasy.[3]

A similar point was made by the diary writer whose diary was analyzed by Peck (1988–1989): "I'm merely talking to this paper with this pen trying to fend off the next wave of despair" (p. 297).

Williams and Douds (2002) have noted that the transference that clients make to counselors, particularly in telephone counseling (and in the present instance, in letter writing) may be useful for them. Perhaps the client can imagine the counselor to be the kind of counselor they need at that moment, rather than having to confront the reality of the counselor as she or he really is. Williams and Douds referred to this as "the power of positive transference."

Research in psychological laboratories has indicated that written emotional expression can result in significantly improved health outcome in *healthy* individuals (usually college students).[4] Emotional expression to others can facilitate the cognitive processing (contemplation and evaluation) of stressful experiences. The situation in which the confrontation with the trauma takes place must be safe and supportive, and intrusive thoughts can impede the assimilation process, especially if the person feels constrained in talking to others about the trauma (Lepore, 1997).

However, in Katie's world, the writing of the diary implies that talking to others about her distress was difficult and had been unhelpful for Katie. The social constraints were perhaps one of the factors that motivated her to express her emotions by writing the diary. Furthermore, the traumas that Katie had to confront were more traumatic than those used in laboratory research (such as preparing for graduate entrance exams in Lepore's [1997] study).

☐ Diaries as Therapeutic Tools

What kinds of diaries might be therapeutically useful? Two types of structured diaries provide good illustrations here. First, Progoff (1975), a Jungian psychotherapist, has provided guidelines for a structured analysis of oneself along Jungian lines. By means of his book, or by attending a workshop on the system, participants are encouraged to pursue self-exploration using a variety of tasks. For example, one task is to write down the stepping-stones of one's life, those critical points in one's life when something happened that provided a shape to one's life path.

A second structured diary is suggested by Burns (1981) based on cognitive therapy. Burns suggests a variety of exercises to engage in, and suggests that they should be recorded in a diary. For example, in one task, before participating in an activity, Burns suggests that the person write down how many pleasure points (on a scale of zero to 100) that she or he expects to get from the activity. After returning, the person records how much pleasure she or he actually got. A person who, for example, believes that he can have pleasure only when accompanied by others, may find that he gets a great deal of pleasure even when going to events by himself.

To see what might be useful and what might be harmful about writing diaries, I surveyed my students who write diaries, and here are some of their comments (paraphrased, combined and edited).

Some of the benefits of writing a diary included:

1. It lets you get your feelings out so you are not holding them inside. You can express the feelings and thoughts that you are ashamed of. It lets you vent and relieve tension. It calms you when you are angry. It relieves stress.
2. It shows how silly you were in the past for thinking like that and how much you have changed over the years.
3. It helps you sort out what you are thinking, clears your mind, puts things in perspective. It allows you to examine your own behavior objectively, after the emotional significance has waned. You are able to analyze your thoughts and determine whether they are rational or irrational.
4. It gives you insight into your past. You can see patterns of behavior and thinking.
5. You find it easier to write your feelings than talk about them.
6. It's like therapy. When talking to a counselor, you can have support. A diary is similar—you feel almost as if something inside of you is listening.

Some of the drawbacks mentioned included:

1. It is bad for you because you may hold back and not tell others how you feel. It keeps you from talking to others; it can increase your isolation.
2. Sometimes you feel you are too anal about things. You tend to analyze people too much when you write. It's hard to stop writing once you start. It makes you nitpick yourself.
3. It makes you dwell on bad experiences. It causes you to focus intently on events that may be best forgotten. When you reread it, it sometimes reminds you of bad events or situations that should be put in the past. It reminds you of grudges that you can then dwell on. You write when something bad happens, and so you have a book full of negative

things that happened to you. It seems that you are always unhappy because, if you are feeling good, you don't always write in your diary.
4. It is a sort of dependency. You can't let go. It gets you frustrated when you plan to write in it and can't. You get upset and feel you're losing it.
5. It is time-consuming.

☐ Katie's Diary

Katie's diary does not appear to have helped her, and a reading of it suggests that it may have been harmful. Let us consider these issues.

Self-reflection can easily turn into rumination—a process of continually going over the same thoughts and ideas without any noticeable change. The person does not achieve any new insights and emotions do not get "worked through." People can, of course, improve psychologically without the help of psychotherapists, but this is where a psychotherapist can be most useful—preventing rumination and stimulating the person to new insights.

In a similar fashion, although Gestalt therapy encourages the complete experiencing of emotions in the expectation that, once fully experienced, the emotions will dissipate, the presence of a Gestalt therapist can help ensure that the emotions are fully experienced rather than blocked and that the individual is allowing himself or herself to experience the real emotion. For example, the emotion of anger is sometimes a "cover" for other emotions, such as anxiety (as when a parent screams at a child who puts himself or herself into a dangerous situation) or shame (as when a person attacks others as a defensive strategy to avoid experiencing blame for some misbehavior).

We are also confronted with the fact that Katie did kill herself. As we have seen in the case of the Sylvia Plath and Anne Sexton, it could be argued that their writing prolonged their lives. By expressing their thoughts and feelings in their poetry, they were forced to distance themselves a little in the act of writing from the emotions involved. In their case, it was also suggested that crafting the poetry gave them even greater distance, similar to that involved in cognitive therapy exercises.

It might be then, in a similar fashion, that writing the diary helped to prolong Katie's life and that, had she not written the diary, she might have killed herself earlier in her life. But Katie's diary has several features that indicate that it might have had a deleterious effect on her.

First, the diary was not designed to be read by others in the way that a letter is. Thus, Katie was not forced to make her thoughts comprehensible to others and, therefore, to herself.

The many juxtapositions of contradictory thoughts and feelings in the same diary (see the examples given in chapter 8) would not appear in a letter, for the writer of the letter would be forced to explain the discrepancies and inconsistencies. In doing so, the writer would have to distance herself from the content and look at the words critically and eliminate the irrationality.

There are many passages in the diary which read as if the writer were disintegrating, perhaps psychotically. The writing becomes fragmented and chaotic, much like the schizophrenic speech that R. D. Laing has documented (Laing, 1960).

July 24: *I feel so dirty—no! I feel so angry! Nothing seems to be going anywhere in my life. It's all so elusive. I don't know why. I feel the cold fingertips all over my body again, but in my heart a special fire burns. I am understanding more—the angels singing—my mother told me about—the darkness was evil—the night was evil—for the night held my Daddy's hands—hands he caressed me with—a scream I choked on—flutters inside me now—like a bird swallowed by a cat. The scream is mine—the bird is not—the cat is not. Here I say what I have to. Words don't mean much to me now. All my words are here to choose from. What are real, which are true? In my Daddy's arms again. I'm looking for home. Where is my home? Railroad tracks—I fly far on—the trees scrape my stomach—my stomach is my scar— hands in a circular motion touch me, rubbing my rape away—on the same day—*

The typed words fail to capture the occasional visual disorganization of the diary as the words are sometimes scrawled on the page, along with nonverbal marks. Of course, perhaps Katie is being poetic in her writing rather than disintegrating. It is difficult to render a judgment.

Second, some of the diary entries are very long, especially in the early months. Katie may have sat writing for hours, time that might have been more profitably employed—socializing with others, working on the courses that she eventually dropped out of, getting employment to ease her financial problems, going to the fitness center or gym, and so on. But Katie, obviously, was not able to do these things.

Thirdly, there is repetition, again and again, of the same themes, thoughts, and emotions, without any apparent movement. There is no monitoring of the conflicts she expresses, no dissection, no rational evaluation, no challenging, no correction. At the end of the year, the diary entries seem no different than those at the beginning. The diary appears to document rumination.

Although Katie is ambivalent, she does occasionally say that the writing helps her:

June 22, year 1: *I hate writing like this in my journals. It doesn't get to the point.*

June 28, year 1: *It's so damn repetitious. I have to move on to a different degree of expressing myself.*

July 17: *Only these pages can carry the weight, nothing else. Only these wonderful pages—they will not hurt me at all—not like people. They always let me down somehow. I'm tired. Good night, Journal.*

July 17 [later]: *My writing isn't helping, perhaps I do not speak to the pen and my hand slow and deep enough.*

July 28: *I get so strung around Mark. I don't know why. I want to go to the bathroom and write in my journal.*

August 7: *This is a book to establish my freedom.*

August 7 [later]: *I wish I could talk more freely in my journal. I go through things I want to remember or make note of, but the big things I minimize. I really hate that. I don't feel like I'm connecting with the natural pace of my own voice. . . . I've sure come a long way in my journal entries since I started writing a few years ago. I've really broke permanently through some (a lot of) ground.*

August 10: *I will talk only to a therapist and my group and diary and most importantly God. . . . I will make sure I still get to express myself freely to this book, as long as I . . . put the past here on paper, it will not touch my life with other people. . . . I commit utter honesty upon these pages.*

August 16: *I love this journal.*

August 22: *I want to finish this book. I don't feel I hit what I needed to talk about, a lot. I feel it was a book of obsessing, well partially.*

November 28: *I want to start a new journal now. I'm so sick of this old one.*

December 6: *A journal is the most therapeutic thing for me.*

December 14: *I've decided to transfer all my insecurities,*

jealousies and anxieties into this book. I do not feel at all that sharing these things with Mark would better our relationship.
January 18: *There is where I feel safe to grow, in my journals. I love the fact that this journal has a lock on it. I want to get a special little chest with all my journals locked in it.*

And she does have the fear (and the hope) that Mark will find and read the diary:

June 22, year 1: *I know Mark must be dying to read my diary.*
July 1: *I want Mark to read some of my journal.*
July 7: *I'm always so afraid he would read this.*
August 28: *I know if Mark will read what I wrote he would possibly hate me.*

Thus, there is a possible reader, and this might have helped her organize her thoughts to some extent. I have said that the diary entries are sometimes fragmented and chaotic, but we cannot know whether or not the written words are an improvement in organization over her thoughts!

☐ Conclusion

Did writing a diary help or harm Katie? A simple question, but difficult to answer. I do not see any therapeutic movement as the entries move through the year in which Katie wrote the five books of her diary. In that respect, I would have to conclude that the diary did not help her. Talking to a competent psychotherapist would have been much better.

But I do not know how Katie would have fared if she had not written the diary. Would her conflicts have grown stronger and more disruptive of her life? Would she have killed herself sooner than she did? Questions that are impossible to answer. Some secrets are taken to the grave.

☐ Notes

1. There are many websites devoted to journaling, including one run by Jane Adams, who has established a Center for Journal Therapy (www.journaltherapy.com).
2. It should be noted in passing that creative writing has been found to be strongly associated with both affective disorder (Andreasen, 1987; Holden, 1987) and with alcohol abuse (Goodwin, 1988), and these disorders may adversely affect the psychological health of writers.

3. Eventually, she did write to me using her name and address, and we did correspond a few times.

4. For a review see Smyth (1998).

☐ References

Andreasen, N. C. (1987). Creativity and mental illness. *American Jounral of Psychiatry, 144*, 1288–1292.

Angyal, A. (1965). *Neurosis and treatment*. New York: Wiley.

Berne, E. (1961). *Transactional analysis in psychotherapy*. New York: Grove.

Burns, D. (1981). *Feeling good*. New York: Signet.

Goodwin, D. W. (1988). *Alcohol and the writer*. Kansas City, MO: Andrews McNeel.

Holden, C. (1987). Creativity and the troubled mind. *Psychology Today, 21*(4), 9–10.

Laing, R. D. (1960). *The divided self*. Chicago: Quadrangle.

Lepore, S. J. (1997). Expressive writing moderates the relation between intrusive thoughts and depressive symptoms. *Journal of Personality and Social Psychology, 73*, 1030–1037.

Lester, D. (2002). Letters to a professor. *Proceedings of the Pavese Society, 12*, 4–22.

Lester, D., & Terry, R. (1992). The use of poetry therapy. *The Arts in Psychotherapy, 19*, 47–52.

Neubauer, J. R. (2001). *The complete idiot's guide to journaling*. Indianapolis, IN: Alpha Books.

Peck, D. L. (1988–1989). Evaluation of a suicide diary. *Omega, 19*, 293–309.

Progoff, I. (1975). *At a journal workshop*. New York: Dialogue House.

Schustov, D., & Lester, D. (1999). Counseling the suicidal client by letter. *Crisis, 20*, 127–131.

Silverman, M. A., & Will, N. P. (1986). Sylvia Plath and the failure of emotional self-repair through poetry. *Psychoanalytic Quarterly, 55*, 99–129.

Simons, G. F. (1978). *Keeping your personal journal*. New York: Paulist Press.

Smyth, J. M. (1998). Written emotional expression. *Journal of Consulting and Clinical Psychology, 66*, 174–184.

Williams, T., & Douds, J. (2002). The unique contribution of telephone therapy. In D. Lester (Ed.), *Crisis intervention and counseling by telephone* (pp. 57–63). Springfield, IL: Charles Thomas.

Wilson, G., & Lester, D. (1998). Crisis intervention by e-mail. *Crisis Intervention and Time-Limited Treatment, 4*, 81–87.

AUTHOR INDEX

SUBJECT INDEX

purchase of the Washington Island place for retreat purposes. I had learned meanwhile that the dreamed-of house was for sale at a price well up in the six-digit bracket. I did not ask the elders to advocate Grace's spending one dollar for it. Rather, the idea was that outside funding would make the purchase possible. With friends helping, I contacted several dozen foundations with potential retreat-house interests. Two years passed. No dice. My dream appeared more and more to be a pipe dream.

Then several unexpected events occurred. Our older son, Christopher, knew of my interest in the concept of a retreat house and had followed events as they unfolded. The property came under the ownership of his law firm colleague. Chris made some personal real-estate transactions that put him a position to make an offer. He approached the owner in full candor, explaining that his offer was all he had, and although he could not come close to the asking price, he nonetheless wanted to purchase it himself and make it available—among other purposes—as a retreat house. That prospect caught on, and after a nail-biting passage of two weeks, the sale was made and a dream fulfilled. A dozen years of annual summer retreats have blessed people from all walks of life, with varied or no religious background, but all finding respite for soul, mind, and body. It has become a dream fulfilled.

Here endeth my dream story. In my heart, I know the dream that night on Iona was more than my unconscious mind working overtime. The confirmation of its heaven-sent origin comes back to me each time I see individuals and groups come, experience great good, and return home refreshed and ready for finer dreams about what their own lives of faith can become. I encourage more attention to dreams as part of the larger picture of our relationship with God. My lone example leaves me without authority to do much more than urge greater curiosity about how God can still communicate through this ancient means. But I can offer this: remember important dreams that connect to ministry. Jot down memories of them before they fade. Test the dream by talking it over with others. Be patient in following a dream to its fruition, fulfilled or not. And when pursuing the Scriptures, take extra interest in dream events that begin, "And an angel of the Lord appeared in a dream, saying…" Who knows? Deeper reflection along that line can turn out to be an unexpected surprise, a welcome asset to the grace of it all.

U-turns

Here is the second most astonishing story I know about U-turns.

A busy mother on Chicago's South Side placed the car seat holding her infant on her automobile roof while she herded her other small children plus grocery bags into the back seat. In a particularly harried moment of forgetfulness she drove off, leaving her youngest strapped into the infant seat—atop the car. The forward motion of the car slid the baby and seat off the car roof, onto the pavement, directly into the path of an oncoming truck that passed directly over the child, still strapped into the seat. The truck driver, white-knuckled and fearing what he might find, made an immediate U-turn. To his immense relief he found that the child was unhurt and—with traffic halted all around him—gathered up the baby from the pavement to deliver it into the arms of the frantic mother, who had seen through her rear-view mirror the near-tragedy she had inadvertently caused.

What outranks that hair-raising U-turn story, however, are accounts of people who have been turned 180 degrees by God's Spirit from sin to grace, from spiritual drift to faithful commitment, from isolation to belonging, from self-preoccupation to purposeful service. Pastors need perceptive eyes to see such U-turns at work, and we do well to stand in awe of them as supreme signs of the life-changing power of the gospel entrusted to us.

One such story begins in an unlikely location, a hospital operating room with two doctors singing as they sewed the final stitches in a patient's chest, completing a major surgery.

Singing! Herbert Greenlee, the senior surgeon, was the tenor, a member of our parish choir. His assistant, Douglas Anderson, was the baritone, a neurosurgery resident. Herb quickly recognized the quality of Douglas's voice and on the spot invited him home for supper and conversation about many things, including music, and particularly the music tradition at Grace Church. That conversation included an invitation to attend choir practice at Grace, which was accepted—and at this point music director Paul Bouman entered the story. He welcomed Anderson to the choir and then did something that took Anderson quite by surprise. He invited the young doctor to drop by the Bouman household after choir practice to get better acquainted—over a glass of beer. Coming from a church tradition in which choir directors did not offer beer as a part of post-rehearsal hospitality, Anderson became increasingly interested to learn more about these musical Lutherans and what made them tick. Unbeknownst to him at the time, and to Bouman and Greenlee as well, a U-turn was in the making.

Douglas Anderson had grown up in a solid family of practicing Christians, giving him early and deep spiritual roots, especially through firm biblical grounding and appreciation for the great hymns and choral music of their Swedish Covenant tradition. His mother was the organist in her congregation and taught piano; his father was equally active in the congregation as a singer and brass instrumentalist. Douglas sang well and often in congregation and school musical events, and with his excellent voice had good reason to envision a career in music. A college athletic scholarship in gymnastics changed that. And another turn of direction occurred when his aspirations toward Olympic-level competition shifted to the study of medicine. He made the switch, excelled in the rigorous neurosurgical course, married a fellow medical student, and seemed well started.

A sharp, painful roadblock loomed unexpectedly, however, in the middle of what seemed promising, and he crashed headlong into it. His young wife left the marriage abruptly. The effects of that turn of events were devastating. Although his medical residency continued, conflicting emotions of grief, anger, shame, self-righteousness, confusion, and rebellion set him toward what Jesus described in a parable as "the far country" (Luke 15:13ff), a state of soul well populated with demons adept in creating U-turns in life that lead over precipices.

Mysteriously, amazingly, that doctor duet in the operating room and the choir invitation following were the first, flickering flares pointing in a new direction. They could not initially be recognized as such. No one could see the faintest glimmerings of divine grace at work in two surgeons finishing surgery by *singing* the operation to its conclusion. That is why eyes of faith are needed to discern such things by hindsight, and eyes filled with hope are needed to believe that such grace-filled U-turns can commence on any given day amidst the most improbable situations. The Greek biblical word for repentance means a radical turning around, as in John the Baptist's call for such a reversal in life to receive the reign of God Jesus brought in (Matt. 3:2).

I heard Douglas before I saw him. On a Sunday morning not many weeks after he had begun attending weekly choir rehearsals, I was sitting in my usual chancel seat, unprepared for the baritone voice that came floating down from the choir balcony above me. Upon hearing the first few lines of the solo, I had to resist getting up and walking out into the chancel to have a look at the person to whom that voice belonged. I met him after that service and arranged a pastoral conversation with him, which included an invitation to a series on faith and practice for adults interested in joining the congregation.

His lively participation in that 10-week course gave me insight into something that was being reclaimed in this young man. The class included some of the most intensely probing adults I can remember; the baritone/neurosurgeon was among those opening life to the renewing power of God's grace. He joined the congregation and put his gifted singing voice to work in the senior choir. From the choir balcony in the south transept at Grace, he could clearly see and hear the preacher in the pulpit. He spoke to me on a later occasion about a particular sermon I had preached on the call to the Christian life, one that—without my knowing—forged another vital link in the continuing U-turn. Like preachers everywhere, I had little idea what the Spirit of God was accomplishing in the hearers of the Word that morning, particularly in one choir singer. And like so many of us who proclaim the Good News, I was later humbled, gratified, and—yes, surprised—when Douglas told me how the seed of Word took root in him that morning.

One thing more. From the choir balcony, Anderson could see not only the preacher in the pulpit but also the worshipers sitting on the pulpit side of the Grace Church sanctuary, including one young blonde parishioner. He noted her with particular interest, met her, courted her, and married her—our older daughter, Ann. Douglas is our son-in-law, helping us all ponder the amazement and live the miracle of our own U-turns.

While I was enlisted in the U-turn as preacher, others had their unique part, certainly his parents and family, whose prayers for their son and brother were unceasing. U-turns are part of the grace of it all as the Spirit works through the Word. They occur in unexpected times and places. Keen spiritual vision can discern them, sharpened by the awareness that one's own daily journey of faith is a turning from sin to grace. Many with different gifts are part of the nurturing of those who make it back home to the Father's waiting arms from the far country. Prayer, patience, waiting, hoping all have their place. The U-turns may not all be dramatic. But every one is a miracle of grace and a sign that God has not given up on the world.

Boldness

Boldness belongs to the calling in which all Christians share, and if we can keep boldness clear of brashness, we're in on something really exciting.

Boldness in the pastoral calling, as I see it, is not a personality trait that some have and others do not. It's a gift of the Spirit stemming from the gospel itself. Paul had a good deal to say about boldness, which he needed in full measure as he took the good news to the Gentile world. And did not our Lord call his people to a revolutionary boldness to be the salt of the earth, the light of the world, and those who are blessed as peacemakers, not only peacekeepers? Declaring the mighty deeds of God does not mean a risk-free life, as all who do it know well.

I've seen so many instances of magnificent boldness in the discipleship of Grace members, too many to incorporate into this theme. Instead of trying to say too much about boldness, I want to cite just two experiences that bracket my years of ministry. I offer them, separated though they are by 50 years, to make one point about boldness that is ever relevant: it makes things happen.

The first has to do with an announcement to our third-year seminary class in the late winter of 1951. Six students were needed for a two-year vicarage in Japan. The seminary dean explained that the Lutheran missionaries expelled from China after the communist takeover were now welcome in postwar Japan. Vicars, the Lutheran term for student interns, were to take over the English-language work so that the missionaries could concentrate on Japanese language study.

I heard that announcement with mixed emotions. On the one hand was the appeal of an exciting challenge to go to a part of the world I had never seen and to learn something about ministry in a culture altogether foreign to me. I was single—in fact, probably the guy in my class least likely to break any hearts by going across the Pacific Ocean for several years. On the other hand, two years is a long time, and Japan is a long distance away. The home ties to family and friends were dear to me.

I spent a weekend in Kansas City with my parents to talk it over. They were admirably neutral, leaving the decision up to me. I can't remember the specific content of my prayers about the decision, or whether I even thought to pray for boldness. But that was given to me without my asking. Boldness provided the nudge to reach for the opportunity before me, despite lingering uncertainties. It helped me hold on to a hope that boldness now could make things happen later.

Those two years were life-changing. They forged a framework broad enough to enrich my entire Grace pastorate with an increasingly global perspective. Under the creative leading of the Spirit, that boldness in 1951 has enabled these things to happen. Because of it, bridges have been built over the past five decades between Japanese Christians and Grace members who travel, work, and study in the Far East. It has resulted in several dozen Japanese students living in our home for varying lengths of time. It began a series of four trips back to Japan for me, as well as three pastoral sabbatical trips around the world to visit, learn, teach, preach, and bring back the fruits of these journeys to Grace members. Those sabbatical journeys, in turn, sparked in me the boldness needed to establish two funds within the congregation that enable Grace staff people to spend study time overseas, as well as bringing overseas Christians to our congregation to broaden our horizons. And so the list lengthens. The point is that boldness in and for the sake of the gospel makes things happen.

The second experience came at the conclusion of my pastoral years at Grace. In its own way, it is an extension of the blessings following my decision in 1951 to take on the two-year vicarage in the Far East.

As 1998 approached, I knew I had to prepare myself to leave Grace as well as to prepare the congregation for the transition to new leadership. Furthermore, I sensed that the break would not be easy. It would call for boldness, so that a clean and healthy parting would serve the good of all involved, not the least of whom would be the incoming pastor. With something of these concerns in mind, Beverly and I traveled to Slovakia in the spring of 1997 to visit her relatives there. Without really giving it much thought beforehand, I remembered that an American theologian, Paul Hinlicky, was teaching in the Slovak Lutheran Church seminary in Bratislava. On a hunch, I phoned him, found him in, and gladly accepted his immediate invitation to meet for coffee. As we spoke, I mentioned my upcoming retirement at Grace in a year. He responded, "Why don't you come over here for some part-time teaching with us?"

Again, a *kairos,* an opportune, promise-filled moment was at hand, the kind that calls for boldness in weighing, praying, and deciding. It did not take long for me, with Beverly's assent, to accept the challenge, take the risk, and say yes. At the time, the principal thing that I hoped boldness would make happen was to get me well out of the way of the new Grace pastor. That was enough. But it wasn't all by any means, as things turned out.

From Bratislava we drove across the Danube to Vienna, just over an hour away. We were guests of Ken and Linda Vander Weele, long-time friends from the days when their boys were students at Grace Lutheran School. While we were sitting in their dining room, the conversation turned to what I was planning to do in my post-Grace life. I described my plans for ongoing ministry in retirement as these were just beginning to appear on the horizon in nearby Slovakia. Ken, who has a keen instinct for visionary service opportunities, began to think aloud about my becoming a pastoral advisor to Eastern Europe regional staff people of Opportunity International. This global organization, begun in 1971, creates employment for impoverished people by making small loans for microenterprise development. Since OI has a Christian basis with the goal of transforming lives and communities, Ken saw a place for me in providing pastoral and biblical support for staff people work-ing in varied locations in eight countries of Eastern Europe. The more he talked, the more we listened, and before supper ended, another avenue of continuing ministry was emerging. Again, boldness was making things happen.

Those seeds were planted in 1997. I now look back on nearly a decade of abundant years of teaching seminary in Bratislava as well as mentoring several dozen master's degree candidates from 16 African countries as an adjunct faculty member of World Vision and Habitat for Humanity. In addi-tion, I continue to participate in conferences and workshops within Russia, Romania, Bulgaria, Macedonia, Poland, Albania, Croatia, and Montenegro. All this flows from the blessings of boldness in seizing the God-given moment in ever-unfolding ways.

Boldness links the Japan challenge in 1951 with my present continuing ministry, and so much that lies between. All this amazes me, for I am not the kind of person whose mailbox is filled with invitations. I am one who has learned and keeps on learning that boldness is part of making things happen, taking hold of prospects for different ways to serve in faith and welcoming new ventures of ministry, risky and daunting though they may be. But the risks are well worth it. They are taken in the name of the Christ who does all things well.

Victories

I once had a victory of sorts, one that I hope is never repeated. When I was returning to the church late one evening, entering by the usual door, a man hurrying out the same door bumped into me. I had inadvertently startled a burglar who had just emptied a church-office desk drawer of 35 cents. In an act more of idiocy than of bravery, I chased him as he ran off across the church lawn, caught up with him at the corner of a busy intersection, and managed to bring him down with a necktie tackle from behind while he took a bite out of my right hand gripping his chin. We wrestled on the ground—no passing driver stopped to heed my shouts for help. During the ruckus a switchblade fell out of his pocket, which, mercifully, he forgot to use on me. A gas-station attendant saw us scuffling and called the police, and the burglar was taken to jail. Later, returning to check out the preacher-intruder fracas, a detective picked up the switchblade left on the ground, showed it to me, and announced gravely: "Reverend, you don't know how lucky you are, because you don't look like the fighting type!" He was dead right. One so-called victory of that order is enough.

It's a long step indeed from that scary moment early in my ministry to the biblical scale of victories. I suffer no illusions of grandeur in mentioning my church-door moment with victories of much greater import. In the Scriptures, interestingly enough, victory is not a common word. When used, it points to the one victory that counts, our Lord's resurrection upon which rests our faith that Jesus is indeed the Son of God (1 John 5:2). We all need victories in the daily life of faith that draw from that supreme deed. All victories, great or small in our eyes, build confidence that faith is not wishful thinking but rests upon Christ's lordship over all. Since it is *faith* that overcomes, I bear witness here to people of faith I know, love, and serve—and victories given them.

A victory comes when *courage wins out over fear.* In a church meeting in 1977 to determine a major step in our parish's future, Jan Uitti spoke with calm conviction to the resolution proposing withdrawal from the denomination that had been our church home for over 70 years. She was well informed on the issues and saw their connection with the main matter at hand, the central authority of the gospel for all faith and life. Her clear message was that we must act so that the gospel would not be hindered by ongoing denominational contention, a battle that had affected her family directly, since her husband was a member of a college faculty accused by synod leaders of false doctrine. Faith would yield its own victories, she challenged us to believe, while fear would cut us off from them. Jan reduced the threat of the unknown to the issue of faith over fear. Her courage was decisive and helped us decide to go forward in faith without knowing the outcome, as did Abraham and Sarah of old (Heb. 11:8).

Pastoral staffing was the setting for a victory of *grace over legalism.* As the decade of the 1990s began, the congregation joined me in thinking through the value of calling a permanent associate rather than assistant pastors every two years. The decision was made to move in that direction, and Karl Boehmke was called. He was my senior by a few years. I had known him in earlier days when he served as vicar in the parish where I had grown up. I had always admired him and was glad when he accepted the call to serve as my partner at Grace. He came to visit and began to lay plans for moving to River Forest, including making the down payment on a house. After returning home, however, Karl knew in his heart that his accepting our call and informing his current congregation was somehow premature.

He had anguished over his dilemma for a few days at home; he finally called me one evening to speak from his heart. He felt foolish, embarrassed, and befuddled, but also convinced deep down that he should continue in service where he was rather than come to Grace Church. Could and would the congregation release him from the call he had accepted? Technically, he acknowledged, he was beholden to come, since he had formally accepted the call in writing. The response from the congregation and me was that Karl should follow the instincts of his heart. We regretted not having him with us, to be sure. And he had to swallow the loss of the down payment on the house. But there was never any doubt about the rightness of both decisions, his and ours. No one regrets the victory of grace over legalistic demands.

I have a mental picture of the victory of *love over bitterness,* a costly victory that involved a father's broken heart. It took place as an elderly man knocked on the door of a house on a wintry night, exhausted both physically and emotionally. After a lengthy search for his daughter, he had finally learned where she was. She had left her husband and family years earlier to live with a man who forbade her contact with the family she deserted. Finally, this aged father had made a last, desperate attempt to at least see and speak to his daughter. And so there he stood at the door. He rang. She answered. He broke the silence with a greeting. She closed the door, having said nothing. He stared momentarily at the closed door before him, and began the long journey home, carrying within him a heart twice broken. His separation from his daughter continued, the deep wound still unhealed. Finally, his years came to their end. All the accumulated tears, dismay, puzzlement, and deep sadness continued to haunt this father's heart, but they did not move him to hate. His closing words in life were words of love for the daughter he never forgot, who had always been in his prayers.

What makes this story so poignant is that there is no happy ending, there are no tears of repentance followed by tears of joyous reconciliation. For that reason, the victory of love over bitterness was all the more profound. The father's love was not permanently rebuffed, however, though the heartbroken man did not live to see what followed. Several years later, the daughter and a brother invited me to join them at a luncheon meeting, and I heard her speak her deep remorse for the pain she had caused her father and the children she had deserted years before. It was a victory of divine love that made her repentance and reconciliation with her brother possible. At that luncheon meeting I thought of the father who, believing that Jesus is the Son of God, handed over his heavy burden to the Father above and trusted that a victory would come finally come, after his eyes were closed in death.

I witnessed the victory of *humility over pride* on a pastoral visit that began with a funny incident but ended on a more important note. I had called on a young couple recently arrived in our neighborhood and was welcomed into a part of the house still under renovation. During our get-acquainted conversation, I noticed a mouse venturing cautiously from a hole in the wall, scurrying along the floor unseen by the hosts. I crossed my legs in the most preposterously awkward way possible, trying to scare the mouse back. It worked once. But when the mouse reappeared and I did my leg act again, both husband and wife gave me a look as if to wonder what was going on. I explained the mouse situation, but later on something far more serious than a cheeky mouse emerged. The husband's behavior was increasingly erratic, and before long his wife's suspicions of alcoholism were confirmed. Then came the titanic struggle that every person suffering alcoholism experiences, admitting total helplessness against the addiction that was destroying his life. The defense mechanisms against that admission are immense. Next to "We confess that we are in bondage to sin and cannot free ourselves"—words of momentous meaning spoken each time we Lutherans offer confession to God—the words of the first among the Twelve Steps, "We admitted we were powerless over alcohol—that our lives had become unmanageable," come as close to any in breaking the grip of denial. The man of that household came to that point, and his recovery of sobriety through Alcoholics Anonymous is now 33 years along. During this time, he has been instrumental in coaching others who have hit bottom and begun the long way back, one day at a time. It is not as though all else in his life had suddenly become trouble-free. But the victory of humility over the hubris of thinking he could do it all himself was one based in his faith and the support of his wife and family with him in the congregation. He lives on, blessed by the daily gift of sobriety.

There is the victory of *persistence over giving up*. On an unforgettable day, a young man of Grace walked into my study. I still see him, dressed smartly in a classy pin-striped suit, but with face flushed, hands nervously fidgeting, unable to sit down to say why he had come. Little wonder he was wound tight as a drum: he blurted out his crime of having put out a contract of murder on another person. The murder had taken place. The police were closing in on him. He came to me as his pastor after a long period of wandering in the far country of self-deception and wrongheaded schemes for remedying the dysfunctional family in which he was raised. But now there was nothing to do but receive his confession of grievous sin and tell him to turn himself in to the Chicago police—which he did. Trial and sentencing followed. And now the long years in prison lengthen. He has learned the hard truth that inmates are easily forgotten. He has taught those of us who have not forgotten him how essential it is to have someone, even if it is only one person, outside the prison walls who remembers, visits, and cares.

This brother in faith is now in his 50s, with a superior mind badly used earlier in his life now educated in the law. He has filed thousands of pages of briefs and appeals for himself and others. His prison life is more retribution than rehabilitation—through loss of his briefs by judges, incompetence of defense lawyers, humiliation by prison officials, carelessness for prisoners' rights by guards, and physical assault by fellow inmates. The temptation to give up living is strong. Persistence in struggling on with his own legal research and appeals is a victory, though the outcomes are not yet known. I have seen the signs of those victories off and on in two decades of writing to and visiting him in the several prisons where he has been incarcerated. In spite of, or maybe because of, the tough going year after year in prison, he has come to appreciate the Lord's invitation for the heavy-burdened to find rest in him. Where will it all end? God alone knows. This is the victory that overcomes the world—our faith (1 John 5:4).

The Stephen Ministry has spread nationwide and beyond in the past four decades; it is a victory of *commitment over expediency.* We began the Stephen Ministry over a decade ago, with various leaders guiding those who sign on for the year's training to become spiritual companions to people with needs of body and soul. The Stephen Ministry is built upon the theological foundation of Ephesians 4:11–13, and has been embraced by Christians of every tradition. Each time a new call goes out for participants, there are, of course, any number of reasons not to respond. Pastors in congregations using the program hear these, among others: It's not convenient for me to commit this much time at this point in life. I've got a full plate of problems myself; why take on others? I doubt if I've got what it takes to be a listener. I'm short of transportation to get where I'm needed. I'm too old. I'm too young. Thus the litany of expediency goes. True, not everyone is gifted or ready for ministry after the Stephen style. But Grace Church and thousands of other congregations across the land are blessed by those who sign on, learn well, stay with it, and find the satisfaction of serving despite all the obstacles. It's a venture of faith, a victory of commitment over expediency, and no one who has ever stayed with it has regretted staying the course instead of never starting it.

A latecomer to our annual summer retreat exemplified the struggle inherent in the victory of *growth over stagnation.* Most of the participants arrived with preparations and reservations made well beforehand But one person's arrival was different. She came in through the retreat house door—burst in, better put—and took her place at the supper table with few noticing the inner agitation she brought with her. I had known her uncertainties about attending and respected her indecision till the last minute as not typical of her, an exceptionally responsible person. Nevertheless, her somewhat breathless arrival cloaked a sizable inner storm—her conflict over whether to hope for marriage to a man with whom she had fallen in love. She had been dealing with the question by not dealing with it, avoiding deeper feelings about herself that were painful to face honestly. Her decision, finally, to make the retreat was a step of growth in understanding herself and her place under God's care. In the course of the retreat days of worship, quiet, conversation on the retreat theme, good fellowship, singing and laughter, and sound sleep at night, she found truth, grace, and peace for her impasse. She left the retreat better equipped to grow by facing hard realities rather than letting them manage her. Continuing pastoral contact with her since has been rewarding. She has shared with me that her faith is growing because she risks venturing into untried waters. Shakespeare had a line for that growth:

> There is a tide in the affairs of men,
> Which, taken at the flood, leads on to fortune;
> Omitted, all the voyage of their life
> Is bound in shallows and miseries.
> William Shakespeare, *Julius Caesar,* IV, iii.

All of us are repulsed by stagnant waters. By contrast, the living, flowing water of Christ's grace supplies growth, which is stronger for being tested.

Pastors need victories, too. As pastors we get our share of knocks, some because we are faithful instead of popular. Others are just part of life's bumps that come to everyone. But seeing the gospel confirmed in the lives of those we serve lifts the heart as nothing else does. The love of God's people comes back to us in overwhelming measure as a sign of the grace that gives us a title we would never choose for ourselves—more than conquerors through Christ who loved us (Rom. 8:37).

Joy

"To find joy in the work." A friend and missionary of many years in India once named joy as a sure sign of grace in the pastoral calling, indeed in any vocation. I value his wisdom and feel wealthier than Bill Gates for the occasions that I've seen in ministry through the years that confirm it.

Some 40 years ago I came across a meditation on the fruits of the Spirit by the India missionary bishop Stephen Neill. *The Difference in Being a Christian* is one of those books to which I keep returning, always with benefit, to renew my acquaintance with the work of the Spirit, including his rare, durable, and treasured gift of joy. Neill contrasts joy with pleasure, experienced through the senses, and happiness, which comes through people. Both are splendid, but neither reaches as deep nor is as lasting as joy. Pleasure is bounded by human sense, after all. Happiness has limits, because people bring trouble as well as delight. He singles out joy, second after love in Paul's listing of the fruits of the Spirit in Galatians 5:22–23, as distinctive, because its object and its source are the Lord. Joy is permanent, because of the One from whom it comes. "Rejoice in the Lord *always*," Paul also writes (Phil. 4:4). The adverb *always* can't apply to pleasure and happiness, great though they are. Jesus's promise of joy reverberates throughout the Gospels, however, including that last night with the disciples before his crucifixion. His Easter victory over all that kills joy is the good news that sin is forgiven and death no longer has the last word. Now comes the Spirit with the gift of joy. To taste it here is to experience already now a fullness yet to come.

I can't remember ever getting out of bed in the morning and deciding, "This day, my goal is joy." My experience is that joy comes not as an end in itself but as the fruit of faith active in love. After a sermon preached, an afterglow of joy can follow. Or when hearing another preach, the same can happen. I recall hearing Martin Luther King, Jr., for the first time, on a Chicago preaching occasion, and the thrill of joy I felt in his preaching, right up to his closing doxology to the God before whom "the morning stars sang together and all the sons of God shouted for joy" (Job 38:7 KJV). After the Eucharist is celebrated, distributed, and received, or after a baptism is administered, the gift of joy can settle in. Not always, since I don't command it, but often and ever as a gift, and more frequently after rather than during.

I sense that joy when joining the congregation in singing hymns with text and music that are thrilling, sometimes so much so that I can't make it through all the verses. Or when listening to the final chorale of Bach's *St. John Passion,* with its petition for God's angels to come at the last. Or when hearing the majestic "Hallelujah Chorus" of Handel's *Messiah.* Or when hearing the Te Deum sung in an early Medieval setting by Music of the Baroque, a Chicago-area professional choral group, in the Grace sanctuary late in Advent each year, those magnificent voices accompanied by the joyful ringing of English handbells.

Some moments of joy are so vivid that I literally can't help but dance a kind of Lutheran jig, as I did in the kitchen of our little house in Kenya when I read a cablegram informing me that the long litigation over our church property had ended at last. I know the joy of the first glimpse of each of our four children, second only to the joy-after-pain of Beverly, who gave them birth. Moments of joy come when breathing deep, fresh Lake Michigan air and feasting my eyes on a sky that is so blue, water even bluer yet, and all around the greenery of the island we hold dear. I know the joy of watching brides walk down the aisle, faces radiant despite hearts racing, and I recall with special joy escorting both our daughters as brides down the aisle of Grace Church. I cherish the joy of Beverly's companionship in love and partnership in ministry through our years together, and the sight of so many holiday tables she has set with an elegance and ease that belies the work involved.

There is joy in heaven over one sinner who repents, our Lord said. That joy is known on earth as well. I think of couples whose marriage seemed shattered beyond repair, but their long, slow, painful work facing problems led to reconciliation and the joy of renewing their vows in the quiet of the Grace sanctuary. Being their shepherd, listening, admonishing, encouraging, and praying with them along that hard way brought moments of joy that make the pastoral calling nothing less than *amazing.* In terms of reward, the most generous paycheck could not come close to the sheer privilege of shepherding as such miracles happened before my eyes.

When pleasure is confined mainly to memories, and happiness is hard to come by, with the whole company of the church in heaven and on earth, I can still hope for joy. There is no date of expiration on this gift of the Spirit. This Lord of ours keeps his promises that underline the grace of it all. In him, as Augustine would remind us, the way is open for every Christian to be "an alleluia from head to foot."

Wonder

A late-April sight that never failed to stir wonder in me was available outside my church study window each spring. It was the row of apple trees in full blossom on each side of the walk leading to the Grace School door, planted there some 40 years before by a parishioner who simply brought a dozen of them over on his company flatbed one day and, without previously having announced his gift, planted them. The burst of color coming from those buds stopped me in my tracks as I savored the magnificence of such a sight and aroma. The overworked adjective *awesome* fit the scene exactly.

Wonder is integral to the life of faith; indeed, some say it is the essential ground to apprehend the divine holiness. Rabbi Abraham Joshua Heschel wrote a beautiful short book, *I Asked for Wonder,* filled with warmth and profundity. There is room for much more attention to this theme of faith resonating in great doxologies such as Paul's exclamation: "O the depth of the riches and wisdom and knowledge of God! How unsearchable are his judgments and inscrutable his ways!" (Rom. 11:33).

Wonder belongs at the heart of pastoral ministry and deserves more attention than is usually given to this subtle, intricate, marvelous gift. Busyness can smother it. Preoccupation with worship attendance, budgets, and other bean-counting aspects of the pastorate can move it too far down the list. But without wonder, we are but a shell of who we are made to be, no matter what our calling. Ministry is thin. Worship is flattened out to mere form, style, or routine. Prayer is reduced to asking, and that in fits and starts. Preaching lacks the resonance of depth in witness to the living God. One of the seven deadly sins, our spiritual forbears recognized long ago, is lassitude, spiritual dryness, sadness in the face of the Holy. Wonder doesn't take root in such soil of the heart.

Whence comes wonder? I see it as another work of God's grace, an open and welcoming gift to the soul, not a product of our doing. It is one thing, and an important thing, to take divine truth seriously and to obey it. But such obedience and fidelity fall short if their end is not reverent wonder before the living God, maker of all that is or was or shall be, the Father of our Lord Jesus Christ.

My amazement at apple blossoms outside my window lies within the biblical tradition as expressed in Psalm 8. The awe-filled gaze of the psalm writer begins with nature, in this case the heavens that are the work of God's fingers, the moon and the stars that God has established. It leads on to greater awe before the crown of the Creator's work, human beings of whom God is mindful, mortals for whom he cares. The sequence points to the supreme wonder: the living God himself and the endless love whereby he gathers us all in and shelters us. That psalm teaches us to wonder when beholding God through his marvelous works and makes wonder the basis for our responsibility as caretakers of the earth. Wonder in this Biblical sense is astonishment that God takes the likes of us into his plans, knows each by name, and calls us to do our part with reverence, joy, and wholeheartedness.

Many astonishing developments in science and technology have appeared throughout the past half-century, although many of them have passed me by unawares. I am not scientifically minded; my whole training and lifework have centered elsewhere. But in pastoral ministry at Grace I have had occasion to respect and appreciate deeply such scientifically minded parishioners as Manuel Bretscher, senior nuclear physicist at Argonne Laboratory. His calling as a scientist is well grounded in a faith beautifully centered in Christ the Savior and generously shared in and beyond the congregation. He and others like him give me hope that scientific and technological accomplishments do not need to come at the expense of wonder but are part of faith at work in their calling. Wonder, with its companion quality of humility, forms the best guard against the idolatry of science and the misuse of technology—and theology as well.

Pastoral ministry offers much occasion for wonder if we are open to it. I recall the wonder in a youngster's eyes when she received her first communion more than 30 years ago. I remember the embrace of two brothers who embraced in reconciling grace after sharp differences. I remember a man's words, few but genuine, as he came to church with a substantial Thanksgiving Day offering for children afar who had little or nothing to eat. I remember the glow of accomplishment on the face of a Grace School graduate for whom just walking to receive her diploma was a triumph of courage in her shrunken body. I remember a pause of respectful silence in a conversation with a Slovak mathematician, when he commented on the mystery of the stratospheric realm of mathematics he occupies. I remember feeling chills up and down my spine when moments of oneness in spirit and service returned after hard times of alienation with a fellow staff member. I have in my mind and heart a permanent picture, wonder-filled, of the people of Grace Church and the love of Christ himself conveyed to me through their faces, words, tears, and warm embraces on that last Sunday of my pastorate, Pentecost Day 1998.

In citing these instances of wonder expressed in ministry with others, I am speaking for the supreme wonder at the heart of all of them, that of being a servant of Christ in his church. Wonder may indeed be solitary on occasions. My experiences with wonder came and still come most often in the community of faith, worship, and service.

Again, in more references that I can recall or recount, the wonder experienced by others and passed on to me through their writing has enriched my storehouse of wonder immeasurably. Among the many that have stirred me and found their

way into my preaching and writing is a recollection by Evg-
eny Yevtushenko, the Russian writer and poet. As a youth he
remembered seeing the column of defeated Germans—some
20,000 of them—marched through the streets of Moscow in
1941. Those who watched them, especially the Russian women
who had lost so many and suffered so much, looked on with
hate and shouted curses as the first contingent of Nazi generals
and officers marched by—jaws set in haughtiness and lips curled
down in contempt for their captors. But then Yevtushenko
remembered the sight of the German foot soldiers, unshaven,
still bloodied, hobbling along with heads down, barely able to
walk. Their miserable plight brought a silence to the streets;
utter silence as they struggled by. Then one old woman in
broken-down boots slipped through the police barricade and
from inside her tattered coat took a crust of black bread. She
stuffed it awkwardly into the pocket of a soldier too exhausted
to thank her. Suddenly from every side women came running
toward the soldiers, giving them bread, cigarettes, or whatever
they could muster from their own meager supplies. By a miracle
of wonder, the soldiers were no longer enemies. They were
fellow human beings. It is a story of wonder that never fails to
grip me as I think of it and pass it on.

Wonder is not bound by the exhilarating emotions that
come with it. It opens the soul and mind to the vastness of
the God we know and love in Christ Jesus, who is able to accomplish abundantly far more than all we can ask or imagine"
(Eph. 3:20). Paul expresses what to me is the capstone truth
about wonder. It is doxology, suffusing all ministry, all faith,
all life, with the grace that frees the heart to sing and makes us
finally what we were created to be. Hear him at his best as he
concludes Romans 11:

> O the depths of the riches and wisdom and knowledge of
> God! How unsearchable are his judgments and how inscru-
> table his ways!
>   "For who has known the mind of the Lord?
>   Or who has been his counselor?"

"Or who has given a gift to him, to receive a gift in
    return?"
For from him and through him and to him are all things. To
him be the glory forever. Amen.

Fifty-plus years of serving the same Lord give me abundant
reason to add my amen to that glorious doxology.

To that joy, I commend every brother and sister in the pastoral calling. If the words and themes of this book can encourage
deeper and more faithful ministry, I will be grateful. I share my
experiences realizing that the pastoral life is broader and richer
than I can express and that many more gifted pastors have
much wisdom to share. My hope is to keep the conversation
going, confirming the Spirit's seal upon each other, affirming
gifts, admonishing and receiving admonition, equipping God's
people for the ministry of the baptized in the world, and finding
enough time along the way to stand back with hope, joy, and
wonder, marveling at the grace of it all.